UNDERSTANDING FINANCIAL STATEMENTS

NINTH EDITION

Lyn M. Fraser

Aileen Ormiston

Prentic

Boston   Columbus   Indianapolis   New York   San Francisco   Upper Saddle River

Amsterdam   Cape Town   Dubai   London   Madrid   Milan   Munich   Paris   Montreal   Toronto

Delhi   Mexico City   Sao Paulo   Sydney   Hong Kong   Seoul   Singapore   Taipei   Tokyo

Editorial Director: Sally Yagan
Editor in Chief: Eric Svendsen
Acquisitions Editor: Julie Broich
Editorial Project Manager: Kierra Kashickey
Editorial Assistant: Christina Rumbaugh
Director of Marketing: Patrice Lumumba Jones
Marketing Manager: Elizabeth Averbeck
Marketing Assistant: Ian Gold
Senior Managing Editor: Judy Leale
Project Manager: Becca Richter
Senior Operations Supervisor: Arnold Vila
Operations Specialist: Ben Smith
Art Director: Jayne Conte

Cover Designer: Margaret Kenselaar
Manager, Rights and Permissions: Charles Morris
Manager, Cover Visual Research & Permissions:
    Karen Sanatar
Cover Art: Hola Images/Getty Images
Lead Media Project Manager: Denise Vaughn
Media Project Manager, Production: Lisa Rinaldi
Full-Service Project Management/Composition:
    TexTech International Pvt Ltd
Printer/Binder: STP Command Web
Cover Printer: STP Command Web
Text Font: 10.5/12 Palatino

Credits and acknowledgments borrowed from other sources and reproduced, with permission, in this textbook appear on appropriate page within text.

Library of Congress Cataloging-in-Publication Data

Fraser, Lyn M.
    Understanding financial statements / Lyn M. Fraser, Aileen Ormiston. —9th ed.
        p.   cm.
    Includes bibliographical references and index.
    ISBN 0-13-608624-1
    1. Financial statements.   2. Corporation reports.   I. Ormiston, Aileen.
    II. Title.
    HF5681.B2F764 2010
    657'.3—dc22   2009000268

10 9 8 7 6 5

Prentice Hall
is an imprint of

www.pearsonhighered.com

ISBN-10:   0-13-608624-1
ISBN-13: 978-0-13-608624-6

For Eleanor

—Lyn M. Fraser

For my father, Mike, Josh, and Jacqui

—Aileen Ormiston

CONTENTS

Preface   xi

Organization of the Ninth Edition   xii

Uses for the Ninth Edition   xiv

Features of the Ninth Edition   xv

Acknowledgments   xvii

About the Authors   xviii

Chapter 1   Financial Statements: An Overview   1

Map or Maze   1

   Usefulness   3

   Volume of Information   3

   Where to Find a Company's Financial Statements   6

   The Financial Statements   7

   Notes to the Financial Statements   7

   Auditor's Report   10

   Sarbanes-Oxley Act of 2002   16

   Management Discussion and Analysis   17

   Five-Year Summary of Selected Financial Data and Market Data   19

   Pandora (A.K.A. "PR Fluff")   19

   Proxy Statement   19

   Missing and Hard-to-Find Information   20

Complexities   21

   Accounting Choices   21

   The Future of Financial Statements   22

Quality of Financial Reporting   22

   Timing of Revenue and Expense Recognition   22

   Discretionary Items   23

The Journey Through the Maze Continues   23

   Self-Test   24

   Study Questions, Problems, and Cases   27

Chapter 2   The Balance Sheet   36

Financial Condition   36

   Consolidation   37

Balance Sheet Date   37

Comparative Data   37

Common-Size Balance Sheet   37

Assets   40

Current Assets   40

Cash and Marketable Securities   41

Accounts Receivable   42

Inventories   44

Inventory Accounting Methods   45

Prepaid Expenses   48

Property, Plant, and Equipment   49

Other Assets   52

Liabilities   52

Current Liabilities   52

Accounts Payable   52

Notes Payable   53

Current Maturities of Long-Term Debt   54

Accrued Liabilities   54

Unearned Revenue or Deferred Credits   55

Deferred Federal Income Taxes   55

Long-Term Debt   59

Capital Lease Obligations   60

Postretirement Benefits Other Than Pensions   60

Commitments and Contingencies   61

Hybrid Securities   61

Stockholders' Equity   62

Common Stock   62

Additional Paid-In Capital   62

Retained Earnings   62

Other Equity Accounts   63

Other Balance Sheet Items   64

Self-Test   *65*

Study Questions, Problems, and Cases   *70*

Chapter 3   Income Statement and Statement of Stockholders' Equity   78

The Income Statement   79

Common-Size Income Statement   81

Net Sales   81

Cost of Goods Sold   83

Gross Profit   83

Operating Expense   85

Depreciation and Amortization   86

Operating Profit   87

Other Income (Expense)   88

Equity Earnings   88

Earnings Before Income Taxes/Effective Tax Rate   90

Special Items   91

Accounting Changes   92

Net Earnings   92

Earnings Per Common Share   92

Comprehensive Income   93

The Statement of Stockholders' Equity   94

Earnings Quality and Cash Flow   96

Self-Test   96

Study Questions, Problems, and Cases   101

Chapter 4   Statement of Cash Flows   107

Preparing a Statement of Cash Flows   108

Calculating Cash Flow from Operating Activities   113

Indirect Method   114

Cash Flow from Investing Activities   116

Cash Flow from Financing Activities   117

Change in Cash   118

Analyzing the Statement of Cash Flows   119

Cash Flow from Operations   119

Nocash Corporation   120

R.E.C. Inc.: Analysis of the Statement of Cash Flows   122

R.E.C. Inc. Analysis: Cash Flow from Operating
Activities   122

Summary Analysis of the Statement of Cash Flows   124

Analysis of Cash Inflows   125

Analysis of Cash Outflows   126

Are We There Yet?   126

Self-Test   127

Study Questions, Problems, and Cases   131

APPENDIX 4A Statement of Cash Flows—Direct Method   144

Direct Method   144

Chapter 5   A Guide to Earnings and Financial Reporting Quality   148

Using the Checklist   150

   I. Sales or Revenues   150

   II. Cost of Goods Sold   156

   III. Operating Expenses   159

   IV. Nonoperating Revenue and Expense   166

   V. Other Issues   169

What Are the Real Earnings?   171

Quality of Financial Reporting—The Balance Sheet   171

Quality of Financial Reporting—The Statement of Cash Flows   172

   Self-Test   173

   Study Questions, Problems, and Cases   178

Chapter 6   The Analysis of Financial Statements   180

Objectives of Analysis   180

Sources of Information   182

   Proxy Statement   182

   Auditor's Report   182

   Management Discussion and Analysis   182

   Supplementary Schedules   182

   Form 10-K and Form 10-Q   183

   Other Sources   183

Tools and Techniques   185

   Common-Size Financial Statements   185

   Key Financial Ratios   186

   Liquidity Ratios: Short-Term Solvency   188

   Cash Conversion Cycle or Net Trade Cycle   191

   Activity Ratios: Asset Liquidity, Asset Management Efficiency   192

   Leverage Ratios: Debt Financing and Coverage   194

   Profitability Ratios: Overall Efficiency and Performance   197

   Market Ratios   199

Analyzing the Data   200

   Background: Economy, Industry, and Firm   202

   Short-Term Liquidity   203

   Operating Efficiency   205

Capital Structure and Long-Term Solvency   205

Profitability   209

Relating the Ratios—The Du Pont System   211

Projections and Pro Forma Statements   212

Summary of Analysis   213

> *Self-Test   215*
>
> *Study Questions, Problems, and Cases   221*

Appendix A   Summary of Financial Ratios   251
Appendix B   Solutions to Self-Tests   254
Appendix C   Glossary   256
Index   265

PREFACE

In each of the previous editions of *Understanding Financial Statements*, my co-author Aileen Ormiston and I have attempted to take the reader behind the numbers, dazzling presentations, and slick annual report marketing to assess the "real" financial condition and performance of U.S. companies. While that remains our objective, we are also looking ahead in this ninth edition to the major changes for U.S. financial statements that will result from the adoption of global financial reporting standards.

Aileen and I were saddened to learn of the death in May 2007 of Lawrence Revsine, Distinguished Professor of Financial Accounting at the Kellogg Graduate School of Management at Northwestern University. We shared Professor Revsine's vision of how to teach financial accounting. On a personal note, I would add that when my daughter was a student at UCLA and using one of his texts, she occasionally called her mom for help; that collaboration and his approach to analyzing financial statements inspired the writing by Aileen and me, following the collapse of Enron, of our book *Understanding the Corporate Annual Report, Nuts, Bolts, and a Few Loose Screws* (Prentice Hall 2003). Along with many others in the accounting profession and in accounting education, we acknowledge and appreciate the tremendous contributions made by Professor Revsine.

Readers also have come to await anxiously a reporting update on the authors' children in each edition. My own daughter Eleanor, who was in grade school when I began this book, currently is Senior Head of TV, Catalogue and IndiVision Film for NBC-Universal in London after completing an MBA at UCLA's Anderson School of Management. Aileen's son Josh, three years old when his mother helped me on the first book, holds an MBA from Texas A&M University and works in Arizona for Piper Jaffray, an investment banking firm. Daughter Jacqui, age one for the first edition, completed a master's degree at Arizona State University and is now a colleague of Aileen's at Mesa Community College where she teaches math.

Lyn M. Fraser

ORGANIZATION OF THE NINTH EDITION

Chapter 1 provides an overview of financial statements and presents approaches to overcoming some of the challenges, obstacles, and blind alleys that may confront the user of financial statements: (1) the volume of information, with examples of specific problems encountered in such areas as the auditor's report and the management discussion and analysis section as well as material that is sometimes provided by management but is not useful for the analyst; (2) the complexity of the accounting rules that underlie the preparation and presentation of financial statements; (3) the variations in quality of financial reporting, including management discretion in some important areas that affect analysis; and (4) the importance of financial information that is omitted or difficult to find in conventional financial statement presentations.

Chapters 2, 3, 4, and 6 describe and analyze financial statements for a mythical but potentially real company, Recreational Equipment and Clothing, Incorporated (R.E.C. Inc.), that sells recreational products through retail outlets in the southwestern United States. The specifics of this particular firm should be helpful in illustrating how financial statement analysis can provide insight into a firm's strengths and weaknesses. But the principles and concepts covered throughout the book apply to any set of published financial statements (other than for specialized industries, such as financial institutions and public utilities).

Because one company cannot provide every account and problem the user will encounter in financial statements, additional company examples are introduced throughout the text where needed to illustrate important accounting and analytical issues.

Chapters 2 through 4 discuss in detail a basic set of financial statements: the balance sheet in Chapter 2; the income (earnings) statement and statement of stockholders' equity in Chapter 3; and the statement of cash flows in Chapter 4. The emphasis in each of these chapters is on what the financial statements convey about the condition and performance of a business firm as well as how the numbers have been derived. Chapter 5 discusses and illustrates issues that relate to the quality, and thus the usefulness, of financial reporting. The chapter contains a step-by-step checklist of key items to help the analyst assess the quality of reporting, and real company examples of each step are provided.

With this material as background, Chapter 6 covers the interpretation and analysis of the financial statements discussed in Chapters 2 through 5. This process involves the calculation and interpretation of financial ratios, an examination of trends over time, a comparison of the firm's condition and performance with its competitors, and an assessment of the future potential of the company based on its historical record. Chapter 6 also reviews additional sources of information that can enhance the analytical process.

Self-tests at the ends of Chapters 1 through 6 provide an opportunity for the reader to assess comprehension (or its absence) of major topics; solutions to the self-tests are given in Appendix B. For more extensive student assignments, study questions and problems are placed at the ends of the chapters. Cases drawn from actual company annual reports are used to highlight in a case-problem format many of the key issues discussed in the chapters.

Appendix A covers the computation and definition of the key financial ratios that are used in Chapter 6 to evaluate financial statements.

Appendix B contains solutions to self-tests for Chapters 1 through 6.

Appendix C presents a glossary of the key terms used throughout the book.

The ultimate goal of this book is to improve the reader's ability to translate financial statement numbers into a meaningful map for business decisions. It is hoped that the material covered in the chapters and the appendixes will enable each reader to approach financial statements with enhanced confidence and understanding of a firm's historical, current, and prospective financial condition and performance.

USES FOR THE NINTH EDITION

Understanding Financial Statements is designed to serve a wide range of readers and purposes, which include:

1. Text or supplementary text for financial statement analysis courses.
2. Text or supplementary text for accounting, finance, and business management classes, which cover financial statement analysis.
3. Study material for short courses on financial statements in continuing education and executive development programs.
4. Self-study guide or course material for bank credit analysis training programs.
5. Reference book for investors and others who make decisions based on the analysis of financial statements.

FEATURES OF THE NINTH EDITION

In revising the text, we have paid close attention to the responses received from faculty who teach from the book, from students who take courses using the book as a primary or supplementary text, and from other readers of the book. Our primary objective remains to convey to readers the conceptual background and analytical tools necessary to understand and interpret business financial statements. Readers and reviewers of earlier editions have commented that the strengths of this book are its readability, concise coverage, and accessibility. We have attempted to retain these elements in the ninth edition.

The ninth edition incorporates the many new requirements and changes in accounting reporting and standards, as well as the following items:

- New examples are provided in all chapters to illustrate accounting concepts and the current accounting environment.
- Chapter 1 has been updated to include discussions of the impact of the Sarbanes–Oxley Act of 2002 as it relates to the auditor's role; and the future of accounting rules and financial reporting standards as the Financial Accounting Standards Board and International Accounting Standards Board work toward a convergence of accounting rules.
- More detail on inventory methods has been added to Chapter 2. The depreciation example that used to be in Chapter 1 has been moved to Chapter 2 where it fits better with the discussion of fixed assets.
- Chapter 3 has been updated to reflect changes in accounting standards.
- The checklist for earnings quality has been updated and new examples for each item on the checklist are included in Chapter 5.
- Study questions and problems have been updated in each of the six chapters.
- The writing skills problems, Internet problems, research problems and Intel problems (using the updated 2007 annual report) have been retained in this edition. The Intel problems offer the student the opportunity to analyze a real company throughout the text and in this edition the highlighted company is Intel, a high-technology firm. Information for the Intel problems is available on the Prentice Hall Web site: *www.pearsonhighered.com/fraser*.
- The comprehensive analysis problem has been retained in the text using the Eastman Kodak 2007 Form 10-K and Annual Report. Problems at the end of each chapter illustrate how to complete a financial statement analysis using the template available on the Prentice Hall Web site: *www.pearsonhighered. com/fraser*.
- More relevant, up-to-date cases based on real-world companies have been added.
- The footnotes provided throughout the text contain resources that may be used by instructors to form the basis of a reading list for students.
- The ninth edition includes other features of earlier editions that readers have found useful: self-tests at the ends of chapters, with solutions provided;

chapter-end study questions and problems; and a glossary of key terms used in the text.

- The Instructor's Manual, which is available at *www.pearsonhighered. com/fraser*, contains solutions to study questions, problems, and cases; a sample course project with assignment outline and a test bank for Chapters 1 through 6. Both objective and short-answer test questions are included.
- The Web site for the text has been updated and includes templates to use for financial calculations and PowerPoint slides that can be downloaded for use in class.

We hope that readers will continue to find material in *Understanding Financial Statements* accessible, relevant, and useful.

ACKNOWLEDGMENTS

We would like to acknowledge with considerable appreciation those who have contributed to the publication of this book.

Many individuals have made critical comments and suggestions for the ninth and previous editions of the text. In particular, we would like to thank: David K. Hensley, The University of Iowa, Robert Roller, LeTourneau University; Corolyn Clark, Saint Joseph's University; Dr. Elisa Muresan, School of Business, Long Island University; Dane Sheldon, University of Miami; Dan Dowdy, Mary Baldwin College; H. Francis Bush, Virginia Military Institute; Bob Gregory, Bellevue University; Patricia Doherty, Boston University School of Management; Wei He, University of Texas of the Permian Basin; Kenton Walker, University of Wyoming; Sean Salter, University of Southern Mississippi; Paul Fisher, Rogue Community College; Ray Whitmire, Texas A&M University–Corpus Christi; Micah Frankel, California State University, Hayward; Seok-Young Lee, The University of Texas at Dallas; Sadhana Alangar, Cleary University; Scott Pardee, Middlebury College; Jill Whitley, University of Sioux Falls; John Baber; Maurice Johnson, Fashion Institute of Technology/SUNY; Melanie Mogg, University of Minnesota, Carlson School of Management; Richard Fendler, Georgia State University; William Seltz, Harvard University; Robert Ewalt, Bergen Community College; Richard Frederics, Lasell College; Tom Geurts, Marist College; Jen Adkins, North Central State College; Irvin Morgan, Bentley College; Jack Cathey, University of North Carolina–Charlotte; and Glenda Levendowski, Arizona State University.

We would also like to express our appreciation for the helpful insights provided by Lynne Renshaw, Managing Director for Internal Audit at Continental Airlines.

We would also like to thank the editorial, production, and marketing departments of Prentice Hall for their assistance at each stage of the writing and production process.

The list would be incomplete without mentioning the pets in our households who helped keep us in good humor throughout the revision of this edition: R.T., Picadilly Circus, Toot, AddieMae, Teddy, Tucker, Toby, Torin and Tisha.

Lyn M. Fraser
Aileen Ormiston

ABOUT THE AUTHORS

Lyn M. Fraser has taught undergraduate and graduate classes in financial statement analysis at Texas A&M University and has conducted numerous seminars on the subject for executive development and continuing education courses. A Certified Public Accountant, she is the co-author with Aileen Ormiston of *Understanding the Corporate Annual Report: Nuts, Bolts, and a Few Loose Screws* (Prentice Hall, 2003) and has published articles in the *Journal of Accountancy*, the *Journal of Commercial Bank Lending*, the *Magazine of Bank Administration*, and the *Journal of Business Strategies*. She has been recognized for Distinguished Achievement in Teaching by the Former Students Association at Texas A&M University and is a member of Phi Beta Kappa.

Aileen Ormiston teaches accounting in the Business Department of Mesa Community College in Mesa, Arizona and has taught in the MBA and the honors program at Arizona State University. She received her bachelor's degree in accounting from Michigan State University and a master's degree in finance from Texas A&M University. Aileen, prior to embarking on her teaching career, worked in cost accounting and also as an auditor in public accounting. Mesa Community College was one of 13 universities and colleges that received a grant from the Accounting Education Change Commission, and Aileen was actively involved in developing the new accounting curriculum. As a result of her pioneering work in changing accounting education, she was the recipient of the "Innovator of the Year" award from the League for Innovation in the Community College.

1

Financial Statements
An Overview

maze (māz), n. 1. An intricate, usually confusing network of passages, some blind
and some leading to a goal. 2. Anything made up of many confused or
conflicting elements. 3. A mental state of confusion or perplexity.

MAP OR MAZE

A *map* helps its user reach a desired destination through clarity of representation.
A *maze*, on the other hand, attempts to confuse its user by purposefully introducing conflicting elements and complexities that prevent reaching the desired goal.
Business financial statements have the potential for being both map and maze
(see Figure 1.1).

As a map, financial statements form the basis for understanding the financial
position of a business firm and for assessing its historical and prospective financial
performance. Financial statements have the capability of presenting clear repre-
sentations of a firm's financial health, leading to informed business decisions.

Unfortunately, there are mazelike interferences in financial statement data
that hinder understanding the valuable information they contain. The sheer
quantity of information contained in financial statements can be overwhelming
and intimidating. Independent auditors attest to the fairness of financial statement presentation, but many lawsuits have been filed and won against accounting firms for issuing "clean" auditors' reports on companies that subsequently
failed. The complexity of accounting policies underlying the preparation of financial statements can lead to confusion and variations in the quality of information presented. In addition, these rules are constantly evolving and changing.
Management discretion in a number of areas influences financial statement

FIGURE 1.1 A Maze of Information.

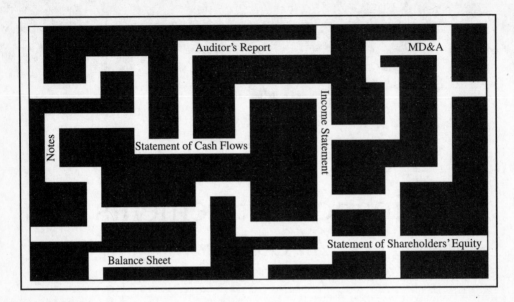

content and presentation in ways that affect and even impede evaluation. Some key information needed to evaluate a company is not available in the financial statements, some is difficult to find, and much is impossible to measure.

One of the main objectives of this book is to ensure that financial statements serve as a map, not a maze—that they lead to a determination of the financial health of a business enterprise that is as clear as possible for purposes of making sound business decisions about the firm.

The material in this book will convey information about how to read and evaluate business financial statements, and the authors will attempt to present the material in a straightforward manner that will be readily accessible to any reader, regardless of background or perspective. The book is designed for use by those who would like to learn more about the content and interpretation of financial statements for such purposes as making investment or credit decisions about a company, evaluating a firm for current or prospective employment, advancing professionally in the current business environment, or even passing an examination or course.

The reader can expect more than a dull exposition of financial data and accounting rules. Throughout these pages we will attempt—using timely examples, illustrations, and explanations—to get behind the numbers, accounting policies, and tax laws to assess how well companies are actually performing. The chapters and appendixes in the book show how to approach financial statements to obtain practical, useful information from their content. Although the examples in the book are based on corporate financial statements, the discussion also applies to the financial statements of small business firms that use generally accepted accounting principles.

The emphasis throughout the book is on analysis. In the first four chapters of the book, we will look at the contents of an annual report and break the financial statements into parts for individual study to better understand the whole of their content as a map to intelligent decision making. To fully analyze a firm, it is important to assess the value of the information supplied by management. This material will be covered in Chapter 5, on the quality of financial reporting. The final chapter of the book combines all parts learned in prior chapters with analytical tools and techniques to illustrate a comprehensive financial statement analysis.

Usefulness

Financial statements and their accompanying notes contain a wealth of useful information regarding the financial position of a company, the success of its operations, the policies and strategies of management, and insight into its future performance. The objective of the financial statement user is to find and interpret this information to answer questions about the company, such as the following:

- Would an investment generate attractive returns?
- What is the degree of risk inherent in the investment?
- Should existing investment holdings be liquidated?
- Will cash flows be sufficient to service interest and principal payments to support the firm's borrowing needs?
- Does the company provide a good opportunity for employment, future advancement, and employee benefits?
- How well does this company compete in its operating environment?
- Is this firm a good prospect as a customer?

The financial statements and other data generated by corporate financial reporting can help the user develop answers to these questions as well as many others. The remainder of this chapter will provide an approach to using effectively the information contained in a corporate annual report. Annual reports in this book will refer to the information package published by U.S. companies primarily for shareholders and the general public. The Securities and Exchange Commission (SEC) requires large, publicly held companies to file annually a 10-K report, which is generally a more detailed document and is used by regulators, analysts, and researchers. The basic set of financial statements and supplementary data is the same for both documents, and it is this basic set of information—financial statements, notes, and required supplementary data—that is explained and interpreted throughout this book.

Volume of Information

The user of a firm's annual report can expect to encounter a great quantity of information that encompasses the required information—financial statements, notes to the financial statements, the auditor's report, a five-year summary of key financial data, high and low stock prices, management's discussion and analysis of operations—as well as material that is included in the report at the imagination and discretion of management. To understand how to navigate the vast amount of information available to financial statement users, background on the accounting rule-making environment is necessary. Financial statements are currently prepared according to generally accepted accounting principles (GAAP) that have been adopted in order to achieve a presentation of financial information that is understandable by users as well as relevant and reliable for decision making. The accounting rules that have been issued in order to achieve these objectives can be complicated and sometimes confusing. The two authorities primarily responsible for establishing GAAP in the United States are the SEC, a public-sector organization, and the Financial Accounting Standards Board (FASB), a private-sector organization.

The SEC regulates U.S. companies that issue securities to the public and requires the issuance of a prospectus for any new security offering. The SEC also requires regular filing of

- Annual reports (10-K)
- Quarterly reports (10-Q)
- Other reports dependent on particular circumstances, such as a change in auditor, bankruptcy, financial restatements, or other important events (all filed as 8-K reports)

The SEC has congressional authority to set accounting policies and has issued rulings called Accounting Series Releases (ASRs) and Financial Reporting Rulings (FRRs). For the most part, however, accounting rule making has been delegated to the FASB. The board issues Statements of Financial Accounting Standards (SFASs) and interpretations, usually after a lengthy process of deliberation.

The SEC and FASB have worked closely together in the development of accounting policy, with the SEC playing largely a supportive role. But at times the SEC has pressured the FASB to move on the issuance of accounting standards or to change its policies (inflation accounting, oil and gas accounting). Pressures on the FASB stem from the private sector and have been highly controversial at times. Figure 1.2 illustrates the relationship between the SEC and the FASB. An example of a measure that was vehemently opposed by the business sector was the FASB's proposal to require companies to deduct from profits compensation to executives in the form of stock options. The FASB first began exploring this issue in 1984, but it was not resolved until 1995 because of business and ultimately

FIGURE 1.2   FASB/SEC Relationship.

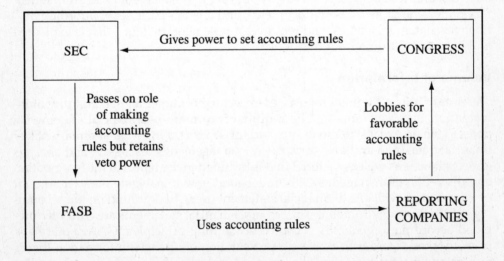

political intervention. Business lobbyists gained congressional support that effectively forced the FASB to compromise its stance on this issue.[1] As a result of the opposition, FASB Statement No. 123, "Accounting for Stock-Based Compensation," only required that companies disclose in the notes to the financial statements the effects on profits of new employee stock options based on the fair value at the date of grant. The controversy that arose with regard to stock-based compensation caused the SEC to take a closer look at the FASB's standard-setting process. In 1996, the SEC made public its concern that the standard-setting process is too slow; however, the SEC rejected suggestions from business executives that the private sector should have more influence in the process. The SEC vowed to maintain the FASB's effectiveness and independence.[2]

Corporate scandals such as Enron and WorldCom have brought to the forefront the challenges and pressures the FASB faces when creating accounting rules. The issue of stock-based compensation was reopened by the FASB in 2002. A new FASB proposal adopted in December 2002 to force the expensing of all employee stock compensation from profits once again resulted in congressional interference, delaying the new rule from taking effect until after June 15, 2005. The SEC and the FASB continue to examine potential rule changes or new rules in a variety of areas such as off–balance-sheet financing and overhauling the financial statements; however, these changes will most likely evolve as a result of joint projects between the U.S. rule-making bodies and the International Accounting Standards Board (IASB).

The globalization of business activity has resulted in the need for a uniform set of accounting rules in all countries. Investors and creditors in international markets would benefit from financial statements that are consistent and comparable regardless of the firm's location. To address this need, the IASB, formerly the International Accounting Standards Committee, was formed in 1973. The eventual goal of the IASB is the adoption of uniform international accounting standards. Accomplishing this objective would allow companies to list securities in any market without having to prepare more than one set of financial statements. The need for international accounting standards has been underscored by global corporate scandals. While Enron was the catalyst for rethinking accounting standards in the United States, Europe also had a comparable scandal when Italian dairy food giant Parmalat filed for bankruptcy after committing financial fraud. Today the FASB and the IASB are working on a convergence of standards. Beginning in 2005, the European Union required publicly traded companies to use the international accounting rules, and it appears the United States could soon follow. The focus throughout this textbook will be on U.S. standards; however, recent changes in GAAP have been made as a beginning step in reconciling the U.S. rules to the international rules (IFRS). In 2006, the FASB and the IASB agreed to work on all major projects jointly. While no date has been set, as this book goes to print, it appears that U.S. companies could begin using IFRS as early as 2013.[3]

---

[1] To learn more about this controversy see Stephen Barr, "FASB Under Siege," *CFO*, September 1994.
[2] "SEC Calls for More Efficient FASB but Rejects Stronger Outside Influence," *Journal of Accountancy*, May 1996.
[3] Sarah Johnson, "Goodbye GAAP," *CFO*, April 2008.

Where to Find a Company's Financial Statements

Corporate financial statements are available from several sources. First, all publicly held companies must file a Form 10-K annually with the SEC. The information in this document is mandated by the SEC and contains uniform content, presented in the same order for all filing companies. Figure 1.3 shows a sample of required 10-K items. Documents filed with the SEC can usually be accessed through the Electronic Data Gathering, Analysis, and Retrieval (EDGAR) database at the SEC's Web site, www.sec.gov. Some companies mail the firm's 10-K

FIGURE 1.3   Form 10-K Components.

Item #	Item Title
Item 1.	Business
Item 2.	Properties
Item 3.	Legal Proceedings
Item 4.	Submission of Matters to a Vote of Security Holders
Item 5.	Market for Registrant's Common Equity and Related Stockholder Matters
Item 6.	Selected Financial Data
Item 7.	Management's Discussion and Analysis of Financial Condition and Results of Operations
Item 7A.	Quantitative and Qualitative Disclosures about Market Risk
Item 8.	Financial Statements and Supplementary Data
Item 9.	Changes in and Disagreements with Accountants on Accounting and Financial Disclosure
Item 9A.	Controls and Procedures
Item 9B.	Other Information
Item 10.	Directors and Executive Officers of the Registrant
Item 11.	Executive Compensation
Item 12.	Security Ownership of Certain Beneficial Owners and Management and Related Stockholder Matters
Item 13.	Certain Relationships and Related Transactions
Item 14.	Principal Accountant Fees and Services
Item 15.	Exhibits, Financial Statement Schedules, and Reports on Form 8-K

report to shareholders, rather than producing a separate annual report. Other firms send a slickly prepared annual report that includes the financial statements as well as other public relations material to shareholders and prospective investors. Finally, most corporations now post their annual report (or provide a link to the EDGAR database) on their corporate Web site.

The Financial Statements

A corporate annual report contains four basic financial statements, illustrated in Exhibit 1.1 for R.E.C. Inc.

1. The *balance sheet or statement of financial position* shows the financial position—assets, liabilities, and stockholders' equity—of the firm on a particular date, such as the end of a quarter or a year.
2. The *income or earnings statement* presents the results of operations—revenues, expenses, net profit or loss, and net profit or loss per share—for the accounting period.
3. The *statement of stockholders' equity* reconciles the beginning and ending balances of all accounts that appear in the stockholders' equity section of the balance sheet. Some firms prepare a statement of retained earnings, frequently combined with the income statement, which reconciles the beginning and ending balances of the retained earnings account. Companies choosing the latter format will generally present the statement of stockholders' equity in a footnote disclosure.
4. The *statement of cash flows* provides information about the cash inflows and outflows from operating, financing, and investing activities during an accounting period.

Each of these statements will be illustrated, described, and discussed in detail in later chapters of the book.

Notes to the Financial Statements

Immediately following the four financial statements is the section entitled Notes to the Financial Statements (Exhibit 1.2). The notes are, in fact, an integral part of the statements and must be read in order to understand the presentation on the face of each financial statement.

The first note to the financial statements provides a summary of the firm's accounting policies. If there have been changes in any accounting policies during the reporting period, these changes will be explained and the impact quantified in a financial statement note. Other notes to the financial statements present details about particular accounts, such as

Inventory

Property, plant, and equipment

Investments

Long-term debt

Equity accounts

EXHIBIT 1.1

R.E.C. Inc. Consolidated Balance Sheets at December 31, 2010 and 2009 (in Thousands)

	2010	2009
Assets		
Current Assets		
Cash	$ 4,061	$ 2,382
Marketable securities (Note A)	5,272	8,004
Accounts receivable, less allowance for doubtful accounts of $448 in 2010 and $417 in 2009	8,960	8,350
Inventories (Note A)	47,041	36,769
Prepaid expenses	512	759
Total current assets	65,846	56,264
Property, Plant, and Equipment (Notes A, C, and E)		
Land	811	811
Buildings and leasehold improvements	18,273	11,928
Equipment	21,523	13,768
	40,607	26,507
Less accumulated depreciation and amortization	11,528	7,530
Net property, plant, and equipment	29,079	18,977
Other Assets (Note A)	373	668
Total Assets	$95,298	$75,909
Liabilities and Stockholders' Equity		
Current Liabilities		
Accounts payable	$14,294	$ 7,591
Notes payable—banks (Note B)	5,614	6,012
Current maturities of long-term debt (Note C)	1,884	1,516
Accrued liabilities	5,669	5,313
Total current liabilities	27,461	20,432
Deferred Federal Income Taxes (Notes A and D)	843	635
Long-Term Debt (Note C)	21,059	16,975
Commitments (Note E)		
Total liabilities	49,363	38,042
Stockholders' Equity		
Common stock, par value $1, authorized, 10,000,000 shares; issued, 4,803,000 shares in 2010 and 4,594,000 shares in 2009 (Note F)	4,803	4,594
Additional paid-in capital	957	910
Retained earnings	40,175	32,363
Total stockholders' equity	45,935	37,867
Total Liabilities and Stockholders' Equity	$95,298	$75,909

The accompanying notes are an integral part of these statements.

EXHIBIT 1.1 (Continued)

R.E.C. Inc. Consolidated Statements of Earnings for the Years Ended December 31, 2010, 2009, and 2008 (in Thousands Except Per Share Amounts)

	2010	2009	2008
Net sales	$215,600	$153,000	$140,700
Cost of goods sold (Note A)	129,364	91,879	81,606
Gross profit	86,236	61,121	59,094
Selling and administrative expenses (Notes A and E)	45,722	33,493	32,765
Advertising	14,258	10,792	9,541
Depreciation and amortization (Note A)	3,998	2,984	2,501
Repairs and maintenance	3,015	2,046	3,031
Operating profit	19,243	11,806	11,256
Other income (expense)			
Interest income	422	838	738
Interest expense	(2,585)	(2,277)	(1,274)
Earnings before income taxes	17,080	10,367	10,720
Income taxes (Notes A and D)	7,686	4,457	4,824
Net earnings	$ 9,394	$ 5,910	$ 5,896
Basic earnings per common share (Note G)	$ 1.96	$ 1.29	$ 1.33
Diluted earnings per common share (Note G)	$ 1.93	$ 1.26	$ 1.31

The accompanying notes are an integral part of these statements.

The notes also include information about

• Any major acquisitions or divestitures that have occurred during the accounting period
• Officer and employee retirement, pension, and stock option plans
• Leasing arrangements
• The term, cost, and maturity of debt
• Pending legal proceedings
• Income taxes
• Contingencies and commitments
• Quarterly results of operations
• Operating segments

Certain supplementary information is also required by the governmental and accounting authorities—primarily the SEC and the FASB—that establish accounting policies. There are, for instance, supplementary disclosure requirements relating to reserves for companies operating in the oil, gas, or other areas of the extractive industries. Firms operating in foreign countries show the effect

EXHIBIT 1.1 (Continued)

R.E.C. Inc. Consolidated Statements of Stockholders' Equity for the Years Ended December 31, 2010, 2009, and 2008 (in Thousands)

	Common Stock		Additional	Retained	
	Shares	Amount	Paid-In Capital	Earnings	Total
Balance at December 31, 2007	4,340	$4,340	$857	$24,260	$29,457
Net earnings				5,896	5,896
Proceeds from sale of shares from exercise of stock options	103	103	21		124
Cash dividends				(1,841)	(1,841)
Balance at December 31, 2008	4,443	$4,443	$878	$28,315	$33,636
Net earnings				5,910	5,910
Proceeds from sale of shares from exercise of stock options	151	151	32		183
Cash dividends				(1,862)	(1,862)
Balance at December 31, 2009	4,594	$4,594	$910	$32,363	$37,867
Net earnings				9,394	9,394
Proceeds from sale of shares from exercise of stock options	209	209	47		256
Cash dividends				(1,582)	(1,582)
Balance at December 31, 2010	4,803	$4,803	$957	$40,175	$45,935

of foreign currency translations. If a firm has several lines of business, the notes will contain a section showing financial information for each reportable segment.

Auditor's Report

Related to the financial statements and notes is the report of an independent or external auditor (Exhibit 1.3). Management is responsible for the preparation of financial statements, including the notes, and the auditor's report attests to the fairness of the presentation. In addition, beginning in 2005, the Sarbanes-Oxley Act of 2002, Section 404, requires that an internal control report be added to the annual report. In this report, management must state its responsibility for establishing and maintaining an adequate internal control structure so that accurate financial statements will be produced each year. Management must also include an assessment of the effectiveness of the internal control structure and procedures in the report. The external auditors are required to audit the internal control assessment of the company as well as the financial statements.

EXHIBIT 1.1 (Continued)

R.E.C. Inc. Consolidated Statements of Cash Flows for the Years Ended December 31, 2010, 2009, and 2008 (in Thousands)

	2010	2009	2008
Cash Flows from Operating Activities— Indirect Method			
Net income	$ 9,394	$ 5,910	$ 5,896
Adjustments to reconcile net income to cash provided (used) by operating activities			
Depreciation and amortization	3,998	2,984	2,501
Deferred income taxes	208	136	118
Cash provided (used) by current assets and liabilities			
Accounts receivable	(610)	(3,339)	(448)
Inventories	(10,272)	(7,006)	(2,331)
Prepaid expenses	247	295	(82)
Accounts payable	6,703	(1,051)	902
Accrued liabilities	356	(1,696)	(927)
Net cash provided (used) by operating activities	$ 10,024	($ 3,767)	$ 5,629
Cash Flows from Investing Activities			
Additions to property, plant, and equipment	(14,100)	(4,773)	(3,982)
Other investing activities	295	0	0
Net cash provided (used) by investing activities	($ 13,805)	($ 4,773)	($ 3,982)
Cash Flows from Financing Activities			
Sales of common stock	256	183	124
Increase (decrease) in short-term borrowings (includes current maturities of long-term debt)	(30)	1,854	1,326
Additions to long-term borrowings	5,600	7,882	629
Reductions of long-term borrowings	(1,516)	(1,593)	(127)
Dividends paid	(1,582)	(1,862)	(1,841)
Net cash provided (used) by financing activities	$ 2,728	$ 6,464	$ 111
Increase (decrease) in cash and marketable securities	($ 1,053)	($ 2,076)	$ 1,758
Cash and marketable securities, beginning of year	10,386	12,462	10,704
Cash and marketable securities, end of year	9,333	10,386	12,462
Supplemental cash flow information:			
Cash paid for interest	$ 2,585	$ 2,277	$ 1,274
Cash paid for taxes	7,478	4,321	4,706

The accompanying notes are an integral part of these statements.

EXHIBIT 1.2

R.E.C. Inc. Notes to Consolidated Financial Statements December 31, 2010, 2009, and 2008

Note A—Summary of Significant Accounting Policies

R.E.C. Inc. is a retailer of recreational equipment and clothing.

Consolidation: The consolidated financial statements include the accounts and transactions of the company and its wholly owned subsidiaries. The company accounts for its investment in its subsidiaries using the equity method of accounting. All significant intercompany transactions have been eliminated in consolidation.

Marketable Securities: Marketable securities consist of short-term, interest-bearing securities.

Inventories: Inventories are stated at the lower of cost—last in, first out (LIFO)—or market. If the first-in, first-out (FIFO) method of inventory accounting had been used, inventories would have been approximately $2,0681,000 and $2,096,000 higher than reported at December 31, 2010 and 2009.

Depreciation and Amortization: Property, plant, and equipment is stated at cost. Depreciation expense is calculated principally by the straight-line method based on estimated useful lives of 3 to 10 years for equipment, 3 to 30 years for leasehold improvements, and 40 years for buildings. Estimated useful lives of leasehold improvements represent the remaining term of the lease in effect at the time the improvements are made.

Expenses of New Stores: Expenses associated with the opening of new stores are charged to expense as incurred.

Other Assets: Other assets are investments in properties not used in business operations.

Note B—Short-Term Debt

The company has a $10,000,000 bank line of credit. Interest is calculated at the prime rate plus 1% on any outstanding balance. Any balance on March 31, 2012, converts to a term note payable in quarterly installments over 5 years.

Note C—Long-Term Debt

Long-term debt consists of the following at the end of each year:

	2010	2009
Mortgage notes collateralized by land and buildings (approximate cost of $7,854,000) payable in aggregate monthly installments of $30,500 plus interest at 8.75–10.5% maturing in 15 to 25 years	$ 3,808,000	$ 4,174,000
Unsecured promissory note due December 2016, payable in quarterly installments of $100,000 plus interest at 8.5%	4,800,000	5,200,000
Promissory notes secured by equipment (approximate cost of $9,453,000) payable in semiannual installments of $375,000 plus interest at 13%, due in January 2018	6,000,000	6,750,000
Unsecured promissory note payable in three installments of $789,000 in 2012, 2013, and 2014, plus interest at 9.25% payable annually	2,367,000	2,367,000
Promissory notes secured by equipment (approximate cost of $8,546,000) payable in annual installments of $373,000 plus interest at 12.5% due in June 2020	5,968,000	—
	22,943,000	18,491,000
Less current maturities	1,884,000	1,516,000
	$21,059,000	$16,975,000

EXHIBIT 1.2 (Continued)

Current maturities for each of the following 5 years are:

December 31, 2011	$2,678,000
2012	2,678,000
2013	2,678,000
2014	1,884,000
2015	1,884,000

Note D—Income Taxes

A reconciliation of income tax expense computed by using the federal statutory tax rate to the company's effective tax rate is as follows:

	2010		2009		2008	
Federal income tax at statutory rate	$7,859,000	46%	$4,769,000	46%	$4,931,000	46%
Increases (decreases)						
State income taxes	489,000	3	381,000	4	344,000	3
Tax credits	(465,000)	(3)	(429,000)	(4)	(228,000)	(2)
Other items, net	(197,000)	(1)	(264,000)	(3)	(223,000)	(2)
Income tax expense reported	$7,686,000	45%	$4,457,000	43%	$4,824,000	45%

Deferred income taxes reflect the net tax effects of temporary differences between the carrying amount of assets and liabilities for financial reporting purposes and the amounts used for income tax purposes.

Significant components of the company's deferred tax assets and liabilities at fiscal year-ends were as follows:

	2010	2009	2008
Excess of tax depreciation over book depreciation	$628,000	$430,000	$306,000
Temporary differences applicable to installment sales	215,000	205,000	112,000
Total	$843,000	$635,000	$418,000

Note E—Commitments

The company conducts some of its operations in facilities leased under noncancellable operating leases. Certain agreements include options to purchase the property and certain agreements include renewal options with provisions for increased rental during the renewal term. Rental expense was $13,058,000 in 2010, $7,111,000 in 2009, and $7,267,000 in 2008.

Minimum annual rental commitments as of December 31, 2010, are as follows:

2011	$ 14,561,000
2012	14,082,000
2013	13,673,000
2014	13,450,000
2015	13,003,000
Thereafter	107,250,000
	$176,019,000

Note F—Common Stock

The company has a stock option plan providing that options may be granted to key employees at an option price of not less than 100% of the market value of the shares at the time the options are granted. As of December 31, 2010, the company has under option 75,640 shares (2009—96,450 shares). All options expire 5 years from date of grant.

EXHIBIT 1.2 (Continued)

Note G—Earnings Per Share

Basic earnings per share are computed by dividing net income by the weighted average of common shares outstanding during each period. Earnings per share assuming dilution are computed by dividing net income by the weighted average number of common shares outstanding during the period after giving effect to dilutive stock options. A reconciliation of the basic and diluted per share computations for fiscal 2010, 2009, and 2008 is as follows:

Fiscal Year Ended

	December 31, 2010			December 31, 2009			December 31, 2008		
	Net Income	Weighted Average Shares	Per Share Amount	Net Income	Weighted Average Shares	Per Share Amount	Net Income	Weighted Average Shares	Per Share Amount
Earnings per common share— basic	$9,394	4,793	$1.96	$5,910	4,581	$1.29	$5,896	4,433	$1.33
Effect of dilutive securities: options		76			96			82	
Earnings per common share— assuming dilution	$9,394	4,869	$1.93	$5,910	4,677	$1.26	$5,896	4,515	$1.31

Sarbanes-Oxley, commonly shortened to SOX, has had a major impact on internal auditing. Section 404 of SOX requires companies to include in their annual reports a statement regarding the effectiveness of internal controls and the disclosure of any material weaknesses in a firm's internal controls system. This requirement has greatly boosted the need for internal auditors and SOX compliance specialists, but more important, has enhanced the value of the internal audit function within companies, as businesses have strengthened internal controls in response to SOX. Internal auditors have become the "rock stars" of the accounting industry.[4]

An *unqualified* report, illustrated for R.E.C. Inc. in Exhibit 1.3, states that the financial statements present fairly, in all material respects, the financial position, the results of operations, and the cash flows for the accounting period, in conformity

---

[4] Rachel Sams, "New Accounting Laws Make Internal Auditors 'Rock Stars,'" *Baltimore Business Journal*, June 2, 2006, and Peter Morton, "The New Rock Stars," *CA Magazine*, October 2006.

EXHIBIT 1.3

Auditor's Report

Board of Directors and Stockholders
R.E.C. Inc.

We have audited the accompanying consolidated balance sheets of R.E.C. Inc., and subsidiaries as of December 31, 2010 and 2009, and the related consolidated statements of earnings, shareholders' equity, and cash flows for each of the three years in the period ended December 31, 2010. These financial statements are the responsibility of the company's management. Our responsibility is to express an opinion on these financial statements based on our audits.

We conducted our audits in accordance with the standards of the Public Company Accounting Oversight Board (United States). Those standards require that we plan and perform the audits to obtain reasonable assurance about whether the financial statements are free of material misstatement. An audit includes examining, on a test basis, evidence supporting the amounts and disclosures in the financial statements. An audit also includes assessing the accounting principles used and significant estimates made by management, as well as evaluating the overall financial statement presentation. We believe that our audits provide a reasonable basis for our opinion.

In our opinion, the consolidated financial statements referred to above present fairly, in all material respects, the consolidated financial position of R.E.C. Inc. and subsidiaries at December 31, 2010 and 2009, and the consolidated results of their operations and their cash flows for each of the three years in the period ended December 31, 2010, in conformity with accounting principles generally accepted in the United States of America.

We also have audited, in accordance with the standards of the Public Company Accounting Oversight Board (United States), the effectiveness of R.E.C. Inc.'s internal control over financial reporting as of December 31, 2010, based on criteria established in Internal Control-Integrated Framework issued by the Committee of Sponsoring Organizations of the Treadway Commission, and our report dated February 15, 2011, expressed an unqualified opinion thereon.

J. J. Michaels and Company
Dime Box, TX
February 15, 2011

with GAAP. Some circumstances warrant reports other than an unqualified opinion and are called *qualified* reports. A departure from GAAP will result in a qualified opinion and the use of the following language in the opinion sentence: "In our opinion, *except* for the (nature of the departure explained), the financial statements present fairly . . ." If the departure from GAAP affects numerous accounts and financial statement relationships, then an *adverse* opinion is rendered, which states that the financial statements have not been presented fairly in accordance with GAAP. A scope limitation means that the extent of the audit work has been limited. This will result in a qualified opinion unless the limitation is so material as to require a *disclaimer of opinion,* which means the auditor cannot evaluate the fairness of the statements and therefore expresses no opinion on them. Lack of independence by the auditor will also result in a disclaimer of opinion.

Many circumstances warrant an *unqualified opinion with explanatory language* such as: a consistency departure due to a change in accounting principle, uncertainty caused by future events such as contract disputes and lawsuits, or events that the auditor wishes to describe because they may present business risk and going-concern problems. Unqualified reports with explanatory language result in additional paragraphs to the standard report.

Sarbanes-Oxley Act of 2002

In theory, the auditing firm performing the audit and issuing the report is "independent" of the firm being audited. The annual report reader should be aware, however, that the auditor is hired by the firm whose financial statements are under review. Over time, a lack of independence and conflicts of interest between companies and their hired auditors led to a series of accounting scandals that eroded investors' confidence in the capital markets. The collapse of Enron and WorldCom was a catalyst for some of the most sweeping corporate reforms since the Securities Act of 1934 was passed. Congress was quick to pass the Sarbanes-Oxley Act of 2002 in hopes of ending future accounting scandals and renewing investor confidence in the marketplace. A discussion of the sections of SOX that directly impact the area of understanding financial reporting follows.[5]

Prior to SOX, auditors followed a self-regulatory model. Title I of the act established the Public Company Accounting Oversight Board (PCAOB), a private, non-profit organization that has been given the authority to register, inspect, and discipline auditors of all publicly owned companies; however, the SEC appoints the board members and has ultimate oversight of the PCAOB. In addition, the PCAOB now has the authority to write auditing rules, and set quality control and ethics standards.

Title II of SOX addresses the area of auditor independence, prohibiting audit firms from providing certain nonaudit services when conducting an external audit of a firm. Prohibited services include bookkeeping, design and implementation of financial information systems, valuation and appraisal services, actuarial services, internal audit services, management or human resource functions, and broker, dealer, or investment banking services. Title II also encourages auditor independence by requiring the rotation of audit partners every five years if the audit partner is the primary partner responsible for a particular audit client. Another issue relating to auditor independence occurs when a company hires its chief financial officer (CFO) or other finance personnel from the ranks of the external audit firm. Section 206 of Title II inserts a one-year waiting period before an employee from the external audit firm may go to work for a client in the position of chief executive officer (CEO), CFO, or controller or any equivalent executive officer position; in any financial oversight role; or preparing any financial statements.

Titles III and IV of SOX focus on corporate responsibility; Title IX attaches harsher penalties for violations. Section 302 requires that the CEO and CFO of a

---

[5] Sarbanes-Oxley Act of 2002.

publicly owned company certify the accuracy of the financial statements. An officer who certifies a report that is later found to be inaccurate could face up to $1 million in fines and/or a jail sentence of up to 10 years according to Section 906. These two sections work in conjunction with Section 404 (discussed previously) to encourage CEOs and CFOs to take responsibility for strong internal controls to prevent accounting fraud and financial statement misrepresentation.

It will take time to determine whether the new laws and enforcement procedures will replace corruption and unethical behavior with integrity and professionalism in the auditing process. Regardless of the outcome, this history of problems underscores the need for users of financial statements to gain a basic understanding of financial statement content and analysis for decision-making purposes.

Management Discussion and Analysis

The *Management Discussion and Analysis* (MD&A) section, sometimes labeled "Financial Review," is of potential interest to the analyst because it contains information that cannot be found in the financial data. The content of this section includes coverage of any favorable or unfavorable trends and significant events or uncertainties in the areas of liquidity, capital resources, and results of operations. In particular, the analyst can expect to find a discussion of the following:

1. The internal and external sources of liquidity
2. Any material deficiencies in liquidity and how they will be remedied
3. Commitments for capital expenditures, the purpose of such commitments, and expected sources of funding
4. Anticipated changes in the mix and cost of financing resources
5. Unusual or infrequent transactions that affect income from continuing operations
6. Events that cause material changes in the relationship between costs and revenues (such as future labor or materials price increases or inventory adjustments)
7. A breakdown of sales increases into price and volume components

See Figure 1.4 for a more detailed explanation of these items.

Alas, there are problems as well with the usefulness of the MD&A section. One goal of the SEC in mandating this section was to make information about future events and trends that might affect future business operations publicly available. One study to determine whether the data in the MD&A section provides useful clues to future financial performance revealed that companies did a good job of describing historical events, but very few provided accurate forecasts. Many companies provided essentially no forward-looking information at all.[6]

The events of 2001, including the economic downturn, September 11, and the collapse of Enron, appear to have affected the quantity of precautionary and explanatory information companies have added to their MD&A sections of

[6] Moses L. Parva and Marc J. Epstein, "How Good Is MD&A as an Investment Tool?" *Journal of Accountancy*, March 1993.

FIGURE 1.4   MD&A Discussion Items: What Do They Mean?

Item	Translation
1. Internal and external sources of liquidity	From where does the company obtain cash—sales of products or services (internal source) or through borrowing and sales of stock (external sources)?
2. Material deficiencies in liquidity and how they will be remedied.	If the firm does not have enough cash to continue to operate in the long term, what is it doing to obtain cash and prevent bankruptcy?
3. Commitments for capital expenditures, the purpose of such commitments, and expected sources of funding.	How much is the company planning to spend next year for investments in property, plant, and equipment or acquisitions? Why? How will it pay for these items?
4. Anticipated changes in the mix and cost of financing resources.	Will the percentage of debt and equity change in the future relative to prior years—i.e., will the company borrow more or less, sell more stock, or generate significant profits or losses?
5. Unusual or infrequent transactions that affect income from continuing operations.	Will revenues or expenses be affected in the future by events not expected in the normal course of business operations?
6. Events that cause material changes in the relationship between costs and revenues.	Will significant changes occur that cause revenues (or expenses) to increase or decrease without a corresponding change in expenses (or revenues)?
7. Breakdown of sales increases into price and volume components.	Did the company's sales increase because it sold more products or services, or was the increase the result of price increases (with even a possible decrease in volume)?

subsequent annual reports. Some firms include a plethora of statements covering every possible negative event that could possibly occur, such as:

> We may not be able to expand, causing sales to decrease.
>
> We may be unable to successfully develop new products.
>
> We may not be successful in our marketing efforts.
>
> Our operating results may fluctuate, causing our stock price to decline.
>
> Our suppliers may not meet our demand for materials.
>
> Our products may have significant defects.

And on and on! These statements may be true, but an assessment of the probability that these events may occur would be more useful to the reader of this information.

More helpful has been the addition to the MD&A of explanations about why changes have occurred in profitability and liquidity. For example, General Electric Company (GE) offers explanations of why certain accounts such as accounts receivable or inventories increased or decreased in its section on liquidity and capital resources. This change is welcome, but GE and other companies still have not offered much in the way of forward-looking information in the MD&A.

Five-Year Summary of Selected Financial Data and Market Data

A five-year summary of selected financial data required by the SEC includes net sales or operating revenues, income or loss from continuing operations, income or loss from continuing operations per common share, total assets, long-term obligations and redeemable preferred stock, and cash dividends per common share. Companies often choose to include more than five years of data and/or additional items. The summary offers the user of financial statements a quick look at some overall trends; however, the discussion in this book will focus on the financial statements themselves, not the summary data.

The market data required by the SEC contains two years of high and low common stock prices by quarter. Since the financial statements do not include market values of common stock, this item is useful when analyzing how well the firm does in the marketplace.

Pandora (A.K.A. "PR Fluff")

In addition to the material required for presentation, many companies add to the annual report an array of colored photographs, charts, a shareholders' letter from the CEO, and other items to make the report and the company attractive to current and prospective investors. Some of these creations also appear on corporate Web sites. Getting to what is needed through the "PR fluff" can be a challenge.

Public relations material, including the shareholders' letter, is often informative but can also be misleading. The chairman and CEO of Pfizer, Inc. paints a positive picture for the future of Pfizer in his 2007 letter to shareholders. He discusses the "solid year" Pfizer had in 2007 as measured by adjusted net income and the fact that costs were reduced by downsizing a total of 11,000 people. In reality, the income statement shows that net income fell from $19,337 million in 2006 to $8,144 million in 2007. A magnifying glass is needed to see the footnote to the shareholders' letter indicating that "adjusted net income" can only be found in the Form 10-K filed with the SEC, not in the annual report that has been sent to the shareholders. The marketplace response to Pfizer's "supposed accomplishments" resulted in a 12% decline of the firm's common stock price between 2006 and 2007.

Proxy Statement

The SEC requires companies to solicit shareholder votes in a document called the *proxy statement*, as many shareholders do not attend shareholder meetings. The proxy statement contains voting procedures and information, background information about the company's nominated directors, director compensation, executive compensation and any proposed changes in compensation plans, the audit committee report, and a breakdown of audit and nonaudit fees paid to the auditing firm. This information is important in assessing who manages the firm and how management is paid and potential conflict-of-interest issues.

The proxy material helps investors and creditors by providing information about the longevity and compensation of top management as well as corporate governance, audit-related matters, director and executive compensation including option grants, and related party transactions.

Missing and Hard-to-Find Information

Some of the facts needed to evaluate a company are not available in the financial statements. These include such intangibles as employee relations with management, the morale and efficiency of employees, the reputation of the firm with its customers, the firm's prestige in the community, the effectiveness of management, provisions for management succession, and potential exposure to changes in regulations—such as environmental or food and drug enforcement. These qualities impact the firm's operating success both directly and indirectly but are difficult to quantify.

Publicity in the media, which affects public perception of a firm, can also impact its financial performance. Pioneers in the "science of reputation management" are now selling their consulting services to firms to help them improve their reputation in the public's eye, and thereby increase the firm's stock price. According to Communications Consulting Worldwide, Inc., Wal-Mart could improve its stock price by 4.9% or $9.7 billion if the company had the reputation of its competitor, Target. Target, while much smaller than Wal-Mart, has been perceived by the public as a firm that adds value to the community in which it does business as a result of its charitable donations, the way it treats its employees, and the atmosphere Target creates in its stores. Wal-Mart has been perceived as the bully that no one wants moving into their neighborhoods and an employer who treats employees poorly through low pay and discrimination.[7]

Some companies are identified with one primary leader or personality, and Apple Inc. is an example of that. Apple's share price is directly affected by any news about Steven Jobs, CEO of Apple Inc., such as issues regarding his health. The global charitable contributions by Microsoft's former CEO, Bill Gates, have had a significantly positive impact on public perception of that firm.

Some relevant facts are available in the financial statements but may be difficult for an average user to find. For example, the amount of long-term debt a firm has outstanding is disclosed on the face of the balance sheet in the noncurrent liability section. However, "long-term" could apply to debt due in 12.5 months or 2 years or 15 years. To determine when cash resources will be required to meet debt principal payments, the user must find and analyze the note to the financial statements on long-term debt with its listing of principal, interest, and maturity of a firm's long-term debt instruments.

Another important form of supplementary information is that reported by diversified companies operating in several unrelated lines of business.

---

[7] Pete Engardio and Michael Arndt, "What Price Reputation?" *Business Week*, July 9 and 16, 2007.

These conglomerates report financial information for the consolidated entity on the face of its financial statements. For a breakdown of financial data by individual operating segments, the analyst must use information in notes to the financial statement. Since 1998, companies have had to comply with FASB Statement No. 131, "Disclosures about Segments of an Enterprise and Related Information."

The Enron collapse highlighted that some companies use complicated financing schemes that may or may not be completely revealed in the notes to the financial statements. Even with notes available, most average users may find these items beyond their comprehension unless they acquire a Ph.D. in accounting or finance or read the authors' discussion of Enron in their other book, *Understanding the Corporate Annual Report—Nuts, Bolts, and a Few Loose Screws.*

COMPLEXITIES

Interpreting financial statements can be challenging because of the complexities inherent in the accounting rules that underlie financial reporting. GAAP, as established by the FASB and SEC, provide a measure of uniformity but also allow corporate management considerable discretion in applying the regulations.

Accounting Choices

Accounting choices and estimates can have a significant impact on the outcome of financial statement numbers. One example is the valuation of inventory (discussed in detail in Chapter 2). Companies can select from several acceptable methods that include, for instance, assuming that the oldest, lowest cost of goods are sold first; or that the most recent, highest cost of goods are sold first. The choice of inventory valuation methods affects both the amount of inventory on the balance sheet and the associated cost of selling inventory in the income statement. Because companies are allowed to select from several possible methods, comparability can be affected if companies within the same industry make different choices. And the quality of financial reporting can also be impacted if the accounting choice does not reflect economic reality.

GAAP-based financial statements are prepared according to the "accrual" rather than the "cash" basis of accounting. The accrual method means that the revenue is recognized in the accounting period when the sale is made rather than when the cash is received. The same principle applies to expense recognition; the expense associated with the product may occur before or after the cash is paid out. The purpose of the accrual method is to attempt to "match" expenses with revenues in appropriate accounting periods. If a firm sells goods on credit, there is a delay between the time the product is sold and the time the cash is collected. The process of matching expense and revenue to accounting periods involves considerable estimation and judgment and, like the inventory example, affects the outcome of the financial statement numbers.

Furthermore, financial statements are prepared on certain dates at the end of accounting periods, such as a year or a quarter. Whereas the firm's life is continuous, financial data must be appropriated to particular time periods.

The Future of Financial Statements

The accounting principles that underlie the preparation of financial statements have been complex historically. U.S. accounting rules established by the FASB have been perceived as being more complex than international standards developed by the IASB. The tendency of FASB has been to develop rules with a significant amount of detail, whereas the IASB has used a broader principles-based approach. As the FASB and the IASB work jointly toward one set of accounting standards, the set of rules that evolves may change significantly. The FASB and IASB have already agreed on some rule changes, but there are controversial issues yet to be resolved. Significant changes being worked on in 2009 (as the book goes to print) include lease accounting, classification of financial instruments, inventory accounting, and revenue recognition. Another important project is the reformatting of the financial statements. FASB has not yet decided on a new format for financial statements, but has made public a proposed format that would require the income statement, balance sheet, and cash flow statement to show five general categories: business, discontinued operations, financing, income taxes, and equity. Each category would have its own subtotal. Within each of the categories, a breakdown of operating versus investing assets and liabilities is also being considered. These subcategories would also have their own subtotals.[8] Obviously, if these changes are agreed to and implemented, financial statements will look different from current GAAP-based statements.

QUALITY OF FINANCIAL REPORTING

It has already been pointed out that management has considerable discretion within the overall framework of GAAP. As a result, the potential exists for management to "manipulate" the bottom line (profit or loss) and other accounts in financial statements. Ideally, financial statements should reflect an accurate picture of a company's financial condition and performance. The information should be useful both to assess the past and predict the future. The sharper and clearer the picture presented through the financial data and the closer that picture is to financial reality, the higher is the quality of the financial statements and reported earnings.

Many opportunities exist for management to affect the quality of financial statements. While Chapter 5 covers the quality of financial reporting in detail, some illustrations follow.

Timing of Revenue and Expense Recognition

One of the generally accepted accounting principles that provides the foundation for preparing financial statements is the matching principle: Expenses are matched with the generation of revenues to determine net income for an accounting period. Reference was made earlier to the fact that published financial statements are based on the accrual rather than the cash basis of accounting,

---

[8] Marie Leone, "The Sums of All Parts: Redesigning Financials," *CFO.com*, November 14, 2007.

which means that revenues are recognized when earned and expenses are recognized when incurred, regardless of when the cash inflows and outflows occur. This matching process involves judgments by management regarding the timing of expense and revenue recognition. Although accounting rules provide guidelines helpful in making the necessary and appropriate allocations, these rules are not always precise.

For example, suppose that a company learns near the end of an accounting period that a material accounts receivable is probably uncollectible. When will the account be written off as a loss—currently, or in the next accounting period when a final determination is made? Pose the same question for obsolete inventory sitting on the warehouse shelves gathering dust. These are areas involving sometimes arbitrary managerial decisions. Generally speaking, the more conservative management is in making such judgments (conservatism usually implies the choice that is least favorable to the firm), the higher the quality of earnings resulting from the matching of revenues and expenses in a given accounting period.

Discretionary Items

Many expenditures made by a business firm are discretionary in nature. Management exercises control over the budget level and timing of expenditures for the repair and maintenance of machinery and equipment, marketing and advertising, research and development, and capital expansion. Policies are also flexible with respect to the replacement of plant assets, the development of new product lines, and the disposal of an operating division. Each choice regarding these discretionary items has both an immediate and a long-term impact on profitability, perhaps not in the same direction. A company might elect to defer plant maintenance in order to boost current period earnings; ultimately, the effect of such a policy could be detrimental.

For some industries, such as beverages and retail marketing, advertising and marketing expenditures are essential to gaining and maintaining market share. Research and development can be critical for ongoing success of industries such as computing and electronics, health, and auto.

The financial analyst should carefully scrutinize management's policies with respect to these discretionary items through an examination of expenditure trends (absolute and relative amounts) and comparison with industry competitors. Such an analysis can provide insight into a company's existing strengths and weaknesses and contribute to an assessment of its ability to perform successfully in the future.

THE JOURNEY THROUGH THE MAZE CONTINUES

Numerous other examples exist to illustrate the difficulty in finding and interpreting financial statement information. Many such examples are discussed in the chapters that follow. Annual reports provide a wealth of useful information, but finding what is relevant to financial decision making may involve overcoming mazelike challenges. The remaining chapters in this book are intended to help readers find and effectively use the information in financial statements and supplementary data.

Self-Test

Solutions are provided in Appendix B.

_____ 1. Why should an individual learn to read and interpret financial statements?
   (a) Understanding financial statements will guarantee at least a 20% return on investments.
   (b) An individual need not learn to read and interpret financial statements because auditors offer a report indicating whether the company is financially sound or not.
   (c) Learning to read and interpret financial statements will enable individuals to gain employment.
   (d) Individuals cannot necessarily rely on auditors and management of firms to offer honest information about the financial well-being of firms.

_____ 2. Which of the following organizations write accounting rules?
   (a) FASB and Congress.
   (b) EDGAR and IASB.
   (c) FASB, SEC, and IASB.
   (d) SOX, SEC, and IASB.

_____ 3. What is the goal of the IASB?
   (a) To have worldwide acceptance of a set of international financial reporting standards.
   (b) To create a set of accounting rules that Europe and the United States will follow.
   (c) To create a set of accounting rules for countries other than the United States.
   (d) To work with the SEC to create a set of accounting rules for publicly held companies.

_____ 4. What are the basic financial statements provided in an annual report?
   (a) Balance sheet and income statement.
   (b) Statement of financial earnings and statement of stockholders' equity.
   (c) Balance sheet, income statement, and statement of cash flows.
   (d) Balance sheet, income statement, statement of cash flows, and statement of stockholders' equity.

_____ 5. What items are included in the notes to the financial statements?
   (a) Summary of accounting policies.
   (b) Changes in accounting policies, if any.
   (c) Detail about particular accounts.
   (d) All of the above.

_____ 6. What does an unqualified auditor's report indicate?
- (a) The financial statements unfairly and inaccurately present the company's financial position for the accounting period.
- (b) The financial statements present fairly the financial position, the results of operations, and the changes in cash flows for the company.
- (c) There are certain factors that might impair the firm's ability to continue as a going concern.
- (d) Certain managers within the firm are unqualified and, as such, are not fairly or adequately representing the interests of the shareholders.

_____ 7. Which of the following statements is false?
- (a) The Sarbanes-Oxley Act of 2002 was the cause of the demise of Enron.
- (b) The FASB and the IASB are working closely to develop a set of accounting rules that would ultimately be used by all publicly traded companies worldwide.
- (c) The Public Company Accounting Oversight Board is responsible for monitoring auditors of all publicly owned companies.
- (d) The Sarbanes-Oxley Act of 2002 requires the chief executive officer and the chief financial officer of a publicly traded company to certify the accuracy of the financial statements.

_____ 8. What does Section 404 of the Sarbanes-Oxley Act of 2002 require?
- (a) A ten-year jail sentence and $1 million fine for violations of the act.
- (b) Rotation of audit partners every five years.
- (c) A statement by the company regarding the effectiveness of internal controls and a disclosure of any material weaknesses in a firm's internal control system.
- (d) Auditor independence, which prohibits audit firms from offering any services other than audit services.

_____ 9. What subject(s) should the management discussion and analysis section discuss?
- (a) Liquidity.
- (b) Commitments for capital expenditures.
- (c) A breakdown of sales increases into price and volume components.
- (d) All of the above.

_____ 10. Which of the following statements is true?
- (a) Annual reports only contain glossy pictures.
- (b) Public relations material should be used cautiously.
- (c) Market data refers to the advertising budget of a firm.
- (d) The shareholders' letter should be ignored.

_____ 11. What information can be found in a proxy statement?
- (a) Information on voting procedures.
- (b) Information on executive compensation.
- (c) Information on the breakdown of audit and nonaudit fees paid to the audit firm.
- (d) All of the above.

———— **12.** Which information is hard to find or missing from the financial statements?

(a) Total long-term debt.

(b) Net income.

(c) Five-year summary of selected financial data.

(d) Reputation of the firm with its customers.

———— **13.** What is the accrual basis of accounting?

(a) Recognition of revenue when it is received in cash.

(b) Recognition of revenue in the accounting period when the sale is made rather than when cash is received.

(c) Matching expenses with revenue in the appropriate accounting period.

(d) Both (b) and (c).

———— **14.** Which of the following are methods by which management can manipulate earnings and possibly lower the quality of reported earnings?

(a) Changing an accounting policy to increase earnings.

(b) Refusing to take a loss on inventory in an accounting period when the inventory is known to be obsolete.

(c) Decreasing discretionary expenses.

(d) All of the above.

15. Where would you find the following information?

———— (1) An attestation to the fairness of financial statements.

———— (2) Summary of significant accounting policies.

———— (3) Cash flow from operating, financing, and investing activities.

———— (4) A qualified opinion.

———— (5) Information about principal, interest, and maturity of long-term debt.

———— (6) Financial position on a particular date.

———— (7) Discussion of the company's results of operations.

———— (8) Description of pension plans.

———— (9) Anticipated commitments for capital expenditures.

———— (10) Reconciliation of beginning and ending balances of equity accounts.

(a) Financial statements.

(b) Notes to the financial statements.

(c) Auditor's report.

(d) Management discussion and analysis.

Study Questions, Problems, and Cases

1.1 What types of questions can be answered by analyzing financial statements?

1.2 What is the difference between an annual report and a 10-K report?

1.3 What are the particular items an analyst should review and study in an annual report, and what material should be read with caution?

1.4 What organization has legal authority to set accounting policies in the United States? Does this organization write most of the accounting rules in the United States? Explain.

1.5 Describe the financial statements that are contained in an annual report or Form 10-K.

1.6 Explain the importance of the notes to the financial statements.

1.7 What causes an auditor's report to be qualified? adverse? a disclaimer of opinion? unqualified with explanatory language?

1.8 Why is the management discussion and analysis useful to the financial analyst?

1.9 What is a proxy statement, and why is it important to the analyst?

1.10 What are the intangible factors that are important in evaluating a company's financial position and performance but are not available in the annual report?

1.11 Writing Skills Problem

Staff members from the marketing department of your firm are doing a splendid job selling products to customers. Many of the customers are so pleased, in fact, they are also buying shares in the company's stock, which means that they receive a copy of the firm's annual report. Unfortunately, questions sometimes arise that the marketing staff members are woefully inadequate at answering. Technical questions about the firm's financial condition and performance are referred to the chief financial officer, but the director of marketing has asked you to write a memo in which you explain the key elements in an annual report so that marketing representatives are better prepared to respond to questions of a more general nature.

Required: Write a memo no longer than one page (single-spaced, double-spaced between paragraphs) in which you describe the contents of an annual report so that marketing personnel can understand the basic requirements. The memo should be dated and addressed to B. R. Neal, Director of Marketing, from you; the subject is "Contents of an Annual Report."

To the Student: In business writing, the primary elements are *clarity* and *conciseness*. You must keep in mind the audience you are addressing and the objective of the communication.

1.12 Research Problem

Research the FASB project to redesign the format of the financial statements. Write a short essay outlining the current status of the project and the expected changes to financial statements.

1.13 Internet Problem

Access the SEC Web site: http://www.sec.gov/. Write a one-page summary explaining the items that a financial analyst might find useful at this Web site.

1.14 Intel Case

The 2007 Intel Annual Report can be found at the following Web site: www
.prenhall.com/fraser. Using the annual report, answer the following
questions:

(a) Describe the type of business in which Intel operates.

(b) Read the letters from the CEO and the chairman and discuss any information learned from this letter that might be useful to an analyst.

(c) What type of audit opinion was given for the financial statements and
the internal financial controls of Intel? Explain the key items discussed
in the audit report.

(d) Read the Management Discussion and Analysis (MD&A). Discuss
whether the items that should be addressed in the MD&A are included.
Support your answer with examples from the Intel MD&A.

(e) After reading the MD&A, discuss the future prospects of Intel. Do you
have any concerns? If so, describe those concerns.

1.15 Eastman Kodak Comprehensive Analysis Case Using the Financial Statement Analysis Template

Each chapter in the textbook contains a continuation of this problem. The
objective is to learn how to do a comprehensive financial statement analysis
in steps as you learn the content of each chapter.

(a) The financial statement analysis template can be found at the following
Web site: www.prenhall.com/fraser. Once you have linked to the template you should see a window that asks whether you want to enable the
macros. You must click on "Enable Macros" to use the template. (You may
have to change the security setting on your computer in order to use this
feature.) Familiarize yourself with the instructions. The tab for the instructions is at the bottom of your screen and is labeled "ReadMe." Print out a
copy of the instructions to be used for all Eastman Kodak problems in
each chapter of the text. Click on the link at the bottom of the screen
labeled "Cover." Enter all of the required data in the template for Eastman
Kodak. Use the instructions to help you locate the necessary information.
The amount for "Rent Expense" can be found in Note 11 under the head-
ing "Other Commitments and Contingencies." When filling in the cash
flow data use the cash flow numbers for continuing operations only. Print
the cover sheet when it is completed. Save the template on your computer
or a disk in order to use it with subsequent problems in later chapters.

(b) Access newspaper and periodical articles about Eastman Kodak to learn
of any information that would be helpful in understanding the company's financial condition as well as future plans. Summarize what you
learn in a short paper.

(c) Access the 2007 Eastman Kodak Annual Report and Form 10-K at www
.prenhall.com/fraser and use these two reports to do the following:

Review Items 1, 3, and 4 of the Form 10-K as well as the Report of
Independent Registered Public Accounting Firm found in Item 8. Write a
concise summary of the important items learned from reading these items.

Note: Keep all information from this problem in a notebook or folder to be
used with the Eastman Kodak problems in later chapters.

1.16 Hasbro, Inc. Case
Required
Locate the Form 10-K for Hasbro, Inc. using the EDGAR database at the SEC Web site: www.sec.gov/. Answer the following questions using Hasbro's Form 10-K.
1. What is Hasbro's fiscal year-end date in 2007?
2. Briefly state the line of business within which Hasbro, Inc. operates.
3. Find the following items in Hasbro's Form 10-K and indicate the page number(s) where the items can be found:

a. Balance sheet
b. Income statement
c. Statement of cash flows
d. Statement of stockholders' equity
e. Notes to the financial statements

f. Management Discussion and Analysis
g. Summary of selected financial data
h. Market data (stock prices)
i. Auditor's report
j. Auditor's report on internal controls

4. What public accounting firm conducted the audit for Hasbro, Inc.?
5. Using the most recent year's information, fill in the amounts for the following items from the financial statements:
   a. Assets = Liabilities + Stockholders' equity
   b. Net sales or net revenues
   c. Net income or loss
   d. Cash increase or decrease
   e. Retained earnings balance

1.17 Biolase Technology, Inc. Case
Excerpts from the Management Discussion and Analysis of Financial Condition and Results of Operations (MD&A) of Biolase Technology, Inc., 2007 Form 10-K are found on pages 30–35.
Required
1. Why is the MD&A section of the annual report useful to the financial analyst? What types of information can be found in this section?
2. Using the excerpts from the MD&A of Biolase Technology, Inc. 2007 Form 10-K, discuss whether each of the items that should be discussed in an MD&A are, in fact, presented in this section. Give examples to support your answer.
3. Evaluate the overall quality of the information presented by Biolase Technology, Inc. in the MD&A.
4. Based on this section only, what is your assessment of the prospects for this company?

Excerpts From Management's Discussion and Analysis of Financial Condition and Results of Operations

Overview

We are a medical technology company that develops, manufactures and markets lasers and related products focused on technologies for improved applications and procedures in dentistry and medicine. In particular, our principal products provide dental laser systems that allow dentists, periodontists, endodontists, oral surgeons and other specialists to perform a broad range of dental procedures, including cosmetic and complex surgical applications. Our systems are designed to provide clinically superior performance for many types of dental procedures, with less pain and faster recovery times than are generally achieved with drills, scalpels and other dental instruments. We have clearance from the U.S. Food and Drug Administration, or FDA, to market our laser systems in the United States and also have the necessary approvals to sell our laser systems in Canada, the European Union and certain other international markets. Since 1998, we have sold approximately 6,300 Waterlase systems including over 2,700 Waterlase MD systems and more than 9,500 laser systems in total in over 50 countries.

We offer two categories of laser system products: (i) Waterlase system and (ii) Diolase system. Our flagship product category, the Waterlase system, uses a patented combination of water and laser to perform most procedures currently performed using dental drills, scalpels and other traditional dental instruments for cutting soft and hard tissue. We also offer our Diolase family of diode laser system products to perform soft tissue and cosmetic procedures, including tooth whitening.

On August 8, 2006, we entered into a License and Distribution Agreement with Henry Schein, Inc., or HSIC, a large distributor of healthcare products to office-based practitioners, pursuant to which we granted HSIC the exclusive right to distribute our complete line of dental laser systems, accessories and services in the United States and Canada.

Year Ended December 31, 2007 Compared With Year Ended December 31, 2006

Net Revenue.   Net revenue for the year ended December 31, 2007 was $66.9 million, a decrease of $2.8 million, or 4%, as compared with net revenue of $69.7 million for the year ended December 31, 2006. Laser system net revenues decreased by approximately 7% in 2007 compared to 2006.

Non-laser system net revenue, which includes consumable products, advanced training programs and extended service contracts and shipping revenue, decreased by approximately 18% for the year ended December 31, 2007 as compared to the same period of 2006. The decrease in non-laser system net revenue is primarily attributed to the recognition in 2006 of $1.3 million of revenue related to training credits that expired during 2006 compared with $164,000 of similar revenue in 2007. Additionally, consumable product sales decreased approximately 9% in 2007 compared to 2006. Training and shipping revenue also decreased partially offset by an increase in revenue related to the sale of extended service contracts.

Sales of our Waterlase systems comprised 68% and 79% of our net revenue for the years ended December 31, 2007 and 2006, respectively, while sales of our Diolase family of laser systems comprised 14% and 5% of our revenue for the years ended December 31, 2007 and 2006, respectively. The increase in Diolase revenue is mainly attributed to the launch of our *ezlase* soft tissue diode laser system in the first quarter of 2007.

Domestic revenues were $41.6 million, or 62% of net revenue, for the year ended December 31, 2007 versus $43.7 million, or 63% of net revenue, for the year ended December 31, 2006. International revenues for 2007 were $25.3 million, or 38% of net revenues for 2007 compared to $26.0 million, or 37% of net revenue for 2006.

We believe that there were various factors which, in the aggregate, had a negative effect on laser system sales in 2007 compared to 2006. General economic conditions with respect to credit availability may have caused dentists considering the purchase of a Waterlase MD laser system to postpone their purchase decision. Additionally, we believe that a variety of sales and marketing execution issues, which led to a management change in November 2007, negatively affected our Waterlase MD system sales.

License fees and royalty income increased to $3.8 million for 2007 from $848,000 for 2006, reflecting the amortization of license fees and related payments received from HSIC and P&G.

Gross Profit.   Gross profit for the year ended December 31, 2007 was $34.5 million, or 52% of net revenue, a decrease of $2.0 million, as compared with gross profit of $36.5 million, or 52% of net revenue for the year ended December 31, 2006. Gross profit excluding license fees and royalty revenue was 49% of products and service revenue for 2007 compared to 52% for 2006. Fixed expenses included in cost of revenue represented a higher percentage of the comparatively lower revenues year over year, resulting in a lower margin on products and services revenue.

Other Income, Net.   Other income consists of gain (loss) on sale of assets. There was no other income, net for the year ended December 31, 2007 compared to $6,000 for the year ended December 31, 2006.

Operating Expenses.   Operating expenses for the year ended December 31, 2007 were $43.5 million, or 65% of net revenue, a $2.2 million increase as compared with $41.3 million, or 59% of net revenue for the year ended December 31, 2006. The increase was driven mainly by convention, seminar, and travel and entertainment expenses described below under *Sales and Marketing Expense* and severance-related expenses as described below under *Restructuring Charge.*

Sales and Marketing Expense.   Sales and marketing expenses for the year ended December 31, 2007 increased by $2.2 million, or approximately 9%, to $26.6 million, or 40% of net revenue, as compared with $24.4 million, or 35% of net revenue, for the year ended December 31, 2006. Convention and seminar expenses increased by $2.0 million in 2007 compared to 2006, and travel and entertainment expenses increased by $670,000 compared to 2006. These increases were partially offset by a $282,000 decrease in payroll related costs primarily due to lower commission expense on decreased sales. While we expect to continue investing in sales and marketing expenses and programs in order to grow our revenues, we believe it is likely that these expenses, excluding commissions, will decrease in 2008 compared to 2007.

General and Administrative Expense.   General and administrative expenses for the year ended December 31, 2007 decreased by $768,000, or 7%, to $10.9 million, or 16% of net revenue, as compared with $11.7 million, or 17% of net revenue, for the year ended December 31, 2006. The decrease in general and administrative expenses resulted primarily from a $1.2 million decrease in the accounts receivable bad debt expense largely due to improved collections from international customers and a $226,000 decrease in legal, regulatory, and consulting expenses. This decrease was offset partially by an increase in audit fees of $463,000 related to increased 2006 audit fees incurred in 2007 and recruiting fees of approximately $209,000 incurred in connection with our search for a new Chief Executive Officer. We believe that our general and administrative expenses are likely to increase nominally in 2008.

Engineering and Development Expense.   Engineering and development expenses for the year ended December 31, 2007 increased by $228,000, or 5%, to $5.1 million, or 8% of net revenue, as compared with $4.9 million, or 7% of net revenue, for the year ended December 31, 2006. The increase was primarily related to an increase in payroll related expenses of $316,000. We expect to invest in more development projects and personnel in 2008, and accordingly it is probable that our engineering and development expenses will increase in 2008.

Restructuring Charge.   Restructuring expense for the year ended December 31, 2007 amounted to $802,000, or 1% of net revenue. We incurred no restructuring expense in 2006. The 2007 expense is primarily due to severance-related costs incurred in the fourth quarter of 2007 in connection with the terminations of our President and Chief Executive Officer and our Executive Vice President, Global Sales and Marketing which were both effective November 5, 2007. In the fourth quarter of 2007, we also terminated eleven other employees, across all functions, in an effort to better rationalize resources and streamline operations.

Patent Infringement Legal Settlement.   In January 2005, we acquired the intellectual property portfolio of Diodem, consisting of certain U.S. and international patents of which four were asserted against us, and settled the existing litigation between us and Diodem, for consideration of $3.0 million in cash, 361,664 shares of our common stock, and a five-year warrant to purchase 81,037 shares of common stock at an exercise price of $11.06 per share. In connection with the Diodem patent litigation settlement, 45,208 shares of our common stock were issued to Diodem and placed in an escrow account. In July 2006, we released these shares from escrow and accordingly, we recorded a $348,000 charge based on the fair market value of our common stock.

Non-Operating Income (Loss)

Gain (Loss) on Foreign Currency Transactions.   We realized a $1.4 million gain on foreign currency transactions for the year ended December 31, 2007 due to our treatment of intercompany balances as short-term, compared to a $251,000 gain on foreign currency transactions for the year ended December 31, 2006. The increase is due to changes in exchange rates between the U.S. dollar and the Euro and the Australian and New Zealand dollar and an increase in foreign currency denominated transactions and balances in 2007 compared to 2006. We have not engaged in hedging transactions to offset foreign currency fluctuations. Therefore, we are at risk for changes in the value of the dollar relative to the value of these foreign currencies.

Interest Income.   Interest income results from interest earned on our cash and investments balances. Interest income for the year ended December 31, 2007 was $580,000 as compared to $448,000 for the year ended December 31, 2006.

Interest Expense.   Interest expense consists primarily of interest on outstanding balances on our line of credit, standby fees under the line of credit, and the periodic use of the line during the year. Interest expense for the year ended December 31, 2007 was $81,000 as compared to $388,000 for the year ended December 31, 2006, given borrowings were lower in 2007 as compared to 2006.

Income Taxes.   An income tax provision of $163,000 was recognized for the year ended December 31, 2007 as compared to $162,000 for the year ended December 31, 2006. As of December 31, 2007, we had net operating loss carryforwards for federal and state purposes of approximately $55.8 million and $23.2 million, respectively, which will begin expiring in 2008. As of December 31, 2007, we had research and development credit carryforwards for federal and state purposes of approximately $804,000 and $447,000, respectively, which will begin expiring in 2011 for federal purposes and will carryforward indefinitely for state purposes. The utilization of net operating loss and credit carryforwards may be limited under the provisions of Internal Revenue Code Section 382 and similar state provisions.

Liquidity and Capital Resources

At December 31, 2007, we had approximately $11.0 million in net working capital, a decrease of $6.3 million from $17.3 million at December 31, 2006. Our principal sources of liquidity at December 31, 2007 consisted of our cash and cash equivalents balance of $14.6 million and a $10.0 million revolving bank line of credit with Comerica Bank (the "Lender") of which $3.6 million was utilized as of December 31, 2007 at an interest rate of 7.5% (based on prime rate plus 0.25% as of that date). This balance was subsequently paid in full on January 2, 2008. Advances under the revolving bank line of credit may not exceed the lesser of $10.0 million or the Borrowing Base (80% of eligible accounts receivable and 35% of eligible inventory), less any amounts outstanding under letters of credit or foreign exchange contract reserves. Notwithstanding the foregoing, advances of up to $6.0 million may be made without regard to the Borrowing Base. On October 5, 2007, we entered into an Amendment to the Loan Agreement which extends the agreement for an additional year. The entire unpaid principal amount plus any accrued but unpaid interest and all other amounts due under the Loan Agreement are due and payable in full on September 28, 2009, but can be extended by us for an additional year upon Lender approval. Our obligations under the line bear interest on the outstanding daily balance at our choice of either: (i) LIBOR plus 2.50%, or (ii) prime rate plus 0.25%. As security for the payment and performance of our obligations under the Loan Agreement, we granted the Lender a first priority security interest in certain collateral, which excludes intellectual property.

The line of credit requires compliance with certain financial covenants, including: (i) minimum effective tangible net worth; (ii) maximum leverage ratio; (iii) minimum cash amount at the Lender of $6.0 million; and (iv) minimum liquidity ratio. The line also contains covenants that require the Lender's prior written consent for us, among other things, to: (i) transfer any part of our business or property; (ii) make any changes in our location or name, or replace our CEO or CFO; (iii) consummate mergers or acquisitions; (iv) incur liens; or, (v) pay dividends or repurchase stock. The line contains customary events of default, any one of which will result in the right of the Lender to, among other things, accelerate all obligations under the line, set-off obligations under the line against any of our balances or deposits held by the Lender, or sell the collateral. We have obtained the Lender's consent for the termination of our former CEO in November 2007, the resignation of our former CFO in January 2008, the appointment of our successor CEO in January 2008 and the appointment of our interim CFO in February 2008 and were in compliance with all other covenants as of December 31, 2007.

For the year ended December 31, 2007, our operating activities used cash of approximately $3.3 million, compared to cash provided by operations of $425,000 for 2006. Cash flows from operating activities in 2007 were negatively impacted by the higher net loss in 2007 compared to 2006 as explained under *"Results of Operations"*. Operating cash flows in 2006 also benefited from the cash infusion from the Procter & Gamble and HSIC transactions. We received a one-time payment from The Procter & Gamble Company, or P&G, of $3.0 million for a license to certain of our patents pursuant to a binding letter agreement, subsequently replaced by a definitive agreement effective January 24, 2007, and a separate one-time payment from HSIC of $5.0 million. Both amounts were initially recorded as deferred revenue when received. In the event of a material uncured breach of the P&G definitive agreement by us, we could be required to refund certain payments made to us under the agreement, including the $3.0 million payment. We cannot assure you that we will not have to return all or a portion of the $3.0 million payment to P&G.

The most significant change in operating assets and liabilities for the year ended December 31, 2007 as reported in our Consolidated Statements of Cash Flow was a decrease in accounts receivable of $4.4 million (before the change in allowance for doubtful accounts). The benefit from the reduction in accounts receivable was partially offset by a $779,000 increase in prepaid expenses and other current assets, a $1.8 million decrease in deferred revenue and a $1.1 million decrease in accounts payable and accrued liabilities. Net changes in operating assets and liabilities for 2006 were $137,000 primarily comprised of an increase in accounts receivable of $7.7 million largely offset by an increase in deferred revenue of $7.5 million.

Effective November 5, 2007, we terminated the employment of Jeffrey W. Jones, our President and Chief Executive Officer. On January 30, 2008, we entered into a Separation and General Release Agreement with Mr. Jones relating to the termination of his employment. The agreement superseded the Employment Agreement we had with Mr. Jones dated December 29, 2005. Pursuant to the terms of the agreement, we agreed to pay Mr. Jones a severance amount of $374,822 and pay COBRA premiums on his behalf of $1,712 per month for the period from December 2007 through February 2008. The severance amount was subsequently paid on February 2, 2008.

Following the termination of Mr. Jones, we appointed Federico Pignatelli, one of our current directors and Chairman Emeritus, as Interim President and Chief Executive Officer. Mr. Pignatelli subsequently resigned his position as Interim Chief Executive Officer in January 2008 following the appointment of Jake St. Philip as our Chief Executive Officer. Mr. Pignatelli will remain our President in 2008 for which he will receive a salary of $150,000.

Effective November 5, 2007, we terminated the employment of Keith G. Bateman, our Executive Vice President, Global Sales and Marketing. On January 22, 2008, we entered into a Separation and General Release Agreement with Mr. Bateman relating to the termination of his employment. Pursuant to the terms of the agreement, we agreed to pay Mr. Bateman a severance amount of $187,263 and pay COBRA premiums on his behalf of $1,311 per month for the period from December 2007 through May 2008. The severance amount was subsequently paid on January 31, 2008.

Mr. St. Philip has an employment agreement that obligates us to pay him severance benefits under certain conditions, including termination without cause and resignation with good reason. In the event Mr. St. Philip is terminated by us without cause or he resigns with good reason, the total severance benefits payable would be approximately $600,000 based on compensation in effect as of January 2, 2008, the date Mr. St. Philip was appointed as our current CEO. In addition to Mr. St. Philip, certain other members of management are entitled to severance benefits payable upon termination following a change in control, which would approximate $2.2 million. Also, we have agreements with certain employees to pay bonuses based on targeted performance criteria.

We believe we currently possess sufficient resources, including amounts available under our revolving bank line of credit, to meet the cash requirements of our operations for at least the next year. Our capital requirements will depend on many factors, including, among other things, the effects of any acquisitions we may pursue as well as the rate at which our business grows, with corresponding demands for working capital and manufacturing capacity. We could be required or may elect to seek additional funding through public or private equity or debt financing. However, the extended credit facility, or additional funds through public or private equity or other debt financing, may not be available on terms acceptable to us or at all.

2

The Balance Sheet

Old accountants never die; they just lose their balance.

—Anonymous

A balance sheet, also called the *statement of condition* or *statement of financial position,* provides a wealth of valuable information about a business firm, particularly when examined over a period of several years and evaluated in relation to the other financial statements. A prerequisite to learning what the balance sheet can teach us, however, is a fundamental understanding of the accounts in the statement and the relationship of each account to the financial statements as a whole.

Consider, for example, the balance sheet *inventory* account. Inventory is an important component of liquidity analysis, which considers the ability of a firm to meet cash needs as they arise. (Liquidity analysis will be discussed in Chapter 6.) Any measure of liquidity that includes inventory as a component would be meaningless without a general understanding of how the balance sheet inventory amount is derived. This chapter will thus cover such issues as what inventories are, how the inventory balance is affected by accounting policies, why companies choose and sometimes change methods of inventory valuation, where to find disclosures regarding inventory accounting, and how this one account contributes to the overall measurement of a company's financial condition and operating performance. This step-by-step descriptive treatment of inventories and other balance sheet accounts will provide the background necessary to analyze and interpret balance sheet information.

FINANCIAL CONDITION

The balance sheet shows the financial condition or financial position of a company *on a particular date.* The statement is a summary of what the firm *owns* (assets) and what the firm *owes* to outsiders (liabilities) and to internal owners (stockholders' equity). By definition, the account balances on a balance sheet must balance; that is, the total of all assets must equal the sum of liabilities and stockholders' equity. The balancing equation is expressed as:

Assets = Liabilities + Stockholders' equity.

This chapter will cover account by account the consolidated balance sheet of Recreational Equipment and Clothing, Inc. (R.E.C. Inc.) (Exhibit 2.1). This particular firm sells recreational products through retail outlets, some owned and some leased, in cities located throughout the southwestern United States. Although the accounts on a balance sheet will vary somewhat by firm and by industry, those described in this chapter will be common to most companies.

Consolidation

Note first that the statements are "consolidated" for R.E.C. Inc. and subsidiaries. When a parent owns more than 50% of the voting stock of a subsidiary, the financial statements are combined for the companies even though they are separate legal entities. The statements are consolidated because the companies are *in substance* one company, given the proportion of control by the parent. In the case of R.E.C. Inc., the subsidiaries are wholly owned, which means that the parent controls 100% of the voting shares of the subsidiaries. Where less than 100% ownership exists, there are accounts in the consolidated balance sheet and income statement to reflect the minority interest in net assets and income.

Balance Sheet Date

The balance sheet is prepared at a point in time at the end of an accounting period, a year, or a quarter. Most companies, like R.E.C. Inc., use the calendar year with the accounting period ending on December 31. Interim statements would be prepared for each quarter, ending March 31, June 30, and September 30. Some companies adopt a fiscal year ending on a date other than December 31.

The fact that the balance sheet is prepared on a particular date is significant. For example, cash is the first account listed on the balance sheet and represents the amount of cash on December 31; the amount could be materially different on December 30 or January 2.

Comparative Data

Financial statements for only one accounting period would be of limited value because there would be no reference point for determining changes in a company's financial record over time. As part of an integrated disclosure system required by the SEC, the information presented in annual reports to shareholders includes two-year audited balance sheets and three-year audited statements of income and cash flows. The balance sheet for R.E.C. Inc. thus shows the condition of the company at December 31, 2010 and 2009.

Common-Size Balance Sheet

A useful tool for analyzing the balance sheet is a common-size balance sheet. Common-size financial statements are a form of vertical ratio analysis that

EXHIBIT 2.1

R.E.C. Inc. Consolidated Balance Sheets at December 31, 2010 and 2009 (in Thousands)

	2010	2009
Assets		
Current Assets		
Cash	$ 4,061	$ 2,382
Marketable securities (Note A)	5,272	8,004
Accounts receivable, less allowance for doubtful accounts of $448 in 2010 and $417 in 2009	8,960	8,350
Inventories (Note A)	47,041	36,769
Prepaid expenses	512	759
Total current assets	65,846	56,264
Property, Plant, and Equipment (Notes A, C, and E)		
Land	811	811
Buildings and leasehold improvements	18,273	11,928
Equipment	21,523	13,768
	40,607	26,507
Less accumulated depreciation and amortization	11,528	7,530
Net property, plant, and equipment	29,079	18,977
Other Assets (Note A)	373	668
Total Assets	$95,298	$75,909
Liabilities and Stockholders' Equity		
Current Liabilities		
Accounts payable	$14,294	$ 7,591
Notes payable—banks (Note B)	5,614	6,012
Current maturities of long-term debt (Note C)	1,884	1,516
Accrued liabilities	5,669	5,313
Total current liabilities	27,461	20,432
Deferred Federal Income Taxes (Notes A and D)	843	635
Long-Term Debt (Note C)	21,059	16,975
Commitments (Note E)		
Total liabilities	49,363	38,042
Stockholder's Equity		
Common stock, par value $1, authorized, 10,000,000 shares; issued, 4,803,000 shares in 2010 and 4,594,000 shares in 2009 (Note F)	4,803	4,594
Additional paid-in capital	957	910
Retained earnings	40,175	32,363
Total stockholders' equity	45,935	37,867
Total Liabilities and Stockholders' Equity	$95,298	$75,909

The accompanying notes are an integral part of these statements.

allows for comparison of firms with different levels of sales or total assets by introducing a common denominator. Common-size statements are also useful to evaluate trends within a firm and to make industry comparisons. The common-size balance sheet for R.E.C. Inc. is presented in Exhibit 2.2. Information from the

EXHIBIT 2.2

R.E.C. Inc. Common-Size Balance Sheets (Percent)

	2010	2009	2008	2007	2006
Assets					
Current Assets					
Cash	4.3	3.1	3.9	5.1	4.9
Marketable securities	5.5	10.6	14.9	15.3	15.1
Accounts receivable, less allowance for doubtful accounts	9.4	11.0	7.6	6.6	6.8
Inventories	49.4	48.4	45.0	40.1	39.7
Prepaid expenses	0.5	1.0	1.6	2.4	2.6
Total current assets	69.1	74.1	73.0	69.5	69.1
Property, Plant, and Equipment					
Land	0.8	1.1	1.2	1.4	1.4
Buildings and leasehold improvements	19.2	15.7	14.4	14.1	14.5
Equipment	22.6	18.1	17.3	15.9	16.5
Less accumulated depreciation and amortization	(12.1)	(9.9)	(6.9)	(3.1)	(3.0)
Net property, plant, and equipment	30.5	25.0	26.0	28.3	29.4
Other Assets	0.4	0.9	1.0	2.2	1.5
Total Assets	100.0	100.0	100.0	100.0	100.0
Liabilities and Stockholders' Equity					
Current Liabilities					
Accounts payable	15.0	10.0	13.1	11.4	11.8
Notes payable—banks	5.9	7.9	6.2	4.4	4.3
Current maturities of long-term debt	2.0	2.0	2.4	2.4	2.6
Accrued liabilities	5.9	7.0	10.6	7.7	5.7
Total current liabilities	28.8	26.9	32.3	25.9	24.4
Deferred Federal Income Taxes	0.9	0.8	0.7	0.5	0.4
Long-Term Debt	22.1	22.4	16.2	14.4	14.9
Total liabilities	51.8	50.1	49.2	40.8	39.7
Stockholders' Equity					
Common stock	5.0	6.1	6.7	7.3	7.5
Additional paid-in capital	1.0	1.2	1.3	1.6	1.8
Retained earnings	42.2	42.6	42.8	50.3	51.0
Total stockholders' equity	48.2	49.9	50.8	59.2	60.3
Total Liabilities and Stockholders' Equity	100.0	100.0	100.0	100.0	100.0

common-size balance sheet will be used throughout this chapter and also in Chapter 6. A common-size balance sheet expresses each item on the balance sheet as a percentage of total assets. Common-size statements facilitate the internal or structural analysis of a firm. The common-size balance sheet reveals the composition of assets within major categories, for example, cash and cash equivalents relative to other current assets, the distribution of assets in which funds are invested (current, long-lived, intangible), the capital structure of the firm (debt relative to equity), and the debt structure (long-term relative to short-term).

ASSETS

Current Assets

Assets are segregated on a balance sheet according to how they are utilized (Exhibit 2.3). Current assets include cash or those assets expected to be converted into cash within one year or one operating cycle, whichever is longer. The *operating cycle* is the time required to purchase or manufacture inventory, sell the product,

EXHIBIT 2.3

R.E.C. Inc. Consolidated Balance Sheets at December 31, 2010 and 2009 (in Thousands)

	2010	2009
Assets		
Current Assets		
Cash	$ 4,061	$ 2,382
Marketable securities (Note A)	5,272	8,004
Accounts receivable, less allowance for doubtful accounts of $448 in 2007 and $417 in 2006	8,960	8,350
Inventories (Note A)	47,041	36,769
Prepaid expenses	512	759
Total current assets	65,846	56,264
Property, Plant, and Equipment (Notes A, C, and E)		
Land	811	811
Buildings and leasehold improvements	18,273	11,928
Equipment	21,523	13,768
	40,607	26,507
Less accumulated depreciation and amortization	11,528	7,530
Net property, plant, and equipment	29,079	18,977
Other Assets (Note A)	373	668
Total Assets	$95,298	$75,909

and collect the cash. For most companies, the operating cycle is less than one year, but in some industries—such as tobacco and wine—it is longer. The designation "current" refers essentially to those assets that are continually used up and replenished in the ongoing operations of the business. The term *working capital* or *net working capital* is used to designate the amount by which current assets exceed current liabilities (current assets less current liabilities).

Cash and Marketable Securities

These two accounts, shown separately for R.E.C. Inc. in Exhibit 2.3, are often combined as "cash and cash equivalents." The cash account is exactly that, cash in any form—cash awaiting deposit or in a bank account. Marketable securities (also referred to as short-term investments) are cash substitutes, cash that is not needed immediately in the business and is temporarily invested to earn a return. These investments are in instruments with short-term maturities (less than one year) to minimize the risk of interest rate fluctuations. They must be relatively riskless securities and highly liquid so that funds can be readily withdrawn as needed. Instruments used for such purposes include U.S. Treasury bills, certificates, notes, and bonds; negotiable certificates of deposit at financial institutions; and commercial paper (unsecured promissory notes of large business firms). As can be seen on the common-size balance sheet, there has been a change in the amount of cash and marketable securities held by R.E.C. Inc. from 20% in 2006 to less than 10% in 2010. This has resulted in increases to other asset accounts.

The valuation of marketable securities on the balance sheet as well as other investments in debt and equity securities requires the separation of investment securities into three categories depending on the intent of the investment:

1. *Held to maturity* applies to those debt securities that the firm has the positive intent and ability to hold to maturity; these securities are reported at amortized cost. Debt securities are securities representing a creditor relationship, including U.S. Treasury securities, municipal securities, corporate bonds, convertible debt, and commercial paper.[1]
2. *Trading securities* are debt and equity securities that are held for resale in the short term, as opposed to being held to realize longer-term gains from capital appreciation. Equity securities represent an ownership interest in an entity, including common and preferred stock. These securities are reported at *fair value* with unrealized gains and losses included in earnings. Fair value is the price that would be received to sell an asset or the price paid to transfer a liability in an orderly transaction between market participants at the measurement date.[2]
3. *Securities available for sale* are debt and equity securities that are not classified as one of the other two categories, either held to maturity or trading securities.

---

[1] Amortized cost refers to the fact that bonds (a debt security) may sell at a premium or discount because the stated rate of interest on the bonds is different from the market rate of interest; the premium or discount is amortized over the life of the bonds so that at maturity the cost equals the face amount.
[2] "Fair Value Measurements," Statement of Financial Accounting Standards No. 157, 2006.

Securities available for sale are reported at fair value with unrealized gains and losses included in comprehensive income. The cumulative net unrealized gains or losses are reported in the accumulated other comprehensive income section of stockholders' equity.

Statement of Financial Accounting Standards No. 159, "The Fair Value Option for Financial Assets and Financial Liabilities," issued in 2007, permits entities to measure many financial instruments and certain other items at fair value. The statement does not apply, however, to investments in consolidated subsidiaries nor to investments in equity securities that, absent the election of the fair value option under Statement No. 159, would be required to be accounted for under the equity method (discussed in Chapter 3).

This accounting requirement most significantly affects financial institutions and insurance companies, which trade heavily in securities as part of their operating activities. The kinds of securities held by companies such as R.E.C. Inc. under the category "marketable securities" or "cash equivalents" are selected for ready conversion into cash, and they have market values that are equal to or very close to cost, as reported in Note A (see Exhibit 1.2) to the R.E.C. Inc. financial statements. ("Marketable securities consist of short-term, interest-bearing securities stated at cost, which approximates market.") Should values be different from cost, however, the company then would have to determine which category of investment applies. For example, if these kinds of securities were considered to be "available for sale," they would be marked to current value, and cumulative unrealized gains and losses would be carried as a component of stockholders' equity in the balance sheet.

Accounts Receivable

Accounts receivable are customer balances outstanding on credit sales and are reported on the balance sheet at their net realizable value, that is, the actual amount of the account less an *allowance for doubtful accounts*. Management must estimate—based on such factors as past experience, knowledge of customer quality, the state of the economy, the firm's collection policies—the dollar amount of accounts they expect will be uncollectible during an accounting period. Actual losses are written off against the allowance account, which is adjusted at the end of each accounting period.

The allowance for doubtful accounts can be important in assessing earnings quality. If, for instance, a company expands sales by lowering its credit standards, there should be a corresponding percentage increase in the allowance account. The estimation of this account will affect both the valuation of accounts receivable on the balance sheet and the recognition of bad debt expense on the income statement. The analyst should be alert to changes in the allowance account—both relative to the level of sales and the amount of accounts receivable outstanding—and to the justification for any variations from past practices.

The allowance account for R.E.C. Inc. represents approximately 5% of total customer accounts receivable. To obtain the exact percentage figure, the amount of the allowance account must be added to the net accounts receivable balance shown on the face of the statement:

	2010	2009
$\dfrac{\text{Allowance for doubtful accounts}}{\text{Accounts receivable (net) + Allowance}}$	$\dfrac{448}{8,960 + 448} = 4.8\%$	$\dfrac{417}{8,350 + 417} = 4.8\%$

The allowance account, which is deducted from the balance sheet accounts receivable account, should reflect the volume of credit sales, the firm's past experience with customers, the customer base, the firm's credit policies, the firm's collection practices, economic conditions, and changes in any of these. There should be a consistent relationship between the rate of change or growth rates in sales, accounts receivable, and the allowance for doubtful accounts. If the amounts are changing at significantly different rates or in different directions—for example, if sales and accounts receivable are increasing, but the allowance account is decreasing or is increasing at a much smaller rate—the analyst should be alert to the potential for manipulation using the allowance account. Of course, there could be a plausible reason for such a change.

The relevant items needed to relate sales growth with accounts receivable and the allowance for doubtful accounts are found on the income statement (sales) and balance sheet (accounts receivable and allowance for doubtful accounts). The following information is from the income statement and balance sheet of R.E.C. Inc.

(In Thousands)	2010	2009	Growth Rate* (% Change)
Net sales	$215,600	$153,000	40.9
Accounts receivable (total)	9,408	8,767	7.3
Allowance for doubtful accounts	448	417	7.4

*Growth rates are calculated using the following formula: $\dfrac{\text{Current amount} - \text{Prior Amount}}{\text{Prior Amount}}$

To analyze the preceding information consider the following:

- The relationship among changes in sales, accounts receivable, and the allowance for doubtful accounts—are all three accounts changing in the same directions and at consistent rates of change?
- If the direction and rates of change are not consistent, what are possible explanations for these differences?
- If there is not a normal relationship between the growth rates, what are possible reasons for the abnormal pattern?

For R.E.C. Inc., sales, accounts receivable, and the allowance for doubtful accounts have all increased, but sales have grown at a much greater rate. The percentage increase in accounts receivable and the allowance account seems lower than expected relative to the change in sales. This relationship is probably a positive one for R.E.C. Inc. because it means that the company has collected more sales in cash and thus will have potentially fewer defaults. The allowance account has increased appropriately in relation to accounts receivable, 7.4% and 7.3% respectively; the allowance account, relative to accounts receivable, is constant at 4.8% in both years. Had the allowance account decreased, there would be concern that management might be manipulating the numbers to increase the earnings number.

Additional information helpful to the analysis of accounts receivable and the allowance account is provided in the schedule of "Valuation and Qualifying Accounts" required by the SEC in the Form 10-K. Companies sometimes include this schedule in the notes to the financial statements, but usually it is found under Item 15 of the Form 10-K. R.E.C. Inc.'s schedule from the Form 10-K is shown here:

R.E.C. Inc.
Schedule II—Valuation and Qualifying Accounts
December 31, 2010, 2009, and 2008
(in Thousands)

	Balance at Beginning of Year	Additions Charged to Costs and Expenses	Deductions	Balance at End of Year
Allowance for doubtful accounts				
2010	$417	$271	$240	$448
2009	$400	$217	$200	$417
2008	$391	$259	$250	$400

The column labeled "Additions Charged to Costs and Expenses" is the amount R.E.C. Inc. has estimated and recorded as bad debt expense each year on the income statement. The "Deductions" column represents the actual amount that the firm has written off as accounts receivable they no longer expect to recover from customers. Because the expense is estimated each year, this amount also includes corrections of prior years' over- or underestimations. The analyst should use this schedule to assess the probability that the firm is intentionally over- or underestimating the allowance account to manipulate the net earnings number on the income statement. R.E.C. Inc. appears to estimate an expense fairly close to the actual amount written off each year, although the firm has estimated slightly more expense than has actually been incurred. Further analysis of accounts receivable and its quality is covered in Chapters 5 and 6.

Inventories

Inventories are items held for sale or used in the manufacture of products that will be sold. A retail company, such as R.E.C. Inc., lists only one type of inventory on the balance sheet: merchandise inventories purchased for resale to the public. A manufacturing firm, in contrast, would carry three different types of inventories: raw materials or supplies, work-in-process, and finished goods. For most firms, inventories are the firm's major revenue producer. Exceptions would be

EXHIBIT 2.4

Inventories as a Percentage of Total Assets	%
Manufacturing	
Pharmaceutical preparations	20.4
Household furniture	33.3
Sporting and athletic goods	39.6
Wholesale	
Drugs	30.4
Furniture	30.1
Sporting and recreational goods	44.8
Retail	
Pharmacies and drug stores	34.6
Furniture stores	48.9
Sporting goods stores	57.8

Source: Data from The Risk Management Association, Annual Statement Studies, Philadelphia, PA, 2007. © "2008" by RMA-The Risk Management Association. All Rights Reserved. No part of this table may be reproduced or utilized in any form or by any means without permission in writing. Refer to www.rmahq.org for further information.

service-oriented companies that carry little or no inventory. Exhibit 2.4 illustrates the proportion of inventories at the manufacturing, wholesale, and retail levels. For these industries—drugs, household furniture, and sporting goods—the percentage of inventories to total assets ranges from 20.4% to 39.6% at the manufacturing stage to 34.6% to 57.8% for retail firms. The common-size balance sheet (Exhibit 2.2) for R.E.C. Inc. reveals that inventories comprise 49.4% and 48.4% of total assets, respectively, in 2010 and 2009. As mentioned previously, from 2006 to 2010, cash and marketable securities have decreased by approximately 10%. Inventories have increased by almost 10% in this same time frame, indicating a shift in asset structure. Most likely, R.E.C. Inc. has chosen to spend cash to expand. As new stores are opened, they must be stocked with inventory.

Given the relative magnitude of inventory, the accounting method chosen to value inventory and the associated measurement of cost of goods sold have a considerable impact on a company's financial position and operating results. Understanding the fundamentals of inventory accounting and the effect various methods have on a company's financial statements is essential to the user of financial statement information.

Inventory Accounting Methods

The method chosen by a company to account for inventory determines the value of inventory on the balance sheet and the amount of expense recognized for cost of goods sold on the income statement. The significance of inventory accounting is underlined by the presence of inflation and by the implications for tax payments and cash flow. Inventory valuation is based on an *assumption* regarding the flow of goods and has nothing whatever to do with the *actual* order in which products are sold. The cost flow assumption is made in order to *match* the cost of products sold during an accounting period to the revenue generated from the sales and to assign a dollar value to the inventory remaining for sale at the end of the accounting period.

The three cost flow assumptions most frequently used by U.S. companies are *FIFO* (first in, first out), *LIFO* (last in, first out), and *average cost*. As the terms imply, the FIFO method assumes the first units purchased are the first units sold during an accounting period; LIFO assumes that the items bought last are sold first; and the average cost method uses an average purchase price to determine the cost of products sold. A simple example should highlight the differences in the three methods. A new company in its first year of operations purchases five products for sale in the order and at the prices shown:

Item	Purchase Price
#1	$ 5
#2	$ 7
#3	$ 8
#4	$ 9
#5	$11

The company sells three of these items, all at the end of the year. The cost flow assumptions would be:

Accounting Method	Goods Sold	Goods Remaining in Inventory
FIFO	#1, #2, #3	#4, #5
LIFO	#5, #4, #3	#2, #1
Average cost	[Total cost/5] × 3	[Total cost/5] × 2

The resulting effect on the income statement and balance sheet would be:

Accounting Method	Cost of Goods Sold (Income Statement)	Inventory Valuation (Balance Sheet)
FIFO	$20	$20
LIFO	$28	$12
Average cost	$24	$16

It can be clearly seen that during a period of inflation, with product prices increasing, the LIFO method produces the highest cost of goods sold expense

FIGURE 2.1 Inventory Methods.

Accounting Method	Cost of Goods Sold (Income Statement)	Inventory Valuation (Balance Sheet)
FIFO	First purchases	Last purchases (close to current cost)
LIFO	Last purchases (close of current cost)	First purchases
Average Cost	Average of all purchases	Average of all purchases

($28) and the lowest ending valuation of inventory ($12). Further, cost of goods sold under the LIFO method most closely approximates the current cost of inventory items as they are the most recent purchases. On the other hand, inventories on the balance sheet are undervalued with respect to replacement cost because they reflect the older costs when prices were lower. If a firm uses LIFO to value inventory, no restatement is required to adjust cost of goods sold for inflation because LIFO matches current costs to current sales. Inventory on the balance sheet, however, would have to be revalued upward to account for inflation. FIFO has the opposite effect; during a period of rising prices, balance sheet inventory is valued at current cost, but cost of goods sold on the income statement is understated. (See Figure 2.1.)

In an annual survey of accounting practices followed by 600 industrial and merchandising corporations in the United States in the early 1970s, 146 companies surveyed reported using LIFO to account for all or part of inventory. By the 1990s, this number had increased to 326 but then fell to 228 by 2006.[3] Why did so many companies switch to LIFO in the 1990s? The answer is taxes.

Referring back to the example, note that when prices are rising (inflation), LIFO produces the largest cost of goods sold expense: the greater the expense deduction, the lower the taxable income. Use of LIFO thus reduces a company's tax bill during inflation. Unlike the case for some accounting rules—in which a firm is allowed to use one method for tax and another method for reporting purposes—a company that elects LIFO to figure taxable income must also use LIFO for reported income. The many companies that have switched to LIFO from other methods are apparently willing to trade lower reported earnings for the positive cash benefits resulting from LIFO's beneficial tax effect. The evidence, however, is that the trend toward LIFO is reversing and that the number of firms electing FIFO is gradually increasing. Reasons could include both a lower inflation rate and the desire to report higher accounting earnings.

In the earlier example, LIFO produced lower earnings than FIFO or average cost, but there can be exceptions. Obviously, in a *period of falling prices* (deflation) the results would reverse. Also, some firms experience price movements that are

---

[3] *Accounting Trends and Techniques,* American Institute of Certified Public Accountants, 1971, 1998, 2007.

counter to the general trend—the high-technology industry, where prices on many products have declined, is a case in point.[4]

Because the inventory cost flow assumption has a significant impact on financial statements—the amount of inventory reported on the balance sheet and the cost of goods sold expense in the income statement—it is important to know where to find its disclosure. The method used to value inventory will generally be shown in the note to the financial statements relating to inventory. R.E.C. Inc. has the following explanation in Note A: Inventories are carried at the lower of cost (LIFO) or market. This statement indicates that the LIFO method is used to determine cost. The fact that inventories are valued at the lower of cost or market reflects the accounting convention of conservatism. If the actual market value of inventory falls below cost, as determined by the cost flow assumption (LIFO for R.E.C. Inc.), then inventory will be written down to market price. Notice that the phrase is "lower" of cost or market. The carrying value of inventory would never be written up to market value—only down.

The inventory note for R.E.C. Inc. also provides information regarding the value of inventory had FIFO been used, as the FIFO valuation would be higher than that recorded on the balance sheet and more closely approximates current value: "If the first-in, first-out (FIFO) method of inventory accounting had been used, inventories would have been approximately $2,681,000 and $2,096,000 higher than reported at December 31, 2010 and 2009."

Companies are allowed to use more than one inventory valuation method for inventories. For example, a multinational firm may choose to use the LIFO method for inventories in the United States, while using FIFO for inventories overseas. This would not be unusual: LIFO is actually an income tax concept, and the application of LIFO is set forth in the United States Internal Revenue Code, not in United States GAAP. Some countries do not recognize LIFO as an acceptable inventory valuation method, and as such, a firm may find it more convenient for reporting purposes to use methods acceptable in the country in which it operates. Diversified companies may also choose different inventory methods for different product lines. Using FIFO for high-technology products and LIFO for food products would make sense if the firm is trying to reduce taxes, because the technology industry is usually deflationary, whereas the food industry is generally inflationary.

Prepaid Expenses

Certain expenses, such as insurance, rent, property taxes, and utilities, are sometimes paid in advance. They are included in current assets if they will expire within one year or one operating cycle, whichever is longer. Generally, prepayments are not material to the balance sheet as a whole. For R.E.C. Inc., prepaid expenses represent less than 1% of total current assets in 2010.

---

[4] Another exception that causes higher earnings when using LIFO during inflationary periods is a base LIFO layer liquidation. This occurs when a firm sells more goods than purchased or manufactured during an accounting period, resulting in the least expensive items being charged to cost of goods sold. To avoid the LIFO liquidation problem, some firms use the dollar-value LIFO method, which is applied to goods in designated pools and measures inventory changes in cost dollars—using a price index—rather than physical units.

Property, Plant, and Equipment

This category encompasses a company's fixed assets (also called *tangible, long-lived,* and *capital* assets)—those assets not used up in the ebb and flow of annual business operations. These assets produce economic benefits for more than one year, and they are considered "tangible" because they have a physical substance. Fixed assets other than land (which has a theoretically unlimited life span) are "depreciated" over the period of time they benefit the firm. The process of depreciation is a method of allocating the cost of long-lived assets. The original cost, less any estimated residual value at the end of the asset's life, is spread over the expected life of the asset. Cost is also considered to encompass any expenditures made to ready the asset for operating use. On any balance sheet date, property, plant, and equipment is shown at book value, which is the difference between original cost and any accumulated depreciation to date.

Management has considerable discretion with respect to fixed assets. Assume that R.E.C. Inc. purchases an artificial ski mountain, known as the "mythical mountain," for its Houston flagship store in order to demonstrate skis and allow prospective customers to test-run skis on a simulated black diamond course. The cost of the mountain is $50,000. Several choices and estimates must be made to determine the annual depreciation expense associated with the mountain. For example, R.E.C. Inc. management must estimate how long the mountain will last and the amount, if any, of salvage value at the end of its useful life.

Furthermore, management must choose a method of depreciation: The straight-line method allocates an equal amount of expense to each year of the depreciation period, whereas an accelerated method apportions larger amounts of expense to the earlier years of the asset's depreciable life and lesser amounts to the later years.

If the $50,000 mountain is estimated to have a five-year useful life and $0 salvage value at the end of that period, annual depreciation expense would be calculated as follows for the first year.

Straight line

$$\frac{\text{Depreciable base (cost less salvage value)}}{\text{Depreciation period}} = \text{Depreciation expense}$$

$$\frac{\$50,000 - \$0}{5\text{years}} = \$10,000$$

Accelerated[5]

Cost less accumulated depreciation $\times$ twice the straight-line rate = Depreciaton expense

$$\$50,000 \times (2 \times 0.2) = \$20,000$$

---

[5] The example uses the double-declining balance method of figuring accelerated depreciation, which is twice the straight-line rate times the net book value (cost less accumulated depreciation) of the asset. Depreciation for year 2 would be:

Straight line $50,000/5 = $10,000   Accelerated $30,000 $\times$ 0.4 = $12,000

The choices and estimates relating to the depreciation of equipment affect the amounts shown on the financial statements relating to the asset. The fixed asset account on the balance sheet is shown at historical cost less accumulated depreciation, and the annual depreciation expense is deducted on the income statement to determine net income. At the end of year 1, the accounts would be different according to the method chosen:

Straight line

Balance Sheet		Income Statement	
Fixed assets	$50,000	Depreciation expense	$10,000
Less accumulated depreciation	(10,000)		
Net fixed assets	$40,000		

Accelerated

Balance Sheet		Income Statement	
Fixed assets	$50,000	Depreciation expense	$20,000
Less accumulated depreciation	(20,000)		
Net fixed assets	$30,000		

The amounts would also vary if the estimates were different regarding useful life or salvage value. For example, if R.E.C. Inc. management concludes the mountain could be sold to Denver Mountaineering Co. at the end of five years for use in testing snowshoes, the mountain would then have an expected salvage value that would enter into the calculations.

The total amount of depreciation over the asset's life is the same regardless of method, although the rate of depreciation varies. The straight-line method spreads the expense evenly by periods, and the accelerated methods yield higher depreciation expense in the early years of an asset's useful life, and lower depreciation expense in the later years. Another depreciation choice is the units-of-production method, which bases depreciation expense for a given period on actual use. According to *Accounting Trends and Techniques,* the vast majority of companies use the straight-line method for financial reporting:[6]

Straight line	592
Accelerated	48
Units of production	23

Refer now to the property, plant, and equipment section of the R.E.C. Inc. balance sheet. First note that there are three categories listed separately: land, buildings and leasehold improvements, and equipment. *Land,* as designated in the fixed asset section, refers to property used in the business; this would be land on which there are corporate offices and retail stores. Any land held for investment purposes would be segregated from property used in the business. (For R.E.C. Inc., see the "Other Assets" section.)

---

[6] *Accounting Trends and Techniques,* American Institute of Certified Public Accountants, 2007.

R.E.C. Inc. owns some of its retail outlets, and others are leased. *Buildings* would include those stores owned by the company as well as its corporate offices. *Leasehold improvements* are additions or improvements made to leased structures. Because leasehold improvements revert to the property owner when the lease term expires, they are amortized by the lessee over the economic life of the improvement or the life of the lease, whichever is shorter.[7]

Some companies may also have an account called *construction in progress*. These are the costs of constructing new buildings that are not yet complete. R.E.C. Inc. does not include this account on its balance sheet.

Equipment represents the original cost, including delivery and installation charges, of the machinery and equipment used in business operations. Included are a variety of items such as the centralized computer system; equipment and furnishings for offices, stores, and warehouses; and delivery trucks. The final two lines under the property, plant, and equipment section for R.E.C. Inc. show the amount of accumulated depreciation and amortization (for all items except land) and the amount of net property, plant, and equipment after the deduction of accumulated depreciation and amortization.

The relative proportion of fixed assets in a company's asset structure will largely be determined by the nature of the business. A firm that manufactures products would likely be more heavily invested in capital equipment than a retailer or wholesaler. Exhibit 2.5 shows the relative percentage of net fixed assets

EXHIBIT 2.5

Net Fixed Assets as a Percentage of Total Assets	%
Manufacturing	
Pharmaceutical preparations	24.0
Household furniture	23.6
Sporting and athletic goods	14.9
Wholesale	
Drugs	9.7
Furniture	11.9
Sporting and recreational goods	9.5
Retail	
Pharmacies and drug stores	12.8
Furniture stores	19.5
Sporting goods stores	15.9

Source: Data from The Risk Management Association, *Annuamel Statent Studies,* Philadelphia, PA, 2007. © "2008" by RMA-The Risk Management Association. All Rights Reserved. No part of this table may be reproduced or utilized in any form or by any means without permission in writing. Refer to www.rmahq.org for further information.

---

[7] *Amortization* is the term used to designate the cost allocation process for assets other than buildings, machinery, and equipment—such as leasehold improvements and intangible assets, discussed later in the chapter.

to total assets for the same three industries identified in Exhibit 2.4. Realize, however, that firms with newly purchased fixed assets will have a higher percentage than firms with older, and hence lower, net fixed asset numbers.

Fixed assets are most prominent at the manufacturing level; retailers are next, probably because retailers require stores and buildings in which to sell products; and the wholesale segment requires the least investment in fixed assets.

For R.E.C. Inc., net fixed assets have increased in proportion to total assets between 2009 and 2010 from 25.0% to 30.5% as can be seen on the common-size balance sheet (Exhibit 2.2). Chapter 6 covers the financial ratios used to measure the efficiency of managing these assets.

Other Assets

Other assets on a firm's balance sheet can include a multitude of other noncurrent items such as property held for sale, start-up costs in connection with a new business, the cash surrender value of life insurance policies, and long-term advance payments. For R.E.C. Inc., other assets represent minor holdings of property not used in business operations (as explained in Note A to the financial statements).

Additional categories of noncurrent assets frequently encountered (but not present for R.E.C. Inc.) are long-term investments and intangible assets, such as goodwill recognized in business combinations, patents, trademarks, copyrights, brand names, and franchises. Of the intangible assets, *goodwill* is the most important for analytical purposes because of its potential materiality on the balance sheet of firms heavily involved in acquisitions activity. Goodwill arises when one company acquires another company (in a business combination accounted for as a purchase) for a price in excess of the fair market value of the net identifiable assets (identifiable assets less liabilities assumed) acquired. This excess price is recorded on the books of the acquiring company as goodwill. Goodwill must be evaluated annually to determine whether there has been a loss of value. If there is no loss of value, goodwill remains on the balance sheet at the recorded cost indefinitely. If it is determined that the book value or carrying value of goodwill exceeds the fair value, the excess book value must be written off as an impairment expense.

LIABILITIES

Current Liabilities

Liabilities represent claims against assets, and current liabilities are those that must be satisfied in one year or one operating cycle, whichever is longer. Current liabilities include accounts and notes payable, the current portion of long-term debt, accrued liabilities, unearned revenue, and deferred taxes.

Accounts Payable

Accounts payable are short-term obligations that arise from credit extended by suppliers for the purchase of goods and services. For example, when R.E.C. Inc. buys inventory on credit from a wholesaler for eventual sale to its own customers, the transaction creates an account payable.

This account is eliminated when the bill is satisfied. The ongoing process of operating a business results in the spontaneous generation of accounts payable, which increase and decrease depending on the credit policies available to the firm from its suppliers, economic conditions, and the cyclical nature of the firm's own business operations. Note that R.E.C. Inc. has almost doubled the amount of accounts payable between 2009 and 2010 (Exhibit 2.6). Part of the balance sheet analysis should include an exploration of the causes for this increase. To jump briefly ahead, the reader might also note that the income statement reveals a significant sales increase in 2010. Perhaps the increase in accounts payable is at least partially explained by this sales growth.

Notes Payable

Notes payable are short-term obligations in the form of promissory notes to suppliers or financial institutions. For R.E.C. Inc. these notes (explained in Note B to

EXHIBIT 2.6

R.E.C. Inc. Consolidated Balance Sheets at December 31, 2010 and 2009 (in Thousands)

	2010	2009
Liabilities and Stockholders' Equity		
Current Liabilities		
Accounts payable	$14,294	$ 7,591
Notes payable—banks (Note B)	5,614	6,012
Current maturities of long-term debt (Note C)	1,884	1,516
Accrued liabilities	5,669	5,313
Total current liabilities	27,461	20,432
Deferred Federal Income Taxes (Notes A and D)	843	635
Long-term debt (Note C)	21,059	16,975
Commitments (Note E)		
Total liabilities	49,363	38,042
Stockholders' Equity		
Common stock, par value $1, authorized, 10,000,000 shares; issued, 4,803,000 shares in 2010 and 4,594,000 shares in 2009 (Note F)	4,803	4,594
Additional paid-in capital	957	910
Retained earnings	40,175	32,363
Total stockholders' equity	45,935	37,867
Total Liabilities and Stockholders' Equity	$95,298	$75,909

The accompanying notes are an integral part of these statements.

the financial statements) are payable to a bank and reflect the amount extended under a line of credit. A line of credit permits borrowing from a financial institution up to a maximum amount. The total amount that can be borrowed under R.E.C. Inc.'s line of credit is $10 million, of which about half ($5,614,000) was outstanding debt at the end of 2010.

Current Maturities of Long-Term Debt

When a firm has bonds, mortgages, or other forms of long-term debt outstanding, the portion of the principal that will be repaid during the upcoming year is classified as a current liability. The currently maturing debt for R.E.C. Inc. occurs as the result of several long-term obligations, described in Note C to the financial statements. The note lists the amount of long-term debt outstanding, less the portion due currently, and also provides the schedule of current maturities for the next five years.

Accrued Liabilities

Like most large corporations, R.E.C. Inc. uses the accrual rather than the cash basis of accounting: Revenue is recognized when it is earned, and expenses are recorded when they are incurred, regardless of when the cash is received or paid. Accrued liabilities result from the recognition of an expense in the accounting records prior to the actual payment of cash. Thus, they are liabilities because there will be an eventual cash outflow to satisfy the obligations.

Assume that a company has a $100,000 note outstanding, with 12% annual interest due in semiannual installments on March 31 and September 30. For a balance sheet prepared on December 31, interest will be accrued for three months (October, November, and December):

$$\$100,000 \times 0.12 = \$12,000 \text{ annual interest}$$
$$\$12,000/12 = \$1,000 \text{ monthly interest}$$
$$\$1,000 \times 3 = \$3,000 \text{ accrued interest for three months}$$

The December 31 balance sheet would include an accrued liability of $3,000. Accruals also arise from salaries, rent, insurance, taxes, and other expenses.

Reserve accounts are often set up for the purpose of estimating obligations for items such as warranty costs, sales returns, or restructuring charges, and are recorded as accrued liabilities. Generally, the only way to determine whether a company has set up a reserve account is to read the notes to the financial statements carefully. Prior to 2003, many firms appeared to be abusing the use of reserve accounts for restructuring charges. By overestimating the reserve and recording all potential restructuring costs in the period when the decision to restructure was made, companies could later reverse the charge, thus giving a boost to the net earnings number. The SEC's concern regarding this possible abuse resulted in the FASB requiring firms to implement Statement of Financial Accounting Standard No. 146, "Accounting for Costs Associated with Exit or Disposal Activities," effective January 1, 2003. This standard prohibits companies from recognizing a liability for a cost associated with an exit or disposal activity unless and until a liability has actually been incurred. Reserve accounts are also set up to record declines in asset values; the allowance for doubtful accounts explained earlier in the chapter is an example.

Unearned Revenue or Deferred Credits

Companies that are paid in advance for services or products record a liability on the receipt of cash. The liability account is referred to as *unearned revenue* or *deferred credits*. The amounts in this account will be transferred to a revenue account when the service is performed or the product delivered as required by the matching concept of accounting. R.E.C. Inc. does not have unearned revenue because it is a retail company that does not generally receive payment in advance of selling its products. However, companies in high-technology, publishing, or manufacturing industries are apt to have unearned revenue accounts on their balance sheets. For example, Intel Corporation shows $625 million on its 2007 balance sheet for "Deferred income on shipments to distributors." In the footnotes to the financial statements, this account is explained as follows under the heading "Revenue recognition": "We recognize net revenue when the earnings process is complete, as evidenced by an agreement with the customer, transfer of title and acceptance if applicable, as well as fixed pricing and probable collectibility. We record pricing allowances, including discounts based on contractual arrangements with customers, when revenue is recognized as a reduction to both accounts receivable and net revenue. Because of frequent sales price reductions and rapid technology obsolescence in the industry, we defer sales made to distributors under agreements allowing price protection and/or right of return are deferred until the distributors sell the merchandise. We include shipping charges billed to customers in net revenue, and include the related shipping costs in cost of sales."[8]

Deferred Federal Income Taxes

Deferred taxes are the result of temporary differences in the recognition of revenue and expense for taxable income relative to reported income. The accounting principles for recording and reporting deferred taxes are specified in Statement of Financial Accounting Standards No. 109, "Accounting for Income Taxes," which superseded Statement of Financial Accounting Standards No. 96 and is effective for fiscal years beginning after December 15, 1992. Most large companies use one set of rules for calculating income tax expense, paid to the IRS, and another set for figuring income reported in the financial statements. The objective is to take advantage of all available tax deferrals to reduce actual tax payments, while showing the highest possible amount of reported net income. There are many areas in which firms are permitted to use different procedures for tax and reporting purposes. Most firms use an accelerated method of depreciation (the Modified Accelerated Cost Recovery System) to figure taxable income and the straight-line method for reporting purposes. The effect is to recognize more depreciation expense in the early years of an asset's useful life for tax calculations.

---

[8] Intel, 2007 Form 10-K, p. 58.

Although depreciation methods are the most common source, other temporary differences arise from the methods used to account for installment sales, long-term contracts, leases, warranties and service contracts, pensions and other employee benefits, and subsidiary investment earnings. They are called *temporary differences* (or timing differences) because, in theory, the total amount of expense and revenue recognized will eventually be the same for tax and reporting purposes. There are also *permanent differences* in income tax accounting. Municipal bond revenue, for example, is recognized as income for reporting purposes but not for tax purposes; life insurance premiums on officers are recognized as expense for financial reporting purposes but are not deductible for income tax purposes. These permanent differences do not affect deferred taxes because a tax will never be paid on the income or the expense will never be deducted on the tax return.

The deferred tax account reconciles the temporary differences in expense and revenue recognition for any accounting period. Under FASB Statement No. 109,[9] business firms recognize deferred tax liabilities for all temporary differences when the item causes financial income to exceed taxable income with an expectation that the difference will be offset in future accounting periods. Deferred tax assets are reported for deductible temporary differences and operating loss and tax credit carryforwards. A deductible temporary difference is one that causes taxable income to exceed financial income, with the expectation that the difference will be offset in the future. Measurement of tax liabilities and assets is based on provisions of the enacted tax law; effects of future anticipated changes in tax law are not considered. A *valuation allowance* is used to reduce deferred tax assets to expected realizable amounts when it is determined that it is more likely than not that some of the deferred tax assets will not be realized.

To illustrate the accounting for deferred taxes, assume that a company has a total annual revenue of $500,000; expenses other than depreciation are $250,000; and depreciation expense is $100,000 for tax accounting and $50,000 for financial reporting (eventually this difference would reverse and the reported depreciation expense in later years would be greater than the tax depreciation expense). The income for tax and reporting purposes would be computed two ways, assuming a 34% tax rate:

	Tax	Reporting
Revenue	$500,000	$500,000
Expenses	(350,000)	(300,000)
Earnings before tax	$150,000	$200,000
Tax expense (× 0.34)	(51,000)	(68,000)
Net income	$ 99,000	$132,000

---

[9] For more reading about FASB Statement No. 109, its application and implementation, see W. J. Read and A. J. Bartsch, "Accounting for Deferred Taxes Under FASB 109"; and G. J. Gregory, T. R. Petree, and R. J. Vitray, "FASB 109: Planning for Implementation and Beyond," *Journal of Accountancy*, December 1992.

Taxes actually paid ($51,000) are less than the tax expense ($68,000) reported in the financial statements. To reconcile the $17,000 difference between the expense recorded and the cash outflow, there is a deferred tax liability of $17,000:

Reported tax expense	$68,000
Cash paid for taxes	51,000
Deferred tax liability	$17,000

For an additional example of deferred taxes, including the ultimate reversal of the temporary difference, see Figure 2.2.

Deferred taxes are classified as current or noncurrent on the balance sheet, corresponding to the classification of related assets and liabilities underlying the temporary difference. For example, a deferred tax asset arising from accounting for 90-day warranties would be considered current. On the other hand, a temporary difference based on five-year warranties would be noncurrent; depreciation accounting would also result in a noncurrent deferred tax because of the noncurrent classification of the underlying plant and equipment account. A deferred tax asset or liability that is not related to an asset or liability for financial reporting, including deferred tax assets related to carryforwards, is classified according to anticipated reversal or benefit. At the end of the accounting period, the firm will report one net current amount and one net noncurrent amount unless the liabilities and assets are attributable to different tax-paying components of the enterprise or to different tax jurisdictions. Thus, the deferred tax account can conceivably appear on the balance sheet as a current asset, current liability, noncurrent asset, or noncurrent liability.

R.E.C. Inc. reports deferred federal income taxes as a noncurrent liability. The temporary differences are based on depreciation methods and long-term installment sales.

An illustration of the disclosures related to deferred income taxes follows. Exhibit 2.7 shows an excerpt from Applied Materials, Inc., 2007 footnote on income taxes. The nine temporary differences that have created the net deferred tax asset are listed at the top of the exhibit. The deferred tax assets indicate the company has deducted more items on the income statement compared to the deductions taken on the tax return. Three items have resulted in deferred tax liabilities. This means that Applied Materials, Inc. has taken greater deductions on its tax return for these items than was recorded on its income statement. The overall net deferred tax asset of $486,485 indicates that in the future, Applied Materials, Inc. should pay $486,485 less in taxes when these temporary differences reverse. The main reason for the net deferred tax asset is the "Accrued liabilities." The company has recorded, but is not allowed to deduct, these expenses for tax purposes until the amounts are actually paid. Notice that Applied Materials recognizes deferred tax items in four classifications on the balance sheet: current assets, noncurrent assets, current liabilities, and noncurrent liabilities.

Current deferred tax liabilities are included in accounts payable and accrued expenses on the Consolidated Balance Sheet and noncurrent deferred tax liabilities are included in other liabilities on the Consolidated Balance Sheet.

FIGURE 2.2   Deferred Taxes—An Example.

A company purchases a piece of equipment for $30,000. The equipment is expected to last three years and have no salvage value at the end of the three-year period. Straight-line depreciation is used for financial reporting purposes and an accelerated method is used for tax purposes. The following table shows the amounts of depreciation that would be recorded for both sets of books over the three-year life of the equipment:

Year	Depreciation expense (Financial reporting)	Depreciation expense (Tax reporting)
1	$10,000	$20,000
2	$10,000	$ 6,667
3	$10,000	$ 3,333

Assume that revenues are $90,000 and all expenses other than depreciation are $20,000 each year, the tax rate is 30%, and depreciation is the only temporary difference that creates the deferred tax account. Calculations to determine tax expense for reporting purposes and tax paid are below:

Year 1	Income Statement		Tax Return
Revenues	$90,000		$90,000
Expenses:			
Depreciation	(10,000)		(20,000)
Other	(20,000)		(20,000)
Earnings before taxes	$60,000	Taxable income	$50,000
Tax rate	× 0.30		× 0.30
Tax expense	$18,000		$15,000

The recording of taxes at the end of year 1 will involve a decrease in the cash account of $15,000, an increase in tax expense of $18,000, and an increase in the deferred tax liability account of the difference, $3,000.

Year 2	Income Statement		Tax Return
Revenues	$90,000		$90,000
Expenses:			
Depreciation	(10,000)		(6,667)
Other	(20,000)		(20,000)
Earnings before taxes	$60,000	Taxable income	$63,333
Tax rate	× 0.30		× 0.30
Tax expense	$18,000		$19,000

The recording of taxes at the end of year 2 will involve a decrease in the cash account of $19,000, an increase in tax expense of $18,000, and a decrease in the deferred tax liability account of the difference, $1,000. The deferred tax liability account will now have a balance of $2,000 at the end of year 2.

Year 3	Income Statement		Tax Return
Revenues	$90,000		$90,000
Expenses:			
Depreciation	(10,000)		(3,333)
Other	(20,000)		(20,000)
Earnings before taxes	$60,000	Taxable income	$66,667
Tax rate	× 0.30		× 0.30
Tax expense	$18,000		$20,000

The recording of taxes at the end of year 3 will involve a decrease in the cash account of $20,000, an increase in tax expense of $18,000, and a decrease in the deferred tax liability account of the difference, $2,000. The deferred tax liability account will now have a balance of $0 at the end of year 3, as the temporary difference has completely reversed.

Notice that the total amount of income tax expense ($54,000) recorded for reporting purposes is exactly equal to the tax paid ($54,000) over the three-year period.

EXHIBIT 2.7

Income Taxes—Applied Materials, Inc.

The components of deferred tax assets and liabilities are as follows:

	2006	2007
Deferred tax assets:	**(in thousands)**	
Inventory reserves and basis difference	$ 96,615	$111,297
Installation and warranty reserves	66,909	69,934
Accrued liabilities	288,634	245,307
Restructuring reserves	8,676	9,275
Deferred revenue	62,578	65,597
Tax credit and net operating loss carryforwards	64,108	11,020
Deferred compensation	30,547	31,263
Equity-based compensation	37,751	60,256
Intangibles	24,831	40,145
	680,649	644,094
Deferred tax liabilities:		
Depreciation	(13,889)	(42,597)
Purchased technology	(72,236)	(87,823)
Other	(25,216)	(27,189)
	(111,341	(157,609)
	$569,308	$486,485

The following table presents the breakdown between current and noncurrent net deferred tax assets and liabilities:

Deferred Income Taxes	2006	2007
	(in thousands)	
Current deferred tax asset	$455,473	$424,502
Noncurrent deferred tax asset	113,835	120,654
Current deferred tax liability	—	(5,357)
Noncurrent deferred tax liability	—	(53,314)
	$569,308	$486,485

Long-Term Debt

Obligations with maturities beyond one year are designated on the balance sheet as noncurrent liabilities. This category can include bonded indebtedness, long-term notes payable, mortgages, obligations under leases, pension liabilities, and long-term warranties. In Note C to the financial statements, R.E.C. Inc. specifies the nature, maturity, and interest rate of each long-term obligation. Even though long-term debt increased by over $4,000 from 2009 to 2010, notice that on the common-size balance sheet (Exhibit 2.2), the percentage of long-term debt relative to total assets has declined.

Capital Lease Obligations

A commonly used type of leasing arrangement is a capital lease. Capital leases are, in substance, a "purchase" rather than a "lease." If a lease contract meets any one of four criteria—transfers ownership to the lessee, contains a bargain purchase option, has a lease term of 75% or more of the leased property's economic life, or has minimum lease payments with a present value of 90% or more of the property's fair value—the lease must be capitalized by the lessee according to the requirements of FASB Statement No. 13, "Accounting for Leases." Leases not meeting one of the four criteria are treated as operating leases, discussed under commitments and contingencies later in the chapter. R.E.C. Inc. uses only operating leases.

A capital lease affects both the balance sheet and the income statement. An asset and a liability are recorded on the lessee's balance sheet equal to the present value of the lease payments to be made under the contract. The asset account reflects what is, in essence, the purchase of an asset; and the liability is the obligation incurred in financing the purchase. Each lease payment is apportioned partly to reduce the outstanding liability and partly to interest expense. The asset account is amortized with amortization expense recognized on the income statement, just as a purchased asset would be depreciated. Disclosures about capital leases can be found in the notes to the financial statements, often under both the property, plant, and equipment note and the commitments and contingencies note.

Postretirement Benefits Other Than Pensions

Other liability accounts (not present for R.E.C. Inc.), such as pension and postretirement benefit obligations, can appear under the liability section of the balance sheet.[10] Statement of Financial Accounting Standards No. 106, "Employers' Accounting for Postretirement Benefits Other Than Pensions," adopted by the FASB in 1990, has had a significant impact on many corporate balance sheets. This statement requires companies to disclose as a balance sheet liability the obligation for paying medical bills of retired employees and spouses—in accordance with the accrual method of accounting—by accruing promised future benefits as a form of deferred compensation. Most companies previously deducted medical expenses in the year paid. This accounting rule also impacts profitability for many firms by substantially increasing the recognition of annual postretirement benefit expense. Statement of Financial Accounting Standards No. 112, "Employers' Accounting for Postemployment Benefits," established accounting

---

[10] The disclosures relating to pension obligations are discussed in Chapter 5.

standards for benefits provided to former or inactive employees, their dependents, and beneficiaries and is effective for fiscal years beginning after December 15, 1993.

Commitments and Contingencies

Many companies will list an account titled "Commitments and Contingencies" on the balance sheet even though no dollar amount will appear. This disclosure is intended to draw attention to the fact that required disclosures can be found in the notes to the financial statements. *Commitments* refer to contractual agreements that will have a significant financial impact on the company in the future. R.E.C. Inc. reports commitments in Note E that describe the company's operating leases.

If the leasing contract does not meet one of the four criteria required to record the lease as a capital lease, the lessee will record "rent expense" on the income statement and a corresponding reduction to cash. Operating leases are a form of *off–balance-sheet financing.* In fact, the lessee is contractually obligated to make lease payments, but is not required by generally accepted accounting principles (GAAP) to record this obligation as a debt on the balance sheet. Companies could purposely negotiate a lease as an operating lease so that the long-term commitment does not have to be shown on the balance sheet; however, astute users of financial statements will know to look at the notes to the financial statements to determine any commitment the company may have with regard to operating leases. For R.E.C. Inc., Note E indicates that the company will be required to make lease payments in the amount of $176,019,000 in the future.

Many firms use complicated financing schemes—product financing arrangements, sales of receivables with recourse, limited partnerships, joint ventures—that do not have to be recorded on balance sheets. Disclosures about the extent, nature, and terms of off–balance-sheet financing arrangements are in the notes to the financial statements, but they may be very complex and difficult to understand, and require putting pieces together from several different sections.

Contingencies refer to potential liabilities of the firm such as possible damage awards assessed in lawsuits. Generally, the firm cannot reasonably predict the outcome and/or the amount of the future liability; however, information about the contingency must be disclosed in the notes to the financial statements.

Hybrid Securities

Some companies have *mandatorily redeemable preferred stock* outstanding. R.E.C. Inc. does not issue these securities, but they are explained here because they have the characteristics of both debt and equity. The financial instrument is called *preferred stock* (see discussion in the stockholders' equity section), but the issuing company must retire the shares at a future date, so it is actually debt. Prior to the FASB issuing Statement of Financial Accounting Standard No. 150, "Accounting for Certain Financial Instruments with Characteristics of Both Liabilities and Equity," in May 2003, companies unsure of how to classify this financial instrument disclosed it between debt and equity on the balance sheet. The FASB has cleared up this confusion by requiring mandatorily redeemable preferred stock to be reported as a liability unless redemption is required only on liquidation or termination of the reporting entity.

STOCKHOLDERS' EQUITY

The ownership interests in the company are represented in the final section of the balance sheet, stockholders' equity or shareholders' equity. Ownership equity is the residual interest in assets that remains after deducting liabilities. The owners bear the greatest risk because their claims are subordinate to creditors in the event of liquidation, but owners also benefit from the rewards of a successful enterprise. The relationship between the amount of debt and equity in a firm's capital structure and the concept of financial leverage, by which shareholder returns are magnified, is explored in Chapter 6.

Common Stock

R.E.C. Inc. has only common stock shares outstanding. Common shareholders do not ordinarily receive a fixed return but do have voting privileges in proportion to ownership interest. Dividends on common stock are declared at the discretion of a company's board of directors. Further, common shareholders can benefit from stock ownership through potential price appreciation (or the reverse can occur if the share price declines).

The amount listed under the common stock account is based on the par or stated value of the shares issued. The par or stated value usually bears no relationship to actual market price but rather is a floor price below which the stock cannot be sold initially. At year-end 2010, R.E.C. Inc. had 4,803,000 shares outstanding of $1 par value stock, rendering a total of $4,803,000 in the common stock account.

Additional Paid-In Capital

This account reflects the amount by which the original sales price of the stock shares exceeded par value. If, for example, a company sold 1,000 shares of $1 par value stock for $3 per share, the common stock account would be $1,000, and additional paid-in capital would total $2,000.

Reference to the additional paid-in capital account for R.E.C. Inc. reveals that the firm's common stock initially sold at a price slightly higher than the $1 par value. The additional paid-in capital account is not affected by the price changes resulting from stock trading subsequent to its original issue.[11]

Retained Earnings

The retained earnings account is the sum of every dollar a company has earned since its inception, less any payments made to shareholders in the form of cash or stock dividends. Retained earnings do not represent a pile of unused cash

---

[11] The paid-in capital account can be affected by treasury stock transactions, preferred stock, retirement of stock, stock dividends, and warrants and by the conversion of debt into stock.

stashed away in corporate vaults; retained earnings are funds a company has elected to reinvest in the operations of the business rather than pay out to stock-holders in dividends. Retained earnings should not be confused with cash or other financial resources currently or prospectively available to satisfy financial obligations. Rather, the retained earnings account is the measurement of all undistributed earnings. The retained earnings account is a key link between the income statement and the balance sheet. Unless there are unusual transactions affecting the retained earnings account, the following equation illustrates this link:

Beginning retained earnings ± Net income (loss) − Dividends = Ending retained earnings.

Other Equity Accounts

In addition to the stockholders' equity accounts shown on the R.E.C. Inc. balance sheet, there are other accounts that can appear in the equity section. These include preferred stock, accumulated other comprehensive income, and treasury stock. Exhibit 2.8 illustrates these additional items for Pfizer, Inc.

Preferred stock usually carries a fixed annual dividend payment but no voting rights. Pfizer, Inc. issued preferred stock in connection with an acquisition.

Beginning in 1998, companies must report comprehensive income or loss for the accounting period. Prior to the issuance of FASB Statement No. 130, "Reporting Comprehensive Income," several comprehensive income items bypassed the income statement and were reported as components of equity.

EXHIBIT 2.8

Pfizer, Inc. Shareholders' Equity at December 31 (in Millions)

	2007	2006
Shareholders' Equity		
Preferred stock, without par value, at stated value; 27 shares authorized; issued: 2007—2,302; 2006—3,497	93	141
Common stock, $0.05 par value; 12,000 shares authorized; issued: 2007—8,850; 2006—8,819	442	441
Additional paid-in capital	69,913	69,104
Employee benefit trust	(550)	(788)
Treasury stock, shares at cost; 2007—2,089; 2006—1,695	(56,847)	(46,740)
Retained earnings	49,660	49,669
Accumulated other comprehensive income/(expense)	2,299	(469)
Total shareholders' equity	65,010	71,358

Comprehensive income consists of two parts, net income and other comprehensive income. Other comprehensive income is reported in a separate equity account on the balance sheet generally referred to as *accumulated other comprehensive income/(expense)*. This account includes up to four items: (1) unrealized gains or losses in the market value of investments in available-for-sale securities, (2) any change in the excess of additional pension liability over unrecognized prior service cost, (3) certain gains and losses on derivative financial instruments, and (4) foreign currency translation adjustments resulting from converting financial statements from a foreign currency into U.S. dollars. (Comprehensive income and the four items noted above are discussed in Chapter 3.)

Firms often repurchase shares of their own stock for a variety of reasons that include meeting requirements for employee stock option and retirement plans, building shareholdings for potential merger needs, increasing earnings per share by reducing the number of shares outstanding in order to build investor confidence, preventing takeover attempts by reducing the number of shareholders, and as an investment use of excess cash holdings. If the repurchased shares are not retired, they are designated as *treasury stock* and are shown as an offsetting account in the stockholders' equity section of the balance sheet. Pfizer, Inc. held 2,089 million shares of treasury stock at the end of 2007. The cost of the shares is shown as a reduction of stockholders' equity.[12]

Employee benefit trust, an account shown in the Pfizer, Inc. shareholders' equity section, is explained as follows:

> The Pfizer, Inc. Employee Benefit Trust (EBT) was established in 1999 to fund our employee benefit plans through the use of its holdings of Pfizer, Inc. stock. The consolidated balance sheets reflect the fair value of the shares owned by the EBT as a reduction of Shareholders' Equity.[13]

OTHER BALANCE SHEET ITEMS

Corporate balance sheets are not limited to the accounts described in this chapter for R.E.C. Inc. and other companies. The reader of annual reports will encounter additional accounts and will also find many of the same accounts listed under a variety of different titles. Those discussed in this chapter, however, should be generally sufficient for understanding the basics of most balance sheet presentations in a set of published financial statements. The balance sheet will recur throughout the remaining chapters of this book given the interrelationship among the financial statements and its important role in the analysis of financial data.

---

[12] The two methods used to account for treasury stock transactions are the cost method (deducting the cost of the purchased shares from equity) and the par value method (deducting the par or stated value of the shares from equity). Most companies use the cost method.
[13] Pfizer, Inc., 2007 Annual Report, p. 64.

Self-Test

Solutions are provided in Appendix B.

_____ 1. What does the balance sheet summarize for a business enterprise?
  (a) Operating results for a period.
  (b) Financial position at a point in time.
  (c) Financing and investment activities for a period.
  (d) Profit or loss at a point in time.

_____ 2. What is the balancing equation for the balance sheet?
  (a) Assets = Liabilities + Stockholders' equity.
  (b) Assets + Stockholders' equity = Liabilities.
  (c) Assets + Liabilities = Stockholders' equity.
  (d) Revenues − Expenses = Net income.

_____ 3. What is a common-size balance sheet?
  (a) A statement that expresses each account on the balance sheet as a percentage of net income.
  (b) A statement that is common to an industry.
  (c) A statement that expresses each account on the balance sheet as a percentage of total assets.
  (d) A statement that expresses each asset account on the balance sheet as a percentage of total assets and each liability account on the balance sheet as a percentage of total liabilities.

_____ 4. Which of the following securities would be classified as marketable securities in the current asset section of the balance sheet?
  (a) Commercial paper, U.S. Treasury bills, land held for investment.
  (b) Commercial paper, U.S. Treasury bills, negotiable certificates of deposit.
  (c) Commercial paper, land held for investment, bonds with maturities in 10 years.
  (d) U.S. Treasury bills, long-term stock investment, bonds with maturities in 10 years.

_____ 5. What items should be calculated when analyzing the accounts receivable and allowance for doubtful accounts?
  (a) The growth rates of sales and inventories.
  (b) The growth rates of sales, accounts receivable, and the allowance for doubtful accounts, as well as the percentage of the allowance account relative to the total or gross accounts receivable.
  (c) The common-size balance sheet.
  (d) The growth rates of all assets and liabilities.

_____ 6. What type of firm generally has the highest proportion of inventory to total assets?
  (a) Retailers.
  (b) Wholesalers.
  (c) Manufacturers.
  (d) Service-oriented firms.

_____ **7.** Why is the method of valuing inventory important?

   (a) Inventory valuation is based on the actual flow of goods.

   (b) Inventories always account for more than 50% of total assets and therefore have a considerable impact on a company's financial position.

   (c) Companies desire to use the inventory valuation method that minimizes the cost of goods sold expense.

   (d) The inventory valuation method chosen determines the value of inventory on the balance sheet and the cost of goods sold expense on the income statement, two items having considerable impact on the financial position of a company.

_____ **8.** What are three major cost flow assumptions used by U.S. companies in valuing inventory?

   (a) LIFO, FIFO, average market.

   (b) LIFO, FIFO, actual cost.

   (c) LIFO, FIFO, average cost.

   (d) LIFO, FIFO, double-declining balance.

_____ **9.** Assuming a period of inflation, which statement is true?

   (a) The FIFO method understates balance sheet inventory.

   (b) The FIFO method understates cost of goods sold on the income statement.

   (c) The LIFO method overstates balance sheet inventory.

   (d) The LIFO method understates cost of goods sold on the income statement.

_____ **10.** Why would a company switch to the LIFO method of inventory valuation?

   (a) By switching to LIFO, reported earnings will be higher.

   (b) A new tax law requires companies using LIFO for reporting purposes also to use LIFO for figuring taxable income.

   (c) LIFO produces the largest cost of goods sold expense in a period of inflation and thereby lowers taxable income and taxes.

   (d) A survey by _Accounting Trends and Techniques_ revealed that the switch to LIFO is a current accounting "fad."

_____ **11.** Where can one most typically find the cost flow assumption used for inventory valuation for a specific company?

   (a) In The Risk Management Association, _Annual Statement Studies_.

   (b) In the statement of retained earnings.

   (c) On the face of the balance sheet with the total current asset amount.

   (d) In the notes to the financial statements.

_____ **12.** What type of firm generally has the highest proportion of fixed assets to total assets?

   (a) Manufacturers.

   (b) Retailers.

   (c) Wholesalers.

   (d) Retailers and wholesalers.

_____ **13.** How is goodwill evaluated?
   (a) Goodwill must be amortized over a 40-year period.
   (b) Goodwill should be written up each year.
   (c) Companies should determine whether goodwill has lost value, and if so, the loss in value should be written off as an impairment expense.
   (d) Goodwill is to be written off at the end of the tenth year.

_____ **14.** Which group of items would most likely be included in the other assets account on the balance sheet?
   (a) Inventories, marketable securities, bonds.
   (b) Land held for investment purposes and long-term prepayments.
   (c) One-year prepaid insurance policy, stock investments, copyrights.
   (d) Inventories, franchises, patents.

_____ **15.** What do current liabilities and current assets have in common?
   (a) Current assets are claims against current liabilities.
   (b) If current assets increase, then there will be a corresponding increase in current liabilities.
   (c) Current liabilities and current assets are converted into cash.
   (d) Current liabilities and current assets are those items that will be satisfied and converted into cash, respectively, in one year or one operating cycle, whichever is longer.

_____ **16.** How can a reserve account be abused by management?
   (a) Management can intentionally overestimate the reserve account to decrease earnings or underestimate the reserve account to increase earnings.
   (b) Management can charge the estimates of obligations to be paid in the future to a reserve account.
   (c) There is no way for management to abuse this account.
   (d) None of the above.

_____ **17.** Which of the following items could cause the recognition of accrued liabilities?
   (a) Sales, interest expense, rent.
   (b) Sales, taxes, interest income.
   (c) Salaries, rent, insurance.
   (d) Salaries, interest expense, interest income.

_____ **18.** Which statement is false?
   (a) Deferred taxes are the product of temporary differences in the recognition of revenue and expense for taxable income relative to reported income.
   (b) Deferred taxes arise from the use of the same method of depreciation for tax and reporting purposes.
   (c) Deferred taxes arise when taxes actually paid are less than tax expense reported in the financial statements.
   (d) Temporary differences causing the recognition of deferred taxes may arise from the methods used to account for items such as depreciation, installment sales, leases, and pensions.

_____ **19.** Which of the following would be classified as long-term debt?
   (a) Mortgages, current maturities of long-term debt, bonds.
   (b) Mortgages, long-term notes payable, bonds due in 10 years.
   (c) Accounts payable, bonds, obligations under leases.
   (d) Accounts payable, long-term notes payable, long-term warranties.

_____ **20.** What accounts are most likely to be found in the stockholders' equity section of the balance sheet?
   (a) Common stock, long-term debt, preferred stock.
   (b) Common stock, additional paid-in capital, liabilities.
   (c) Common stock, retained earnings, dividends payable.
   (d) Common stock, additional paid-in capital, retained earnings.

_____ **21.** What does the additional paid-in capital account represent?
   (a) The difference between the par and the stated value of common stock.
   (b) The price changes that result for stock trading subsequent to its original issue.
   (c) The market price of all common stock issued.
   (d) The amount by which the original sales price of stock exceeds the par value.

_____ **22.** What does the retained earnings account measure?
   (a) Cash held by the company since its inception.
   (b) Payments made to shareholders in the form of cash or stock dividends.
   (c) All undistributed earnings.
   (d) Financial resources currently available to satisfy financial obligations.

23. Listed below are balance sheet accounts for Elf's Gift Shop. Mark current accounts with "C" and noncurrent accounts with "NC."
   _____ (a) Long-term debt.
   _____ (b) Inventories.
   _____ (c) Accounts payable.
   _____ (d) Prepaid expenses.
   _____ (e) Equipment.
   _____ (f) Accrued liabilities.
   _____ (g) Accounts receivable.
   _____ (h) Cash.
   _____ (i) Bonds payable.
   _____ (j) Patents.

24. Dot's Delicious Donuts has the following accounts on its balance sheet:
   (1) Current assets.
   (2) Property, plant, and equipment.
   (3) Intangible assets.
   (4) Other assets.
   (5) Current liabilities.
   (6) Deferred federal income taxes.
   (7) Long-term debt.
   (8) Stockholders' equity.

How would each of the following items be classified?

_____ (a) Land held for speculation.
_____ (b) Current maturities on mortgage.
_____ (c) Common stock.
_____ (d) Mortgage payable.
_____ (e) Balances outstanding on credit sales to customers.
_____ (f) Accumulated depreciation.
_____ (g) Buildings used in business.
_____ (h) Accrued payroll.
_____ (i) Preferred stock.
_____ (j) Debt outstanding from credit extended by suppliers.
_____ (k) Patents.
_____ (l) Land on which warehouse is located.
_____ (m) Allowance for doubtful accounts.
_____ (n) Liability due to difference in taxes paid and taxes reported.
_____ (o) Additional paid-in capital.

25. Match the following terms to the correct definitions.

____ (a) Consolidated financial statements.
____ (b) Current assets.
____ (c) Depreciation.
____ (d) Deferred taxes.
____ (e) Allowance for doubtful accounts.
____ (f) Prepaid expenses.
____ (g) Current maturities.
____ (h) Accrued expense.
____ (i) Capital lease.
____ (j) Market value of stock.

(1) Used up within one year or operating cycle, whichever is longer.
(2) Expenses incurred prior to cash outflow.
(3) An agreement to use assets that is in substance a purchase.
(4) Estimation of uncollectible accounts receivable.
(5) Cost allocation of fixed assets other than land.
(6) Expenses paid in advance.
(7) Combined statements of parent company and controlled subsidiary companies.
(8) Price at which stock trades.
(9) Difference in taxes reported and taxes paid.
(10) Portion of debt to be repaid during the upcoming year.

Study Questions, Problems, and Cases

2.1 What information is provided in a balance sheet?

2.2 How is a common-size balance sheet created?

2.3 Discuss how marketable securities are valued on the balance sheet.

2.4 How can the allowance for doubtful accounts be used to assess earnings quality?

2.5 Why is the valuation of inventories important in financial reporting?

2.6 Why would a company switch to the LIFO method of inventory valuation in an inflationary period?

2.7 Which inventory valuation method, FIFO or LIFO, will generally produce an ending inventory value on the balance sheet that is closest to current cost?

2.8 Discuss the difference between the straight-line method of depreciation and the accelerated methods. Why do companies use different depreciation methods for tax reporting and financial reporting?

2.9 What is the purpose of listing the account "Commitments and contingencies" on the balance sheet even though no dollar amounts appear?

2.10 How is it possible for a company with positive retained earnings to be unable to pay a cash dividend?

2.11 The King Corporation has total annual revenue of $800,000; expenses other than depreciation of $350,000; depreciation expense of $200,000 for tax purposes; and depreciation expense of $130,000 for reporting purposes. The tax rate is 34%. Calculate net income for reporting purposes and for tax purposes. What is the deferred tax liability?

2.12 Explain how treasury stock affects the stockholders' equity section of the balance sheet and the calculation of earnings per share.

2.13 Using the following amounts (in thousands) reported in Agilysys, Inc. and Subsidiaries consolidated balance sheets and statements of income at March 31, 2007 and 2006, and the valuation schedule, analyze the receivables and allowance account for all years.

(in thousands)	2007	2006
Net Revenues	$474,570	$468,984
Accounts receivable, net of allowances for customer adjustments and doubtful accounts of $1,186 in 2007, $3,311 in 2006	116,735	111,903

Schedule II—Valuation and Qualifying Accounts Years ended March 31, 2007, 2006, and 2005

		Balance at beginning of period	Charged to costs and expenses	Charged to other accounts	Deduction	Balance at end of period
2007	Allowance for doubtful accounts	$3,311	$(1,547)	$ –	$(578)	$1,186
2006	Allowance for doubtful accounts	$2,588	$ 881	$305 (a)	$(463)	$3,311
2005	Allowance for doubtful accounts	$3,283	$ (430)	$ –	$(265)	$2,588

(a) The $305 represents allowance for doubtful accounts acquired in business combinations.

2.14 Tisha's Toys had the following goods available for sale in the last accounting period:

Beginning inventory	600 units @ $10
Purchases (in order from first to last):	1,000 units @ $11
	900 units @ $12
	700 units @ $14

Sales for the period were 1,900 units.

(a) Compute the inventory balance and the cost of goods sold at the end of the accounting period using average cost, FIFO, and LIFO.
(b) Which method shows the highest ending inventory?
(c) Which method shows the highest cost of goods sold?
(d) Explain why ending inventory and cost of goods sold differ under the three methods of inventory valuation.

2.15 The F.L.A.C. Corporation sells a single product. The following is information on inventory, purchase, and sales for the current year:

		Number of units	Unit cost	Sale price
January 1	Inventory	10,000	$ 3.00	
January 10	Purchase	4,000	3.50	
January 1–March 31	Sales	8,000		$ 5.00
April 25	Purchase	10,000	4.00	
April 1–June 30	Sales	11,000		5.50
July 10	Purchase	6,000	4.50	
July 1–September 30	Sales	3,000		6.00
October 15	Purchase	8,000	5.00	
October 1–December 31	Sales	9,000		6.50

(a) Compute the inventory balance and the cost of goods sold expense reported at the end of the year using the following methods: FIFO, LIFO, and average cost.
(b) Discuss the effect of each method on the balance sheet and income statement during periods of inflation.

2.16 The following information is available for Kennametal Inc.'s inventories as of June 30, 2007:

(in Thousands)	2007	2006
Finished goods	$234,828	$184,349
Work in process and powder blends	161,815	167,475
Raw materials and supplies	72,941	53,454
Inventories at current cost	469,584	405,278
Less LIFO valuation	(65,971)	(70,329)
Total inventories	$403,613	$334,949

We used the LIFO method of valuing our inventories for approximately 50% and 53% of total inventories at June 30, 2007 and 2006, respectively.

(a) What method of inventory is used for the other 50% and 47% of total inventories?

(b) Explain the meaning of each of the numbers listed in the table.

2.17 The Lazy O Ranch just purchased equipment costing $60,000. The equipment is expected to last five years and have no salvage value.

(a) Calculate the depreciation expense using the straight-line method for the first two years the equipment is owned.

(b) Calculate the depreciation expense using the double-declining balance method for the first two years the equipment is owned.

2.18 Using the information below for Dean Corporation, calculate the amount of dividends Dean most likely paid to common stockholders in 2008, 2009, and 2010.

Retained earnings balances		Year	Net income
January 1, 2008	$ 700		
December 31, 2008	890	2008	$250
December 31, 2009	1,045	2009	225
December 31, 2010	1,010	2010	40

2.19 From the following accounts, prepare a balance sheet for Chester Co. for the current calendar year.

Accrued interest payable	$ 1,400
Property, plant, and equipment	34,000
Inventory	12,400
Additional paid-in capital	7,000
Deferred taxes payable (noncurrent)	1,600
Cash	1,500
Accumulated depreciation	10,500
Bonds payable	14,500
Accounts payable	4,300
Common stock	2,500
Prepaid expenses	700
Land held for sale	9,200
Retained earnings	?
Current portion of long-term debt	1,700
Accounts receivable	6,200
Notes payable	8,700

2.20 Writing Skills Problem. At fiscal year-end February 2, 2008, Target Corporation had the following assets and liabilities on its balance sheet (in millions):

Current liabilities	$11,782
Long-term debt	15,126
Other liabilities	2,345
Total assets	44,560

Target reported the following information on leases in the notes to the financial statements:

Total rent expense was $165 million in 2007, $158 million in 2006, and $154 million in 2005, including percentage rent expense of $5 million in 2007, 2006, and 2005. Most long-term leases include one or more options to renew, with renewal terms that can extend the lease term one to more than fifty years. Certain leases also include options to purchase the leased property.

Future minimum lease payments required under noncancellable lease agreements existing at February 2, 2008, were:

Future Minimum Lease Payments (in Millions)	Operating Leases	Capital Leases
2008	$ 239	$ 12
2009	187	16
2010	173	16
2011	129	16
2012	123	17
After 2012	2,843	155
Total future minimum lease payments	$3,694 (a)	$232
Less: Interest (b)		(105)
Present value of minimum capital lease payments		$127 (c)

(a) Total contractual lease payments include $1,721 million related to options to extend lease terms that are reasonably assured of being exercised, and also include $98 million of legally binding minimum lease payments for stores that will open in 2008 or later.
(b) Calculated using the interest rate at inception for each lease.
(c) Includes current portion of $4 million.

Required: Your friend, Liz, loves to shop at Target and is now interested in investing in the company. Tom, another friend of Liz, has told her that Target's debt structure is risky with obligations nearly 74% of total assets. Liz sees that debt on the balance sheet is 65% of total assets and is confused by Tom's comment. Write an explanation to Liz discussing the debt structure of Target and why Tom thinks Target is risky. Be sure to explain clearly to Liz what information appears on financial statements, as well as what information does not appear directly on the financial statements.

2.21 Research Problem

Locate a library that carries "The Risk Management Association, Annual Statement Studies." Choose three industries from Annual Statement Studies (different from those illustrated in Exhibits 2.4 and 2.5 in Chapter 2) and create a table with the percentages for the following items: accounts receivable, inventories, fixed assets, accounts payable, and long-term debt as a percentage of total assets.

2.22 Internet Problem

Choose a publicly held corporation (unless your teacher assigns a particular corporation for this assignment) and find the balance sheet and notes to the financial statements in the most recent Form 10-K. The Form 10-K can be located by going to the home page of the Securities and Exchange Commission and locating the SEC EDGAR Database. The address for the home page is www.sec.gov/.

Using the information you find, answer the following questions:

(a) What current assets are included on the balance sheet?

(b) If the company lists accounts receivable and an allowance account, analyze these accounts.

(c) What method does the company use to value inventory?

(d) What depreciation method does the company use?

(e) What assets other than current assets and property, plant, and equipment are included on the balance sheet?

(f) What current liabilities are included on the balance sheet?

(g) How many deferred tax accounts are included on the balance sheet? Under which classification(s) are deferred taxes found? What temporary differences caused the creation of the deferred tax account(s)?

(h) Does the company have long-term debt? How much?

(i) Does the company have commitments and contingencies? If so, what commitments does the company have and for what amount is the company committed? Explain any contingencies.

(j) What stockholders' equity accounts are included on the balance sheet?

2.23 Intel Case

The 2007 Intel Annual Report can be found at the following Web site: www.prenhall.com/fraser. Using the annual report, answer the following questions:

(a) Prepare a common-size balance sheet for Intel for all years presented.

(b) Describe the types of assets Intel owns. Which assets are the most significant to the company? Using the notes to the financial statements, discuss the accounting methods used to value assets. What other information can be learned about the asset accounts from the notes? Have there been significant changes to the asset structure from 2006 to 2007?

(c) Analyze the accounts receivable and allowance accounts.

(d) Describe the types of liabilities Intel has incurred. Which liabilities are the most significant to the company? Have there been significant changes to the liability and equity structure from 2006 to 2007?

(e) Describe the commitments and contingencies of Intel.

(f) Under which classification(s) are deferred taxes listed? What item is the most significant component of deferred taxes?

2.24 Eastman Kodak Comprehensive Analysis Case Using the Financial Statement Analysis Template

Each chapter in the textbook contains a continuation of this problem. The objective is to learn how to do a comprehensive financial statement analysis in steps as the content of each chapter is learned. Using the 2007 Eastman Kodak Annual Report and Form 10-K that can be found at www.prenhall .com/fraser, complete the following requirements:

(a) Open the financial statement analysis template that you saved from the Chapter 1 Eastman Kodak problem and input the data from the Eastman Kodak balance sheet. Eastman Kodak has combined many of its asset and liability accounts into one comprehensive account on the balance sheet. Be sure to read the notes to determine the correct numbers to input on the template. For example, the company has combined many items in the account "Other long-term assets" that should be separated into appropriate accounts. When you have finished inputting the data, review the balance sheet to make sure there are no red blocks indicating that your numbers do not match the cover sheet information you input from the Chapter 1 problem. Make any necessary corrections before printing out both your input and the common-size balance sheet that the template automatically creates for you.

(b) Analyze the balance sheet. Write a summary that includes important points that an analyst would use in assessing the financial condition of Eastman Kodak.

2.25 Del Monte Foods Case

The following are excerpts from Del Monte Foods' 2007 Form 10-K Notes to the Consolidated Financial Statements:

Business

Del Monte Foods Company and its consolidated subsidiaries ("Del Monte," or the "Company") is one of the country's largest producers, distributors and marketers of premium quality, branded food and pet products for the U.S. retail market, with leading food brands, such as *Del Monte*, *StarKist*, *S&W*, *Contadina*, *College Inn* and other brand names and premier foods and snacks for pets, with brands including *Meow Mix*, *Kibbles 'n Bits*, *Nine Lives*, *Milk-Bone*, *Pup-Peroni*, *Meaty Bone*, *Snausages*, *Pounce* and other brand names. The Company acquired *Meow Mix* and *Milk-Bone* brands during the three months ended July 30, 2006, in connection with the acquisitions discussed in Note 4. The Company also produces private label food and pet products. The majority of its products are sold nationwide in all channels serving retail markets, mass merchandisers, the U.S. military, certain export markets, the foodservice industry and food processors.

Note 4. Acquisitions

The acquisitions were accounted for under the purchase method of accounting. The purchase prices were allocated to the net assets acquired based upon estimated fair market values at the respective dates of acquisition. The Company utilized independent valuation firms to assist in estimating the fair value of the acquired businesses' real estate, machinery and equipment and identifiable intangible assets. The Company's allocation of purchase price to the net tangible and intangible assets acquired and liabilities assumed is as follows as of April 29, 2007:

	Meow Mix	Milk-Bone
Cash and cash equivalents	$ 3.6	$ —
Trade accounts receivable, net	18.8	—
Inventories	25.9	18.0
Prepaid expenses and other current assets	11.0	9.8
Property, plant and equipment, net	34.3	37.3
Goodwill	420.8	219.5
Intangible assets, net	307.0	330.0
Other assets, net	1.3	—
Total assets, acquired	822.7	614.6
Accounts payable and accrued expenses	28.3	10.9
Deferred tax liabilities	69.5	5.8
Other noncurrent liabilities	3.3	4.9
Total liabilities assumed	101.1	21.6
Net assets acquired	$ 721.6	$ 593.0

Required

1. Using the Consolidated Balance Sheets for Del Monte Foods for April 29, 2007, and April 30, 2006, prepare a common-size balance sheet.
2. Evaluate the asset, debt, and equity structure of Del Monte Foods, as well as trends and changes found on the common-size balance sheet.
3. What concerns would investors and creditors have based on only this information?
4. What additional financial and nonfinancial information would investors and creditors need to make investing and lending decisions for Del Monte Foods?

Del Monte Foods Company and Subsidiaries
Consolidated Balance Sheets
(In millions, except share and per share data)

	April 29, 2007	April 30, 2006
Assets		
Cash and cash equivalents	$ 13.0	$ 459.9
Restricted cash	—	43.3
Trade accounts receivable, net of allowance	261.1	237.8
Inventories	809.9	764.2
Prepaid expenses and other current assets	132.5	111.9
Total current assets	1,216.5	1,617.1
Property, plant, and equipment, net	718.6	641.4
Goodwill	1,389.3	758.7
Intangible assets, net	1,198.6	572.5
Other assets, net	38.5	33.2
Total assets	$4,561.5	$3,622.9
Liabilities and Stockholders' Equity		
Accounts payable and accrued expenses	$ 508.7	$ 450.9
Short-term borrowings	21.8	1.7
Current portion of long-term debt	29.4	58.6
Total current liabilities	559.9	511.2
Long-term debt	1,951.9	1,242.5
Deferred tax liabilities	368.0	228.1
Other noncurrent liabilities	229.5	327.1
Total liabilities	3,109.3	2,308.9
Stockholders' Equity:		
Common stock— ($0.01 par value per share; shares authorized: 500,000,000; 214,208,733 issued and 202,211,661 outstanding at April 29, 2007; and 212,114,276 issued and 200,117,204 outstanding at April 30, 2006)	2.1	2.1
Additional paid-in capital	1,021.7	989.5
Treasury stock, at cost	(133.1)	(126.5)
Accumulated other comprehensive income (loss)	24.4	(7.9)
Retained earnings	537.1	456.8
Total stockholders' equity	1,452.2	1,314.0
Total liabilities and stockholders' equity	$4,561.5	$3,622.9

See Accompanying Notes to Consolidated Financial Statements.

3

Income Statement and Statement of Stockholders' Equity

Learning about earnings, the bottom line,
Is very important most of the time.
A phony number
Just may encumber
Those folks trying to make more than a dime.[1]

—A. ORMISTON

The operating performance of a business firm has traditionally been measured by its success in generating earnings—the "bottom line." Investors, creditors, and analysts eagerly await companies' earnings reports. One objective of this book is to broaden the reader's perspective of operating success to consider such yardsticks as "cash flow from operations" as well as net income. In this chapter, however, the focus will be on the income statement and how a company arrives at its "bottom line." Chapter 5 presents examples of ways in which companies manipulate their "bottom line" and what readers can look for to detect and adjust for these strategies.

---

[1] According to the *New Book of Knowledge* (1985) by Grolier Incorporated, limericks are difficult to write. Limericks, a form of nonsense-verse, consist of five lines, of which lines one, two, and five rhyme and have from eight to eleven syllables each; lines three and four rhyme, with five to seven syllables each. Although thousands exist in literature, it is estimated that only 200 are probably genuine, flawless examples. Readers may submit limericks for possible inclusion in future editions!

The *income statement,* also called the *statement of earnings,* presents revenues, expenses, net income, and earnings per share for an accounting period, generally a year or a quarter. (The terms *income, earnings,* and *profit* are used interchangeably throughout the book.) The statement of stockholders' equity is an important link between the balance sheet and the income statement. This statement documents the changes in the balance sheet equity accounts from one accounting period to the next. Companies may choose to report the information on the statement of stockholders' equity in a supplementary schedule or in a note to the financial statements rather than preparing a formal financial statement. Annual reports include three years of income statements and stockholders' equity information.

R.E.C. Inc. prepares a formal statement of stockholders' equity. Both the income statement and statement of stockholders' equity will be discussed in this chapter using the R.E.C. Inc. statements as the basis for a description of each statement and the accounts that typically appear in the statements.

THE INCOME STATEMENT

Regardless of the perspective of the financial statement user—investor, creditor, employee, competitor, supplier, regulator—it is essential to understand and analyze the earnings statement. But it is also important that the analyst realize that a company's report of earnings and other information presented on the income statement are not complete and sufficient barometers of financial performance. The income statement is one of many pieces of a financial statement package, and, like the other pieces, the income statement is partially the product of a wide range of accounting choices, estimates, and judgments that affect reported results, just as business policies, economic conditions, and many other variables affect results.

It has previously been explained that earnings are measured on an accrual rather than a cash basis, which means that income reported on the income statement is not the same as cash generated during the accounting period. Cash flow from operations and its importance to analysis are covered in Chapter 4. The purpose of this chapter is not to minimize the importance of the income statement, however, but to provide a clear context for its interpretation.

The income statement comes in two basic formats and with considerable variation in the degree of detail presented. The earnings statement for R.E.C. Inc. is presented in a *multiple-step* format, which provides several intermediate profit measures—gross profit, operating profit, and earnings before income tax—prior to the amount of net earnings for the period. (See Exhibit 3.1.) The *single-step* version of the income statement groups all items of revenue together, then deducts all categories of expense to arrive at a figure for net income. Exhibit 3.2 illustrates the single-step approach if R.E.C. Inc. used that method to report earnings. For purposes of analysis, the multiple-step format should be used. If a company presents income statement information in single-step or a modified multiple-step format, the user of the financial statements should redo the income statement in multiple-step format before beginning an analysis.

Certain special items, if they occur during an accounting period, must be disclosed separately on an income statement, regardless of format. These include *discontinued operations* and *extraordinary transactions* discussed later in this chapter.

EXHIBIT 3.1

R.E.C. Inc. Consolidated Statements of Earnings for the Years Ended December 31, 2010, 2009, and 2008 (in Thousands Except per Share Amounts)

	2010	2009	2008
Net Sales	$215,600	$153,000	$140,700
Cost of goods sold (Note A)	129,364	91,879	81,606
Gross profit	86,236	61,121	59,094
Selling and administrative expenses (Notes A and E)	45,722	33,493	32,765
Advertising	14,258	10,792	9,541
Depreciation and amortization (Note A)	3,998	2,984	2,501
Repairs and maintenance	3,015	2,046	3,031
Operating profit	19,243	11,806	11,256
Other income (expense)			
Interest income	422	838	738
Interest expense	(2,585)	(2,277)	(1,274)
Earnings before income taxes	17,080	10,367	10,720
Income taxes (Notes A and D)	7,686	4,457	4,824
Net Earnings	$ 9,394	$ 5,910	$ 5,896
Basic earnings per common share (Note G)	$ 1.96	$ 1.29	$ 1.33
Diluted earnings per common share (Note G)	$ 1.93	$ 1.26	$ 1.31

The accompanying notes are an integral part of these statements.

EXHIBIT 3.2

R.E.C. Inc. Consolidated Statements of Earnings for Years Ended December 31, 2010, 2009, and 2008 (in Thousands Except per Share Amounts)

	2010	2009	2008
Income			
Net sales	$215,600	$153,000	$140,700
Interest income	422	838	738
	216,022	153,838	141,438
Costs and Expenses			
Cost of goods sold	129,364	91,879	81,606
Marketing, administrative, and other expenses	66,993	49,315	47,838
Interest expense	2,585	2,277	1,274
Income taxes	7,686	4,457	4,824
Net Earnings	$ 9,394	$ 5,910	$ 5,896
Basic Earnings per Common Share	$ 1.96	$ 1.29	$ 1.33
Diluted Earnings per Common Share	$ 1.93	$ 1.26	$ 1.31

As noted in Chapter 2, the Financial Accounting Standards Board (FASB) passed a new rule, effective in 1998, requiring companies to report *comprehensive income*. According to FASB Statement of Financial Accounting Concepts No. 6, "Elements of Financial Statements," comprehensive income is the change in equity of a company during a period from transactions, other events, and circumstances relating to nonowner sources. It includes all changes in equity during a period except those resulting from investments by owners and distributions to owners. Companies are required to report total comprehensive income in one of three ways:

- on the face of its income statement,
- in a separate statement of comprehensive income, or
- in its statement of stockholders' equity.

Data are presented in corporate income statements for three years to facilitate comparison and to provide evidence regarding trends of revenues, expenses, and net earnings. Because R.E.C. Inc. has only net earnings and no other comprehensive income, the company does not have a statement of comprehensive income. The statements for R.E.C. Inc. are consolidated, which means that the information presented is a combination of the results for R.E.C. Inc. and its wholly owned subsidiaries. The disclosure of comprehensive income and the accounting methods used for subsidiary investments will be discussed later in the chapter under the headings "Comprehensive Income" and "Equity Earnings."

Common-Size Income Statement

As discussed in Chapter 2, common-size financial statements are a useful analytical tool to compare firms with different levels of sales or total assets, facilitate internal or structural analysis of a firm, evaluate trends, and make industry comparisons. The common-size income statement expresses each income statement item as a percentage of net sales. The common-size income statement shows the relative magnitude of various expenses relative to sales, the profit percentages (gross profit, operating profit, and net profit margins), and the relative importance of "other" revenues and expenses. Exhibit 3.3 presents the common-size income statement for R.E.C. Inc. that will be used in this chapter and Chapter 6 to analyze the firm's profitability.

Net Sales

Total sales revenue for each year of the three-year period is shown net of returns and allowances. A *sales return* is a cancellation of a sale, and a *sales allowance* is a deduction from the original sales invoice price. Sales are the major revenue source for most companies; therefore, the trend of this figure is a key element in performance measurement. Although most of the analysis of R.E.C. Inc.'s financial statements will be conducted in Chapter 6, the reader can look for clues on the income statement.

It would appear, for instance, that R.E.C. Inc. had a much better sales year in 2010 than 2009: Sales increased 40.9% ($62.6 million) between 2009 and 2010, compared with an 8.7% ($12.3 million) growth between 2008 and 2009. If a company's sales are increasing (or decreasing), it is important to determine whether the

EXHIBIT 3.3

R.E.C. Inc. Common-Size Income Statements (Percent)

	2010	2009	2008	2007	2006
Net Sales	100.0	100.0	100.0	100.0	100.0
Cost of Goods Sold	60.0	60.1	58.0	58.2	58.2
Gross Profit	40.0	39.9	42.0	41.8	41.8
Operating Expenses					
Selling and administrative expenses	21.2	21.8	23.2	20.3	20.0
Advertising	6.6	7.1	6.8	6.4	6.3
Depreciation and amortization	1.9	2.0	1.8	1.4	1.2
Repairs and maintenance	1.4	1.3	2.2	2.7	2.7
Operating Profit	8.9	7.7	8.0	11.0	11.6
Other Income (Expense)					
Interest income	0.2	0.5	0.5	0.3	0.3
Interest expense	(1.2)	(1.5)	(0.9)	(0.9)	(1.0)
Earnings before income taxes	7.9	6.7	7.6	10.4	10.9
Income Taxes	3.6	2.9	3.4	5.4	5.7
Net Earnings	4.3	3.8	4.2	5.0	5.2

change is a result of price, volume, or a combination of both. Are sales growing because the firm is increasing prices or because more units are being sold, or both? It would seem that, in general, higher-quality earnings would be the product of both volume and price increases (during inflation). The firm would want to sell more units and keep prices increasing at least in line with the rate of inflation. The reasons for sales growth (or decline) are covered in a firm's Management Discussion and Analysis section of the annual or 10-K report (see Chapter 1).

A related issue is whether sales are growing in "real" (inflation-adjusted) as well as "nominal" (as reported) terms. The change in sales in nominal terms can be readily calculated from the figures reported on the income statement. An adjustment of the reported sales figure with the Consumer Price Index (CPI) (or some other measure of general inflation) will enable the analyst to make a comparison of the changes in real and nominal terms. To make the calculation to compare real with nominal sales, begin with the sales figures reported in the income statement, and adjust years prior to the current year with the CPI or some other price index. For R.E.C. Inc., the nominal growth rate was already calculated to be 40.9%. Assuming the CPIs for 2010 and 2009 are 207.3 and 201.6, respectively, the adjusted or real sales figure for 2009 is $157,326 (207.3/201.6) × $153,000. Sales when adjusted for inflation still increased 37.0% from 2009 to 2010, but at a smaller rate. Note A (see Exhibit 1.2) to the R.E.C. Inc. financial statements indicates that new store openings have occurred that could explain the large sales growth in the past year.

The remainder of the income statement reveals management's ability to translate sales dollars into profits. The sales or revenue number is the common denominator in the common-size income statement (Exhibit 3.3) and is, therefore, 100% for all companies when preparing this statement. The calculations are shown for other important items on the common-size income statement as they are discussed in this chapter.

Cost of Goods Sold

The first expense deduction from sales is the cost to the seller of products or services sold to customers. This expense is called *cost of goods sold* or *cost of sales*. The amount of cost of goods sold for any accounting period, as explained in Chapter 2, will be affected by the cost flow assumption used to value inventory. R.E.C. Inc. uses the last-in, first-out (LIFO) method, which means that the last purchases made during the year have been charged to expense. The LIFO method generally results in the matching of current costs with current revenues and therefore produces higher-quality earnings than either first-in, first-out (FIFO) or average cost.

The relationship between cost of goods sold and net sales—called the *cost of goods sold percentage*—is an important one for profit determination because cost of goods sold is the largest expense item for many firms.

	2010	2009	2008
$\dfrac{\text{Cost of goods sold}}{\text{Net sales}}$	$\dfrac{129,364}{215,600} = 60.0\%$	$\dfrac{91,879}{153,000} = 60.1\%$	$\dfrac{81,606}{140,700} = 58.0\%$

The cost of goods sold percentage for R.E.C. Inc. increased between 2008 and 2009. This is a result of the firm lowering prices or increasing costs. See Figure 3.1 for a more detailed explanation. Since then, the firm either has controlled costs more effectively and/or has been able to pass along price increases to customers. The cost of goods sold percentage will vary significantly by industry, according to markup policies and other factors. For example, the cost of goods sold percentage for jewelry retailers averages 57.3%, compared with 74.8% for retailers of groceries.[2]

Gross Profit

The difference between net sales and cost of goods sold is called *gross profit* or *gross margin*. Gross profit is the first step of profit measurement on the multiple-step income statement and is a key analytical tool in assessing a firm's operating performance. The gross profit figure indicates how much profit the firm is generating after deducting the cost of products or services sold. Gross profit, expressed as a percentage of net sales, is the gross profit margin.

---

[2] The Risk Management Association, *Annual Statement Studies*, Philadelphia, PA, 2007.

FIGURE 3.1   Understand the Math!

If the cost of goods sold (COGS) percentage increases or decreases, this does not necessarily mean that costs have increased or decreased. The change in the percentage may be caused by decreases or increases in the selling price. Here's an example:

> Assume it costs a company $4 to make to toy that sells for $10 in year 1. In year 2, competition is fierce, and the company must drop the selling prices to $8 to sell the toy.

	Year 1		Year 2	
Sales	$10	100%	$8	100%
COGS	4	40%	4	50%
Gross Profit	$ 6	60%	$4	50%

Notice that the COGS percentage has increased, but the cost to manufacture the toy has not. The decrease in selling price is the cause of the higher COGS percentage and lower gross profit margin.

Always pay attention to the numbers—know the difference between raw dollars and percentages!

	2010	2009	2008
Gross profit / Net sales	$\dfrac{86,236}{215,600} = 40.0\%$	$\dfrac{61,121}{153,000} = 39.9\%$	$\dfrac{59,094}{140,700} = 42.0\%$

The gross profit margin and cost of goods sold percentage are complements of each other (the two percentages always add to 100%); therefore, the analysis of these ratios will be the same. Generally, firms want to maintain the relationship between gross profit and sales, or, if possible, increase gross profit margin. In stable industries, such as groceries, one can expect to find the same gross profit margin from year to year because companies will raise prices proportionately as cost of goods sold increases. In volatile industries such as high technology, gross profit margin may increase or decrease significantly from year to year. For example, Target Corporation's gross profit margin for 2005, 2006, and 2007 was 32% whereas Candela Corporation had a 54.6%, 60.6%, and 66.3% gross profit margin, respectively, in the same three years. In capital intensive industries such as manufacturing, sales volume changes will cause volatility in the gross profit margin because there are fixed costs included in cost of goods sold. Fixed costs do not vary proportionately with volume changes but remain the same within a relevant range of activity.

Companies having more than one revenue source will show each revenue line separately and also show the corresponding cost of goods sold or cost of sales for each revenue source. An illustration of how to calculate and analyze gross profit margin when there are multiple revenue sources is shown in Figure 3.2.

FIGURE 3.2   Gross Profit Margin for Multiple Revenue Sources.

ABC Company has two distinct revenue sources, food and tobacco. The following information is from ABC Company's income statement:

	2007	%	2006	%
Food sales	$ 800		$ 750	
Tobacco sales	900		900	
Total sales	$1,700	100.0	$1,650	100.0
Cost of goods sold—food	$ 560		$ 525	
Cost of goods sold—tobacco	450		360	
Total cost of goods sold	$1,010	59.4	$ 885	53.6
Gross profit	$ 690	40.6	$ 765	46.4

To analyze the overall gross profit margin change from 46.4% to 40.6% the gross profit margins of each revenue source should be calculated as follows:

	2007	%	2006	%
Food sales	$800	100.0	$750	100.0
Less: Cost of goods sold—food	(560)	70.0	(525)	70.0
Gross profit—food	$240	30.0	$225	30.0
Tobacco sales	$900	100.0	$900	100.0
Less: Cost of goods sold—tobacco	(450)	50.0	(360)	40.0
Gross profit—tobacco	$450	50.0	$540	60.0

The overall decline in gross profit margin has been caused by the tobacco product line, not food product line. By analyzing each revenue source individually the analyst can better understand which divisions of a company are successful and which may be facing challenges.

Operating Expense

R.E.C. Inc. discloses four categories of operating expense: selling and administrative, advertising, depreciation and amortization, and repairs and maintenance. In addition, a fifth category, operating lease payments, is disclosed in Note E. These are all areas over which management exercises discretion and that have considerable impact on the firm's current and future profitability. Thus, it is important to track these accounts carefully in terms of trends, absolute amounts, relationship to sales, and relationship to industry competitors.

Selling and administrative expenses are expenses relating to the sale of products or services and to the management of the business. They include salaries, rent, insurance, utilities, supplies, and sometimes depreciation and advertising expense. R.E.C. Inc. provides separate disclosures for advertising and for depreciation and amortization. Note A to the R.E.C. Inc. financial statements indicates that the firm includes the expenses related to the opening of new stores in selling and administrative expense.

Advertising costs are or should be a major expense in the budgets of companies for which marketing is an important element of success. This topic was discussed in

Chapter 1. As a retail firm operating in a competitive industry, recreational products, R.E.C. Inc. spends 6 to 7 cents of every sales dollar for advertising, as indicated by the ratio of advertising to net sales:

	2010	2009	2008
Advertising —————— Net sales	$\dfrac{14,258}{215,600} = 6.6\%$	$\dfrac{10,792}{153,000} = 7.1\%$	$\dfrac{9,541}{140,700} = 6.8\%$

Lease payments include the costs associated with operating rentals of leased facilities for retail outlets. Note E to the financial statements explains the agreements that apply to the rental arrangements and presents a schedule of minimum annual rental commitments. Observation of the sharp rise in lease payments for R.E.C. Inc. between 2009 and 2010, from $7.1 million to $13.1 million—an increase of 84%—would indicate an expansion of the firm's use of leased space.

Depreciation and Amortization

The cost of assets other than land that will benefit a business enterprise for more than a year is allocated over the asset's service life rather than expensed in the year of purchase. Land is an exception to the rule because land is considered to have an unlimited useful life. The cost allocation procedure is determined by the nature of the long-lived asset. *Depreciation* is used to allocate the cost of tangible fixed assets such as buildings, machinery, equipment, furniture and fixtures, and motor vehicles. *Amortization* is the process applied to capital leases, leasehold improvements, and the cost expiration of intangible assets such as patents, copyrights, trademarks, and franchises. The cost of acquiring and developing natural resources—oil and gas, other minerals, and standing timber—is allocated through *depletion*. The amount of expense recognized in any accounting period will depend on the level of investment in the relevant asset; estimates with regard to the asset's service life and residual value; and for depreciation, the method used.

R.E.C. Inc. recognizes annual depreciation expense for the firm's buildings and equipment and amortization expense for the leasehold improvements on rental property. Note A to the R.E.C. Inc. financial statements explains the company's procedures relating to depreciation and amortization: "Depreciation and Amortization: Property, plant, and equipment is stated at cost. Depreciation expense is calculated principally by the straight-line method based on estimated useful lives for buildings. Estimated useful lives of leasehold improvements represent the remaining term of the lease in effect at the time the improvements are made." Remember that for tax purposes, most firms use the Modified Accelerated Cost Recovery System for depreciation.

With any expense on the income statement, the analyst should evaluate the amount and trend of the expenditure as well as its relationship to the volume of firm activity that is relevant to the expense. For a firm like R.E.C. Inc., one would expect a fairly constant relationship between the investment in buildings, leasehold improvements, and equipment on the balance sheet and the annual expense recorded for depreciation and amortization on the income statement.

	2010	2009
Depreciation and amortization ───────────────────────────── Buildings, leasehold improvements, equipment	$\dfrac{3,998}{39,796} = 10.0\%$	$\dfrac{2,984}{25,696} = 11.6\%$

The percentage of depreciation and amortization expense has decreased somewhat, possibly due to the fact that new assets were placed in service during 2010 for only a part of the year, rendering less than a full year's depreciation and amortization.

Repairs and maintenance are the annual costs of repairing and maintaining the firm's property, plant, and equipment. Expenditures in this area should correspond to the level of investment in capital equipment and to the age and condition of the company's fixed assets. Similar to research and development and advertising and marketing expenses, inadequate allowance for repair and maintenance can impair the ongoing success of an organization. This category, like depreciation, should be evaluated in relation to the firm's investments in fixed assets. The percentage decrease in this account for R.E.C. Inc. could be a result of having newer fixed assets needing fewer repairs, or it could be a choice to delay repairs in order to increase operating profit in the short-term.

	2010	2009
Repairs and maintenance ───────────────────────────── Buildings, leasehold improvements, equipment	$\dfrac{3,015}{39,796} = 7.6\%$	$\dfrac{2,046}{25,696} = 8.0\%$

Firms in industries other than retail will have different expenses that should also be evaluated. For example, the trend of research and development expenses relative to net sales is an important measurement to evaluate for high-technology and pharmaceutical companies. By preparing a common-size income statement, each operating expense can be easily analyzed for any company. When evaluating operating expenses, good judgment must be used to decide whether increases or decreases in expenses are warranted. For example, reducing advertising or research and development may be detrimental in the long term if sales decrease; however, unnecessary increases in operating expense accounts could indicate inefficiencies in the company's operations.

Operating Profit

Operating profit (also called *EBIT* or *earnings before interest and taxes*) is the second step of profit determination on the R.E.C. Inc. earnings statement and measures the overall performance of the company's operations: sales revenue less the expenses associated with generating sales. The figure for operating profit provides a basis for assessing the success of a company apart from its financing and investing activities and separate from tax considerations. The *operating profit margin* is calculated as the relationship between operating profit and net sales:

	2010	2009	2008
$\dfrac{\text{Operating profit}}{\text{Net sales}}$	$\dfrac{19{,}243}{215{,}600} = 8.9\%$	$\dfrac{11{,}806}{153{,}000} = 7.7\%$	$\dfrac{11{,}256}{140{,}700} = 8.0\%$

The ratio indicates that R.E.C. Inc. strengthened its return on operations in 2010 after a dip in 2009. Looking at the common-size income statement (Exhibit 3.3) it is easy to see that despite the increase in cost of goods sold over the past two years, R.E.C. Inc. has reduced selling and administrative and advertising expenses enough to increase operating profit.

Other Income (Expense)

This category includes revenues and costs other than from operations, such as dividend and interest income, interest expense, gains (losses) from investments, equity earnings (losses), and gains (losses) from the sale of fixed assets. Equity earnings (losses) are discussed in the next section. R.E.C. Inc. recognizes as other income the interest earned on its investments in marketable securities and as other expense the interest paid on its debt. The relative amounts will be dependent on the level of investments and the amount of debt outstanding, as well as the prevailing level of interest rates.

Under the requirements of FASB Statement No. 115, discussed in Chapter 2, firms (primarily financial institutions and insurance companies) that carry debt and equity securities classified as "trading securities" report these investments on the balance sheet at market value with any unrealized gains and losses included in earnings.

In the assessment of earnings quality (discussed in Chapter 5), it is important that the analyst consider the materiality and the variability of the nonoperating items of income—for example, gains and losses on the sale of major capital assets, accounting changes, extraordinary items, investment income from temporary investments in cash equivalents, and investment income recognized under the equity method.

Equity Earnings

An additional issue that users sometimes encounter in attempting to evaluate financial statement data is the method—cost or equity—employed to account for investments in the voting stock of other companies. This method is not an issue for R.E.C. Inc. because the parent owns 100% of the voting stock in its subsidiaries; R.E.C. Inc. and its subsidiaries are, in substance, one consolidated entity. Where one firm owns more than 50% of the voting stock of another company, the parent company can obviously control the business operations, financial policies, and dividend declarations of the subsidiary, and consolidated financial statements are prepared with the disclosures relating to consolidation policies provided in the financial statement notes. The accounting rules underlying the preparation of consolidated financial statements, though similar to the equity method, are extremely complicated and beyond the scope of this book.[3] Questions regarding use of cost or equity come into play for stock investments of less than 50%, where consolidated financial statements are not prepared.

Accounting rules permit two different methods to account for stock investments of less than 50%. The equity method allows the investor proportionate recognition of the investee's net income, irrespective of the payment or nonpayment of cash dividends; under the cost method, the investor recognizes investment income only to the extent of any cash dividends received. At issue in the choice of accounting methods is whether the investor exercises control over the investee.

Accounting Principles Board Opinion No. 18 specifies that the equity method of accounting should be used when the investor can exercise significant influence over the investee's operating and financing policies. No problem exists where there is ownership of 50% or more because, clearly, one company can control the other. But at what level below 50% ownership can one firm substantially influence the affairs of another firm? Although there can be exceptions, 20% ownership of voting stock is generally considered to be evidence of substantial influence. There are, however, circumstances in which less than 20% ownership reflects control and cases in which more than 20% does not. Such factors as the extent of representation on the investee's board of directors, major intercompany transactions, technological dependence, and other relationships would be considered in the determination.

Use of the equity method is justified on a theoretical basis because it fits the requirements of the accrual basis of accounting. The investor's share in investee income is recorded by the investor in the period in which it is earned, rather than as cash is received. Analysts, however, should be aware of whether a company uses the cost or the equity method. What difference does it make whether a company uses the cost or equity method? An illustration should help provide the answer.

Assume that Company A acquires exactly 20% of the voting common stock of Company B for $400,000. Company B reports $100,000 earnings for the year and pays $25,000 in cash dividends. For Company A, the income recognition in the earnings statement and the noncurrent investment account on the balance sheet would be entirely different depending on the accounting method used for the investment.

	Cost	Equity
Income statement: investment income	$ 5,000	$ 20,000
Balance sheet: investment account	$400,000	$415,000

The cost method allows recognition of investment income only to the extent of any cash dividends actually received ($25,000 × 0.20), and the investment account is carried at cost.[4] The equity method permits the investor to count as income the percentage interest in the investee's earnings.

---

[3] Accounting for consolidated financial statements is fully discussed and explained in advanced accounting textbooks.

[4] Or market, depending on the provisions of FASB Statement No. 115; this statement does not apply to investments accounted for under the equity method.

Company B's earnings	$100,000
Company A's percent ownership	× 0.20
Company A's investment income	$ 20,000

Under the equity method, the investment account is increased by the amount of investment income recognized and is reduced by the amount of cash dividends received.

Investment at cost	$400,000
Investment income	+20,000
Cash dividends received	−5,000
Investment account	$415,000

Use of the equity method somewhat distorts earnings in the sense that income is recognized even though no cash may ever be received. The theoretical justification for the equity method is that it is presumed that the investor (Company A), through its control of voting shares, could cause Company B to pay dividends. In reality, this may not be true, and Company A is permitted to recognize more income than is received in cash.

One adjustment to net income (illustrated in Chapter 4) to calculate cash flow from operations is to deduct the amount by which income recognized under the equity method of accounting exceeds cash received from dividends. For Company A this amount would be $15,000 (investment income $20,000 less cash dividends $5,000). It is also equal to the increase in the balance sheet investment account (ending balance $415,000 less original cost $400,000). For comparative purposes it would be appropriate to eliminate this noncash portion of earnings.

Earnings Before Income Taxes/Effective Tax Rate

Earnings before income taxes is the profit recognized before the deduction of income tax expense. Income taxes are discussed in notes to the financial statements describing the difference between the reported figure for income taxes and the actual amount of income taxes paid (see the discussion of deferred income taxes in Chapter 2). For R.E.C. Inc., refer to Note A, which explains why the differences occur, and Note D, which quantifies the reconciliation between taxes paid and tax expense reported on the income statement. R.E.C. Inc.'s *effective tax rate* would be calculated by dividing income taxes on the income statement by earnings before taxes.

	2010	2009	2008
$\dfrac{\text{Income taxes}}{\text{Earnings before income taxes}}$	$\dfrac{7,686}{17,080} = 45.0\%$	$\dfrac{4,457}{10,367} = 43.0\%$	$\dfrac{4,824}{10,720} = 45.0\%$

In recent years, as revenues have been sluggish or decreasing, some companies have resorted to techniques to reduce taxes in order to increase earnings. Legitimately cutting taxes should always be applauded; however, firms cannot rely on tax-cutting techniques to continually increase earnings. Users of financial statements need to distinguish between earnings increasing due to core operations versus items such as tax rate deductions. (See Chapter 5 for more on this topic.)

Noteworthy items that may affect the effective tax rate are net operating losses (NOLs) and foreign taxes. Companies operating at a loss are allowed to carry back the loss two years and/or carry forward the loss 20 years, offsetting prior or future tax payments. If the NOL is carried back, the company may receive a refund of taxes previously paid.

Companies often have operations in foreign countries and must pay taxes based on that country's tax law. By reading the notes to the financial statements, the user can determine the effect foreign taxes have on the overall effective tax rate. General Electric Company (GE) reported earnings growth from 2005 to 2007 of 32.8%, yet its provision for income taxes declined from 18.1% to 15.5%. GE has one of the lowest effective tax rates in the United States (the U.S. federal statutory income tax rate for corporations was 35.0% in 2007). How has GE accomplished this? GE primarily was able to reduce its statutory tax rate (by 15.7% in 2007) through lower foreign tax rates.

Special Items

If companies are affected by the following two items, they must be disclosed separately on the income statement, net of income tax effects:

- Discontinued operations
- Extraordinary items

Special items are often one-time items that will not recur in the future. Because of the special disclosure requirements, it is easier for the analyst to determine whether these items should be included when predicting future earnings amounts. R.E.C. Inc. is not affected by any special items; however, each item will be explained in this chapter and examples are discussed further in Chapter 5.

Discontinued operations occur when a firm sells or discontinues a clearly distinguishable portion of its business. The results of continuing operations are shown separately from the operating results of the discontinued portion of the business. Any gain or loss on the disposal is also disclosed separately.

Extraordinary gains and losses are items that meet two criteria: unusual in nature and not expected to recur in the foreseeable future, considering the firm's operating environment. In an interesting decision in 2001, the FASB declared that the terrorist attack on September 11 was not an extraordinary event. Although the FASB agreed that in layman's terminology the event was extraordinary, it concluded that recording revenues or expenses related to September 11 as extraordinary would not improve the financial reporting system. The FASB's task force realized the dilemma as it tried to apply extraordinary treatment to the airline industry. Separating losses caused by the attack from losses already incurred by the economic downturn was an impossible task.[5]

---

[5] Steve Liesman, "Accountants, in a Reversal, Say Costs from the Attack Aren't 'Extraordinary,'" *Wall Street Journal*, October 1, 2001.

Accounting Changes

Prior to 2006, the cumulative effect of a change in accounting principle was disclosed when a firm changed an accounting policy. Changes in accounting policy may be voluntary; for example, a company changes inventory methods from FIFO to the average cost method. Other changes are mandated by the FASB or the Securities and Exchange Commission (SEC) when new rules must be implemented. The issuance of FASB Statement No. 154, "Accounting Changes and Error Corrections—a replacement of APB Opinion No. 20 and FASB Statement No. 3," effective for fiscal years beginning after December 15, 2005, has changed the disclosure requirements for accounting changes. This ruling is a result of the FASB's efforts to develop standards that are in agreement with current international accounting standards. Retrospective application to prior periods' financial statements is required for changes in accounting principles.[6] Retrospective application is defined as the application of a different accounting principle to prior accounting periods as if that principle had always been used or as the adjustment of previously issued financial statements to reflect a change in the reporting entity. The term *restatement* was also redefined in FASB Statement No. 154 as the revising of previously issued financial statements to reflect correction of an error. In addition, the statement specifies that changes to depreciation, amortization, or depletion methods be accounted for as a change in accounting estimate affected by a change in accounting principle.

Net Earnings

Net earnings, or "the bottom line," represents the firm's profit after consideration of all revenue and expense reported during the accounting period. The *net profit margin* shows the percentage of profit earned on every sales dollar.

	2010	2009	2008
Net earnings	$\dfrac{9,394}{215,600} = 4.4\%$	$\dfrac{5,910}{153,000} = 3.9\%$	$\dfrac{5,896}{140,700} = 4.2\%$
Net sales			

Earnings Per Common Share

Earnings per common share is the net earnings available to common stockholders for the period divided by the average number of common stock shares outstanding. This figure shows the return to the common stock shareholder for every share owned. R.E.C. Inc. earned $1.96 per share in 2010, compared with $1.29 per share in 2009 and $1.33 per share in 2008.

Companies with complex capital structures—which means existence of convertible securities (such as bonds convertible into common stock), stock options,

---

[6] If it is impracticable to determine the period-specific effects of an accounting change on one or more individual prior periods presented, then the new accounting principle should be applied to the balances of assets and liabilities as of the beginning of the earliest period for which retrospective application is practicable and a corresponding adjustment should be made to the opening balance of retained earnings for that period rather than be reported in the income statement.

and warrants—must calculate two amounts for earnings per share: *basic* and *diluted*. If convertible securities were converted into common stock and/or the options and warrants were exercised, there would be more shares outstanding for every dollar earned, and the potential for dilution is accounted for by the dual presentation. R.E.C. Inc. has a complex capital structure and therefore presents both basic and diluted earnings per share. In Note G to the financial statements, R.E.C. Inc. discloses the reconciliation of the basic and diluted earnings per share computations for the three-year period ended December 31, 2010. The diluted earnings per share number is slightly lower each year compared to the basic earnings per share because of the dilutive effect of stock options that employees could exercise in the future.

Another issue that an analyst should consider in assessing earnings quality is any material changes in the number of common stock shares outstanding that will cause a change in the computation of earnings per share. Changes in the number of shares outstanding result from such transactions as treasury stock purchases, the purchase and retirement of a firm's own common stock, stock splits, and reverse stock splits. (Stock splits and reverse stock splits are explained in a later section of this chapter.)

Comprehensive Income

As discussed in Chapter 2 and earlier in this chapter, companies must now report total comprehensive income either on the face of the income statement, in the statement of stockholders' equity, or in a separate financial statement. For example, even though Applied Materials, Inc. chooses to report total comprehensive income in the statement of shareholders' equity, if a separate statement had been used, it would appear as illustrated in Exhibit 3.4.

EXHIBIT 3.4

Applied Materials, Inc. Statements of Comprehensive Income for the Years Ended October 30, 2005, October 29, 2006, and October 28, 2007 (in thousands)

	2005	2006	2007
Net income	$1,209,900	$1,516,663	$1,710,196
Components of comprehensive income/(expense):			
Translation adjustments	(5,305)	6,757	9,583
Change in unrealized net gain/loss on investments	(33,053)	16,486	21,887
Change in unrealized net gain on derivative instruments	8,561	(4,888)	(5,728)
Change in medical retiree benefit			(1,132)
Change in minimum pension liability	(17,868)	(117)	3,462
Other	—	—	2,291
Total comprehensive income	$1,162,235	$1,534,901	$1,740,559

Currently, there are four items that may comprise a company's other comprehensive income: *foreign currency translation effects, unrealized gains and losses, additional pension liabilities,* and *cash flow hedges.* These items are outlined below; however, a detailed discussion of these topics is beyond the scope of this text. A more complete discussion of these four areas can be found in most intermediate or advanced accounting textbooks.

Foreign currency translation effects are the result of disclosures specified in FASB Statement No. 52, "Foreign Currency Translation." When U.S. firms operate abroad, the foreign financial statements must be translated into U.S. dollars at the end of the accounting period. Because the value of the dollar changes in relation to foreign currencies, gains and losses can result from the translation process. These exchange gains and losses, which fluctuate from period to period, are "accumulated" in the stockholders' equity section in most cases.[7]

According to the provisions of FASB Statement No. 115, discussed in Chapter 2, *unrealized gains and losses* on investments in debt and equity securities classified as available-for-sale are reported in comprehensive income. Cumulative net unrealized gains and losses are reported in the accumulated other comprehensive income section of stockholders' equity on the balance sheet.

Additional pension liabilities are reported as other comprehensive income when the accumulated benefit obligation is greater than the fair market value of plan assets less the balance in the accrued pension liability account or plus the balance in the deferred pension asset account. Pension accounting is discussed in Chapter 5.

Companies using *cash flow hedges* (derivatives designated as hedging the exposure to variable cash flows of a forecasted transaction) are required to initially report any gain or loss from a change in the fair market value of the cash flow hedge in other comprehensive income and subsequently reclassify the amount into earnings when the forecasted transaction affects earnings.[8]

THE STATEMENT OF STOCKHOLDERS' EQUITY

The statement of stockholders' equity details the transactions that affect the balance sheet equity accounts during an accounting period. Exhibit 3.5 shows the changes that have occurred in the equity accounts of R.E.C. Inc. Changes to the common stock and additional paid-in capital accounts are due to employees exercising their stock options. The retained earnings account has been increased each year by the net earnings and reduced by the cash dividends that R.E.C. Inc. has paid to their common stockholders. (R.E.C. Inc.'s dividend payment policy is discussed in Chapter 6.)

In 2010, R.E.C. Inc. paid cash dividends of $0.33 per share on average shares outstanding (Note G) of 4,792,857 for a total of $1,581,643. The amount of the dividend payment was reduced from $0.41 per share in 2009 and 2008.

---

[7] Exceptions are when the U.S. company designates the U.S. dollar as the "functional" currency for the foreign entity—such is the case, for example, when the foreign operations are simply an extension of the parent company's operations. Under this circumstance, the foreign translation gains and losses are included in the calculation of net income on the income statement.

[8] FASB Statement of Financial Accounting Standards No. 133, "Accounting for Derivative Instruments and Hedging Activities," 1998.

EXHIBIT 3.5

R.E.C. Inc. Consolidated Statements of Stockholders' Equity for the Years Ended December 31, 2010, 2009, and 2008 (in Thousands)

| | Common Stock | | Additional | Retained | |
	Shares	Amount	Paid-in Capital	Earnings	Total
Balance at December 31, 2007	4,340	$4,340	$857	$24,260	$29,457
Net earnings				5,896	5,896
Proceeds from sale of shares from exercise of stock options	103	103	21		124
Cash dividends				(1,841)	(1,841)
Balance at December 31, 2008	4,443	$4,443	$878	$28,315	$33,636
Net earnings				5,910	5,910
Proceeds from sale of shares from exercise of stock options	151	151	32		183
Cash dividends				(1,862)	(1,862)
Balance at December 31, 2009	4,594	$4,594	$910	$32,363	$37,867
Net earnings				9,394	9,394
Proceeds from sale of shares from exercise of stock options	209	209	47		256
Cash dividends				(1,582)	(1,582)
Balance at December 31, 2010	4,803	$4,803	$957	$40,175	$45,935

Some companies have *stock dividends, stock splits,* or *reverse stock splits* during an accounting period. With stock dividends, the company issues to existing shareholders additional shares of stock in proportion to current ownership. Stock dividends reduce the retained earnings account. Unlike a cash dividend, which results in the receipt of cash, a stock dividend represents nothing of value to the stockholder. The stockholder has more shares, but the proportion of ownership is exactly the same, and the company's net assets (assets minus liabilities) are exactly the same. The market value of the stock should drop in proportion to the additional shares issued.

Stock splits also result in the issuance of additional shares in proportion to current ownership and represent nothing of value to the stockholder; they are generally used to lower the market price of a firm's shares to make the common stock more affordable for the average investor. For example, if a company declares a 2–1 stock split, a stockholder with 100 shares ends up with 200 shares and the market price of the stock should fall by 50%. The company makes no accounting entry but does have a memorandum item noting the change in par value of the stock and the change in the number of shares outstanding. A reverse stock split is the opposite of a stock split and occurs when a company decreases, rather than increases, its out-standing shares. A 1–10 reverse stock split would have the effect of reducing 100 shares to 10 shares and the market price should increase 10 times. A reverse stock split usually occurs when a company is struggling financially.

Transactions other than the recognition of net profit/loss and the payment of dividends can cause changes in the retained earnings balance. These include prior period adjustments and certain changes in accounting principles. Prior pe-riod adjustments result primarily from the correction of errors made in previous accounting periods; the beginning retained earnings balance is adjusted for the year in which the error is discovered. Some changes in accounting principles, such as a change from LIFO to any other inventory method, also cause an adjust-ment to retained earnings for the cumulative effect of the change. Retained earn-ings can also be affected by transactions in a firm's own shares.

EARNINGS QUALITY AND CASH FLOW

Additional topics that are directly related to the income statement are covered in other sections of the book. The assessment of the quality of reported earnings is an essential element of income statement analysis. Many firms now report more than just the generally accepted accounting principles (GAAP) earnings numbers in their annual reports and quarterly press releases. These additional numbers are referred to as pro forma earnings, earnings before interest, taxes, depreciation, and amortization (EBITDA), core earnings, or adjusted earnings and have added not only to the confusion of investors, but have in many cases affected the quality of financial reporting. This important topic is discussed in Chapter 5.

The earnings figure reported on the income statement is rarely the same as the cash generated during an accounting period. Because it is cash that a firm needs to service debt, pay suppliers, invest in new capital assets, and pay cash dividends, cash flow from operations is a key ingredient in analyzing operating performance. The calculation of cash flow from operations, how it differs from reported earnings, and the interpretation of cash flow as a performance measure are discussed in Chapter 4.

Self-Test

Solutions are provided in Appendix B.

_____   **1.** What does the income statement measure for a firm?
   (a) The changes in assets and liabilities that occurred during the period.
   (b) The financing and investment activities for a period.
   (c) The results of operations for a period.
   (d) The financial position of a firm for a period.

_____   **2.** How are companies required to report total comprehensive income?
   (a) On the face of the income statement.
   (b) In a separate statement of comprehensive income.
   (c) In its statement of stockholders' equity.
   (d) All of the above.

_____ 3. Which of the following items needs to be disclosed separately in the income statement?
(a) Discontinued operations.
(b) Salary expense.
(c) Warranty expense.
(d) Bad debt expense.

_____ 4. What is a common-size income statement?
(a) An income statement that provides intermediate profit measures.
(b) An income statement that groups all items of revenue together, then deducts all categories of expense.
(c) A statement that expresses each item on an income statement as a percentage of net sales.
(d) An income statement that includes all changes of equity during a period.

_____ 5. Which of the following statements is incorrect with regard to gross profit or gross profit margin?
(a) The gross profit margin and cost of goods sold percentage are complements of each other.
(b) Generally, firms want to maintain the relationship between gross profit and sales, or, if possible, increase gross profit margin.
(c) The gross profit margin tends to be more stable in industries such as groceries.
(d) When cost of goods sold increases, most firms do not raise prices.

_____ 6. Why is it important to evaluate increases and decreases in operating expenses?
(a) Increases in operating expenses may indicate inefficiencies and decreases in operating expenses may be detrimental to long-term sales growth.
(b) It is important to determine whether companies are spending at least 10 cents of every sales dollar on advertising expenses.
(c) Increases in operating expenses are always an indication that a firm will increase sales in the future.
(d) None of the above.

_____ 7. Which of the following assets will not be depreciated over its service life?
(a) Buildings.
(b) Furniture.
(c) Land.
(d) Equipment.

_____ 8. How are costs of assets that benefit a firm for more than one year allocated?
(a) Depreciation.
(b) Depletion and amortization.
(c) Costs are divided by service lives of assets and allocated to repairs and maintenance.
(d) Both (a) and (b).

_____ 9. Why should the expenditures for repairs and maintenance correspond to the level of investment in capital equipment and to the age and condition of that equipment?

(a) Repairs and maintenance expense is calculated in the same manner as depreciation expense.

(b) Repairs and maintenance are depreciated over the remaining life of the assets involved.

(c) It is a generally accepted accounting principle that repairs and maintenance expense is generally between 5% and 10% of fixed assets.

(d) Inadequate repairs of equipment can impair the operating success of a business enterprise.

_____ 10. Why is the figure for operating profit important?

(a) This is the figure used for calculating federal income tax expense.

(b) The figure for operating profit provides a basis for assessing the success of a company apart from its financing and investment activities and separate from its tax status.

(c) The operating profit figure includes all operating revenues and expenses as well as interest and taxes related to operations.

(d) The figure for operating profit provides a basis for assessing the wealth of a firm.

_____ 11. Why can the equity method of accounting for investments in the voting stock of other companies cause distortions in net earnings?

(a) Significant influence may exist even if the ownership of voting stock is less than 20%.

(b) Income is recognized where no cash may ever be received.

(c) Income should be recognized in accordance with the accrual method of accounting.

(d) Income is recognized only to the extent of cash dividends received.

_____ 12. Why should the effective tax rate be evaluated when assessing earnings?

(a) It is important to understand whether earnings have increased because of tax techniques rather than from positive changes in core operations.

(b) Effective tax rates are irrelevant because they are mandated by law.

(c) Effective tax rates do not include the effects of foreign taxes.

(d) Net operating losses allow a firm to change its effective tax rates for each of the five years prior to the loss.

_____ 13. Which of the following items should be recorded as other comprehensive income?

(a) Foreign currency translation effects.

(b) Extraordinary gains and losses.

(c) Realized gains and losses.

(d) All of the above.

_____ **14.** What are three profit measures calculated from the income statement?

    (a) Operating profit margin, net profit margin, repairs and mainte-
nance to fixed assets.

    (b) Gross profit margin, cost of goods sold percentage, EBIT.

    (c) Gross profit margin, operating profit margin, net profit margin.

    (d) None of the above.

_____ **15.** When is a dual presentation of basic and diluted earnings per share
required?

    (a) When a company has pension liabilities.

    (b) When convertible securities are in fact converted.

    (c) When a company has a simple capital structure.

    (d) When a company has a complex capital structure.

_____ **16.** What is a statement of stockholders' equity?

    (a) It is the same as a retained earnings statement.

    (b) It is a statement that reconciles only the treasury stock account.

    (c) It is a statement that summarizes changes in the entire stockhold-
ers' equity section of the balance sheet.

    (d) It is a statement reconciling the difference between stock issued at
par value and stock issued at market value.

_____ **17.** What accounts can be found on a statement of stockholders' equity?

    (a) Investments in other companies.

    (b) Treasury stock, accumulated other comprehensive income, and
retained earnings.

    (c) Market value of treasury stock.

    (d) Both (a) and (c).

_____ **18.** Which of the following cause(s) a change in the retained earnings account balance?

    (a) Prior period adjustment.

    (b) Payment of dividends.

    (c) Net profit or loss.

    (d) All of the above.

19. Match the following terms with the correct definitions:

    _____ (a) Depreciation.

    _____ (b) Depletion.

    _____ (c) Amortization.

    _____ (d) Gross profit.

    _____ (e) Operating profit.

    _____ (f) Net profit.

    _____ (g) Equity method.

    _____ (h) Cost method.

    _____ (i) Single-step format.

    _____ (j) Multiple-step format.

    _____ (k) Basic earnings per share.

    _____ (l) Diluted earnings per share.

    _____ (m) Extraordinary events.

    _____ (n) Discontinued operations.

Definitions

(1) Proportionate recognition of investee's net income for investments in voting stock of other companies.

(2) Presentation of income statement that provides several intermediate profit measures.

(3) Unusual events not expected to recur in the foreseeable future.

(4) Allocation of costs of tangible fixed assets.

(5) Difference between sales revenue and expenses associated with generating sales.

(6) Recognition of income from investments in voting stock of other companies to the extent of cash dividend received.

(7) Operations that will not continue in the future because the firm sold a major portion of its business.

(8) Difference between net sales and cost of goods sold.

(9) Allocation of costs of acquiring and developing natural resources.

(10) Earnings per share figure calculated by dividing the average number of common stock shares outstanding into the net earnings available to common stockholders.

(11) Presentation of income statement that groups all revenue items, then deducts all expenses, to arrive at net income.

(12) Earnings per share figure based on the assumption that all potentially dilutive securities have been converted to common stock.

(13) Allocation of costs of intangible assets.

(14) Difference between all revenues and expenses.

20. The following categories appear on the income statement of Joshua Jeans Company:

(a) Net sales.

(b) Cost of sales.

(c) Operating expenses.

(d) Other revenue/expense.

(e) Income tax expense.

Classify the following items according to income statement category:

_____ (1) Depreciation expense.

_____ (2) Interest revenue.

_____ (3) Sales revenue.

_____ (4) Advertising expense.

_____ (5) Interest expense.

_____ (6) Sales returns and allowances.

_____ (7) Federal income taxes.

_____ (8) Repairs and maintenance.

_____ (9) Selling and administrative expenses.

_____ (10) Cost of products sold.

_____ (11) Dividend income.

_____ (12) Lease payments.

Study Questions, Problems, and Cases

3.1 What is the difference between a multiple-step and a single-step format of the earnings statement? Which format is the most useful for analysis?

3.2 How is a common-size income statement created?

3.3 What are the two causes of an increasing or decreasing sales number?

3.4 Discuss all reasons that could explain an increase or decrease in gross profit margin.

3.5 Explain how a company could have a decreasing gross profit margin, but an increasing operating profit margin.

3.6 What is an example of an industry that would need to spend a minimum amount on advertising to be competitive? On research and development?

3.7 Alpha Company purchased 30% of the voting common stock of Beta Company on January 1 and paid $500,000 for the investment. Beta Company reported $100,000 of earnings for the year and paid $40,000 in cash dividends. Calculate investment income and the balance sheet investment account for Alpha Company under the cost method and under the equity method.

3.8 Discuss the four items that are included in a company's comprehensive income.

3.9 Explain what can be found on a statement of stockholders' equity.

3.10 Why is the bottom line figure, net income, not necessarily a good indicator of a firm's financial success?

3.11 An excerpt from the Sun Company's annual report is presented below. Calculating any profit measures deemed necessary, discuss the implications of the profitability of the company.

**Sun Company Income Statements for the Years
Ended December 31, 2010, 2009, and 2008**

	2010	2009	2008
Net sales	$236,000	$195,000	$120,000
Cost of goods sold	186,000	150,000	85,000
Gross profit	$ 50,000	$ 45,000	$ 35,000
Operating expenses	22,000	18,000	11,000
Operating profit	$ 28,000	$ 27,000	$ 24,000
Income taxes	12,000	11,500	10,500
Net income	$ 16,000	$ 15,500	$ 13,500

3.12 Prepare a multiple-step income statement for Jackrabbit, Inc. from the following single-step statement.

Net sales	$1,840,000
Gain on sale of equipment	15,000
Interest income	13,000
	1,868,000
Costs and expenses:	
Cost of goods sold	1,072,000
Selling expenses	270,000
General and admin. expenses	155,000
Depreciation	24,000
Equity losses	9,000
Interest expense	16,000
Income tax expense	96,000
Net income	$ 226,000

3.13 Income statements for Yarrick Company for the years ending December 31, 2010, 2009, and 2008 are shown below. Prepare a common-size income statement and analyze the profitability of the company.

**Yarrick Company Income Statements for the Years
Ending December 31, 2010, 2009, and 2008**

(in millions)	2010	2009	2008
Net sales	$237	$155	$134
Cost of goods sold	138	84	72
Gross profit	$ 99	$ 71	$ 62
Sales, general, and administrative expenses	42	31	39
Research and development	38	33	54
Operating profit	$ 19	$ 7	($ 31)
Income tax expense (benefit)	7	2	(11)
Net profit	$ 12	$ 5	($ 20)

3.14 LA Theatres, Inc. has two distinct revenue sources, ticket and concession revenues. The following information from LA Theatres, Inc. income statements for the past three years is available:

(in millions)	2010	2009	2008
Ticket revenue	$1,731	$1,642	$1,120
Concessions revenue	792	687	411
Total revenue	$2,523	$2,329	$1,531
Cost of goods sold—tickets	$ 951	$ 854	$ 549
Cost of goods sold—concessions	70	69	48
Total cost of goods sold	$1,021	$ 923	$ 597
Gross profit	$1,502	$1,406	$ 934

(a) Calculate gross profit margins for tickets and concessions for all three years. Calculate an overall gross profit margin for LA Theatres, Inc. for all three years.

(b) Analyze the changes in gross profit margin for all three years.

3.15 Writing Skills Problem

Income statements are presented for the Elf Corporation for the years ending December 31, 2010, 2009, and 2008.

Elf Corporation Income Statements for the Years Ending December 31, 2010, 2009, and 2008

(in millions)	2010	2009	2008
Sales	$700	$650	$550
Cost of goods sold	350	325	275
Gross profit	$350	$325	$275
Operating expenses:			
Administrative	100	100	100
Advertising and marketing	50	75	75
Operating profit	$200	$150	$100
Interest expense	70	50	30
Earnings before tax	$130	$100	$ 70
Tax expense (50%)	65	50	35
Net income	$ 65	$ 50	$ 35

Required: Write a one-paragraph analysis of Elf Corporation's profit performance for the period.

To the Student: The focus of this exercise is on analyzing financial data rather than simply describing the numbers and trends. Analysis involves breaking the information into parts for study, relating the pieces, making comparisons, drawing conclusions, and evaluating cause and effect.

3.16 Research Problem

Locate the income statement of a company in each of the following industries: pharmaceutical, technology, retailer—groceries, and automobile manufacturer. (See Chapter 1 for help in locating a company's financial statements.) Calculate the gross profit margin, operating profit margin, and net profit margin for all companies. Write a short essay explaining the differences you find between the profit margins calculated and why you think the profit margins differ.

3.17 Internet Problem

Look up the FASB home page on the Internet at the following address: www.fasb.org/. Find the list of technical projects that are currently on the board's agenda. Choose one of the projects that will impact the income statement. Describe the potential change and how the income statement may be impacted.

3.18 Intel Case

The 2007 Intel Annual Report can be found at the following Web site: www .prenhall.com/fraser.

(a) Using the consolidated statements of operations, analyze the profitability of Intel by preparing a common-size income statement and by calculating any other ratios deemed necessary for the past three years. Be sure to calculate sales growth and operating expense growth for each two-year period presented.

(b) Using the consolidated statements of stockholders' equity for Intel, explain the key reasons for the changes in the common stock, accumulated other comprehensive income, and retained earnings accounts. Evaluate these changes.

3.19 Eastman Kodak Comprehensive Analysis Case Using the Financial Statement Analysis Template

Each chapter in the textbook contains a continuation of this problem. The objective is to learn how to do a comprehensive financial statement analysis in steps as the content of each chapter is learned. Using the 2007 Eastman Kodak Annual Report and Form 10-K, which can be found at www.prenhall.com/fraser, complete the following requirements:

(a) Open the financial statement analysis template that you saved from the Chapter 1 Eastman Kodak problem and input the data from the Eastman Kodak income statement. Use the basic earnings per share from continuing operations when inputting the earnings per share amount. When you have finished inputting the data, review the income statement to make sure there are no red blocks indicating that your numbers do not match the cover sheet information you input from the Chapter 1 problem. Make any necessary corrections before printing out both your input and the common-size income statement that the template automatically creates for you.

(b) Analyze the income statement of Eastman Kodak. Write a summary that includes important points that an analyst would use in assessing the profitability of Eastman Kodak.

3.20 Sara Lee Corporation Case

Sara Lee Corporation is a manufacturer and marketer of high-quality, brand-name products such as *Ambi Pur, Ball Park, Douwe Egberts, Hillshire Farm, Jimmy Dean, Kiwi, Sanex, Senseo,* and its namesake, *Sara Lee.* In February 2005, Sara Lee announced a business transformation plan. Significant organizational changes have been implemented, including the disposition of a significant portion of the corporation's business, as well as actions to improve operational efficiency. Selected information from Sara Lee's 2007 Annual Report is given on pages 105–106.

Required

1. Sara Lee's income statements should be reformatted before beginning an analysis. Explain what format Sara Lee has used and why the income statements should be reconfigured.

2. Redo the income statements for Sara Lee and prepare common-size income statements for all three years presented. Explain your reasoning for how revenues and expenses were reclassified.
3. Analyze the profitability of Sara Lee using the common-size income statements you prepared, as well as any other calculations you deem necessary. Be sure to include an explanation of the effective tax rate and any nonrecurring or nonoperating items.

Consolidated statements of income
Dollars in millions, except per share data

	Years Ended		
	June 30, 2007	July 1, 2006	July 2, 2005
Continuing operations			
Net Sales	$12,278	$11,460	$11,346
Cost of sales	7,552	7,025	6,795
Selling, general, and administrative expenses	4,023	3,848	3,679
Net charges for exit activities, asset and business dispositions	95	86	43
Impairment charges	172	193	—
Contingent sale proceeds	(120)	(114)	(117)
Interest expense	265	305	285
Interest income	(128)	(75)	(85)
	11,859	11,268	10,600
Income from continuing operations before income taxes	419	192	746
Income tax (benefit) expense	(7)	161	131
Income from continuing operations	426	31	615
Discontinued operations			
Net income from discontinued operations, net of tax expense of $30, $19, and $139	62	123	104
Gain on sale of discontinued operations, net of tax (benefit) expense of $(11), $65, and $0	16	401	—
Net Income (Loss)	$ 504	$ 555	$ 719
Net income from continuing operations per share of common stock			
Basic	$ 0.58	$ 0.04	$ 0.78
Diluted	$ 0.57	$ 0.04	$ 0.77
Net income per share of common stock			
Basic	$ 0.68	$ 0.72	$ 0.91
Diluted	$ 0.68	$ 0.72	$ 0.90

The accompanying Notes to Financial Statements are an integral part of these statements.

Note 16—Contingencies

Contingent Asset—The corporation sold its European cut tobacco business in 1999. Under the terms of that agreement, the corporation will receive an annual cash payment of 95 million euros if tobacco continues to be a legal product in the Netherlands, Germany and Belgium through July 15, 2009. The legal status of tobacco in each country accounts for a portion of the total contingency with the Netherlands accounting for 67%, Germany 22% and Belgium 11%. If tobacco ceases to be a legal product within any of these countries, the corporation forfeits the receipt of all future amounts related to that country. The contingencies associated with the 2007, 2006, and 2005 payments passed in the first quarter of each fiscal year and the corporation received the annual payments. The 2007 annual payment was equivalent to $120, the 2006 annual payment was equivalent to $114, and the 2005 payment was equivalent to $117 based upon the respective exchange rates on the dates of receipt. These amounts were recognized in the corporation's earnings when received. The payments increased diluted earnings per share by $0.16 in 2007 and $0.15 in 2006 and 2005.

Note 23—Income Taxes

The provisions for income taxes on continuing operations computed by applying the U.S. statutory rate to income from continuing operations before taxes as reconciled to the actual provisions were:

	2007	2006	2005
Income from continuing operations before income taxes			
United States	(45.4)%	(250.9)%	(22.6)%
Foreign	145.4	350.9	122.6
	100.0%	100.0%	100.0%
Tax expense at U.S. statutory rate	35.0%	35.0%	35.0%
Tax on remittance of foreign earnings	43.4	274.5	30.6
Finalization of tax reviews and audits	(26.3)	(172.2)	(24.8)
Foreign taxes different than U.S. statutory rate	(13.7)	15.8	(8.5)
Valuation allowances	6.2	(18.5)	—
Benefit of foreign tax credits	(7.3)	(5.5)	(6.3)
Contingent sale proceeds	(10.0)	(20.8)	(5.5)
Tax rate changes	(3.8)	(2.4)	(3.2)
Goodwill impairment	8.0	—	—
Sale of capital assets	(36.3)	(14.4)	—
Other, net	3.2	(8.0)	0.3
Taxes at effective worldwide tax rates	(1.6)%	83.5%	17.6%

In 2006, the corporation recognized tax expense of $161 million, or an effective tax rate of 83.5% as the corporation recognized a $529 million tax charge to repatriate to the U.S. approximately $1.7 billion of cash related to current and prior year earnings of certain foreign subsidiaries previously deemed to be permanently invested. Of the $529 million charge, $291 million relates to earnings of prior years. This charge was partially offset by a $332 million credit related to the favorable outcome of certain foreign tax audits and reviews that were completed during the period and a $36 million benefit due to a change in a valuation allowance.

4

Statement of Cash Flows

"Joan and Joe: A Tale of Woe"
Joe added up profits and went to see Joan,
Assured of obtaining a much-needed loan.
When Joe arrived, he announced with good cheer:
"My firm has had an outstanding year,
And now I need a loan from your bank."
Eyeing the statements, Joan's heart sank.
"Your profits are fine," Joan said to Joe.
"But where, oh where, is your company's cash flow?
I'm sorry to say: the answer is 'no'."

—L. FRASER

The statement of cash flows, required by Statement of Financial Accounting Standards No. 95, represents a major step forward in accounting measurement and disclosure because of its relevance to financial statement users. Ample evidence has been provided over the years by firms of every conceivable size, structure, and type of business operation that it is possible for a company to post a healthy net income but still not have the cash needed to pay its employees, suppliers, and bankers. The statement of cash flows, which replaced the statement of changes in financial position in 1988, provides information about cash inflows and outflows during an accounting period. On the statement, cash flows are segregated by *operating activities, investing activities,* and *financing activities.*[1] The mandated focus on cash in this statement results in a more useful document than its predecessor. A positive net income figure on the income statement is ultimately insignificant unless a company can translate its earnings into cash, and the only source in financial statements for learning about cash generation is the statement of cash flows.

The objectives of this chapter are twofold: (1) to explain how the statement of cash flows is prepared and (2) to interpret the information presented in the statement, including a discussion of the significance of cash flow from operations as an analytical tool in assessing financial performance. Readers may legitimately ask at this point why it is necessary to wade through the preparation of this statement to understand and use the information it contains. This chapter provides a more extensive treatment of the preparation of the statement—its underpinnings—than the chapters on the balance sheet, income statement, and statement of stockholders' equity. The reason for this approach is its extreme importance as an analytical tool. Understanding the statement is greatly enhanced by understanding how it is developed from the balance sheet and income statement; knowing the nuts and bolts helps the analyst utilize its disclosures to maximum effect.

The Consolidated Statements of Cash Flows for R.E.C. Inc., shown in Exhibit 4.1, will serve as the background for an explanation of how the statement is prepared and a discussion of its usefulness for financial analysis.

PREPARING A STATEMENT OF CASH FLOWS

Preparing the statement of cash flows begins with a return to the balance sheet, covered in Chapter 2. The statement of cash flows requires a reordering of the information presented on a balance sheet. The balance sheet shows account balances at the end of an accounting period, and the statement of cash flows shows changes in those same account balances between accounting periods (see Figure 4.1). The statement is called a statement of *flows* because it shows *changes over time rather than the absolute dollar amount of the accounts at a point in time.* Because a balance sheet balances, the changes in all of the balance sheet accounts balance, and the changes that reflect cash inflows less the changes that result from cash outflows will equal the changes in the cash account.

The statement of cash flows is prepared in exactly that way: by calculating the changes in all of the balance sheet accounts, including *cash;* then listing the changes in all of the accounts except cash as *inflows* or *outflows;* and categorizing the flows by *operating, financing,* or *investing* activities. The *inflows less the outflows balance to and explain the change in cash.*

To classify the account changes on the balance sheet, first review the definitions of the four parts of a statement of cash flows:

- Cash
- Operating activities

---

[1] Financing and investing activities not involving cash receipts and payments—such as the exchange of debt for stock or the exchange of property—are reported in a separate schedule on the statement of cash flows.

EXHIBIT 4.1

R.E.C. Inc. Consolidated Statements of Cash Flows for the Years Ended December 31, 2010, 2009, and 2008 (in Thousands)

	2010	2009	2008
Cash Flows from Operating Activities— Indirect Method			
Net income	$ 9,394	$ 5,910	$ 5,896
Adjustments to reconcile net income to cash provided (used) by operating activities			
Depreciation and amortization	3,998	2,984	2,501
Deferred income taxes	208	136	118
Cash provided (used) by current assets and liabilities			
Accounts receivable	(610)	(3,339)	(448)
Inventories	(10,272)	(7,006)	(2,331)
Prepaid expenses	247	295	(82)
Accounts payable	6,703	(1,051)	902
Accrued liabilities	356	(1,696)	(927)
Net cash provided (used) by operating activities	$ 10,024	($ 3,767)	$ 5,629
Cash Flows from Investing Activities			
Additions to property, plant, and equipment	(14,100)	(4,773)	(3,982)
Other investing activities	295	0	0
Net cash provided (used) by investing activities	($ 13,805)	($ 4,773)	($ 3,982)
Cash Flows from Financing Activities			
Sales of common stock	256	183	124
Increase (decrease) in short-term borrowings (includes current maturities of long-term debt)	(30)	1,854	1,326
Additions to long-term borrowings	5,600	7,882	629
Reductions of long-term borrowings	(1,516)	(1,593)	(127)
Dividends paid	(1,582)	(1,862)	(1,841)
Net cash provided (used) by financing activities	$ 2,728	$ 6,464	$ 111
Increase (decrease) in cash and marketable securities	($ 1,053)	($ 2,076)	$ 1,758
Cash and marketable securities, beginning of year	10,386	12,462	10,704
Cash and marketable securities, end of year	$ 9,333	$10,386	$12,462
Supplemental cash flow information:			
Cash paid for interest	$ 2,585	$ 2,277	$ 1,274
Cash paid for taxes	7,478	4,321	4,706

The accompanying notes are an integral part of these statements.

FIGURE 4.1 How Cash Flows During an Accounting Period.

Operating Activities

Inflows

Revenue from sales of goods
Revenue from services
Returns on equity securities (dividends)
Returns on interest-earning assets (interest)

Outflows

Payments for purchase of inventory
Payments for operating expenses
   (salaries, rent, etc.)
Payments for purchases from suppliers
   other than inventory
Payments to lenders (interest)
Payments for taxes

Investing Activities

Inflows

Revenue from sales of long-lived assets
Returns from loans (principal) to others
Revenue from sales of debt or equity
   securities of other entities (except
   securities traded as cash equivalents)*

Outflows

Acquisitions of long-lived assets
Loans (principal) to others
Purchases of debt or equity securities
   of other entities*

Financing Activities

Inflows

Proceeds from borrowing
Proceeds from issuing the firm's own
   equity securities

Outflows

Repayments of debt principal
Repurchase of a firm's own shares
Payment of dividends

Total Inflows less Total Outflows = Change in cash for the accounting period

*Cash flows from purchases, sales, and maturities of trading securities shall be classified based on
the nature and purpose for which the securities were acquired.

- Investing activities
- Financing activities

   Cash includes cash and highly liquid short-term marketable securities, also
called *cash equivalents*. Marketable securities are included as cash for R.E.C. Inc.,
because they represent, as explained in Chapter 2, short-term highly liquid
investments that can be readily converted into cash. They include U.S. Treasury
bills, certificates, notes, and bonds; negotiable certificates of deposit at financial
institutions; and commercial paper. Some companies will separate marketable
securities into two accounts: (1) cash and cash equivalents and (2) short-term
investments. When this occurs, the short-term investments are classified as
investing activities.

Operating activities include delivering or producing goods for sale and providing services and the cash effects of transactions and other events that enter into the determination of income.

Investing activities include (1) acquiring and selling or otherwise disposing of (a) securities that are not cash equivalents and (b) productive assets that are expected to benefit the firm for long periods of time and (2) lending money and collecting on loans.

Financing activities include borrowing from creditors and repaying the principal and obtaining resources from owners and providing them with a return on the investment.

With these definitions in mind, consider Exhibit 4.2, a worksheet for preparing the statement of cash flows that shows comparative 2010 and 2009 balance sheet accounts for R.E.C. Inc. Included in this exhibit is a column with the account balance changes and the category (or categories) that applies to each account. Explanations of how each account change is used in a statement of cash flow will be provided in subsequent sections of this chapter.

The next step is to transfer the account changes to the appropriate area of a statement of cash flows.[2] In doing so, a determination must also be made of what constitutes an inflow and what constitutes an outflow when analyzing the change in an account balance. The following table should help:

Inflow	Outflow
– Asset account	+ Asset account
+ Liability account	– Liability account
+ Equity account	– Equity account

The table indicates that a decrease in an asset balance and an increase in liability and equity accounts are inflows.[3] Examples from Exhibit 4.2 are the decrease in other assets (cash inflow from the sale of property not used in the business), the increase in long-term debt (cash inflow from borrowing), and the increase in common stock and additional paid-in capital (cash inflow from sales of equity securities). Outflows are represented by the increase in inventories (cash outflow to purchase inventory) and the decrease in notes payable (cash outflow to repay borrowings).

Note that accumulated depreciation appears in the asset section but actually is a contra-asset or credit balance account because it reduces the amount of total assets. Accumulated depreciation is shown in parentheses on the balance sheet and has the same effect as a liability account.

---

[2] Several alternative formats can be used for presenting the statement of cash flows, provided that the statement is reconciled to the change in cash and shows cash inflows and outflows from operating, financing, and investing activities.

[3] In accounting terminology, an inflow results from the decrease in a debit balance account or an increase in a credit balance account; an outflow results from the increase in a debit balance account or the decrease in a credit balance account.

EXHIBIT 4.2

R.E.C. Inc. Worksheet for Preparing Statement of Cash Flows (in Thousands)

	2010	2009	Change (2010–2009)	Category
Assets				
(1) Cash	$ 4,061	$ 2,382	$ 1,679	Cash
(2) Marketable securities	5,272	8,004	(2,732)	Cash
(3) Accounts receivable (net)	8,960	8,350	610	Operating
(4) Inventories	47,041	36,769	10,272	Operating
(5) Prepaid expenses	512	759	(247)	Operating
(6) Property, plant, and equipment	40,607	26,507	14,100	Investing
(7) Accumulated depreciation and amortization	(11,528)	(7,530)	(3,998)	Operating
(8) Other assets	373	668	(295)	Investing
Liabilities and Stockholders' Equity				
Liabilities				
(9) Accounts payable	14,294	7,591	6,703	Operating
(10) Notes payable—banks	5,614	6,012	(398)	Financing
(11) Current maturities of long-term debt	1,884	1,516	368	Financing
(12) Accrued liabilities	5,669	5,313	356	Operating
(13) Deferred income taxes	843	635	208	Operating
(14) Long-term borrowings				
Additions to long-term borrowings			5,600	
Reductions of long-term borrowings			(1,516)	
Net change in long-term debt	21,059	16,975	$ 4,084	Financing
Stockholders' Equity				
(15) Common stock	4,803	4,594	209	Financing
(16) Additional paid-in capital	957	910	47	Financing
(17) Retained earnings				
(a) Net income			9,394	Operating
(b) Dividends paid			(1,582)	Financing
Net change in retained earnings	$40,175	$32,363	$ 7,812	

Another complication occurs from the impact of *two transactions in one account.* For example, the net increase in retained earnings has resulted from the combination of net income for the period, which increases the account, and the payment of dividends, which reduces the account. Multiple transactions can also affect other accounts, such as property, plant, and equipment if a firm both acquires and sells capital assets during the period, and debt accounts if the firm both borrows and repays principal.

(1)(2) Cash and marketable securities are cash. The changes in these two accounts—a net decrease of $1,053 thousand (decrease in marketable securities of $2,732 thousand less increase in cash of $1,679 thousand)—will be explained by the changes in all of the other accounts. This means that for the year ending 2007, the cash outflows have exceeded the cash inflows by $1,053 thousand.

(3)(4)(5) Accounts receivable, inventories, and prepaid expenses are all operating accounts relating to sales of goods, purchases of inventories, and payments for operating expenses.

(6) The net increase in property, plant, and equipment is an investing activity reflecting purchases of long-lived assets.

(7) The change in accumulated depreciation and amortization is classified as operating because it will be used as an adjustment to operating expenses or net income to determine cash flow from operating activities.

(8) Other assets are holdings of land held for resale, representing an investing activity.

(9) Accounts payable is an operating account because it arises from purchases of inventory.

(10)(11) Notes payable and current maturities of long-term debt result from borrowing (debt principal), a financing activity.

(12) Accrued liabilities are operating because they result from the accrual of operating expenses such as wages, rent, salaries, and insurance.

(13) The change in deferred income taxes is categorized as operating because it is part of the adjustment of tax expense to calculate cash flow from operating activities.

(14) The change in long-term debt, principal on borrowings, is a financing activity.

(15)(16) Common stock and paid-in capital are also financing activities because the changes result from sales of the firm's own equity shares.

(17) The change in retained earnings, as explained in Chapter 3, is the product of two activities: (a) net income for the period, which is operating; and (b) the payment of cash dividends, which is a financing activity.

CALCULATING CASH FLOW FROM OPERATING ACTIVITIES

The R.E.C. Inc. Consolidated Statements of Cash Flows begins with cash flow from operating activities. This represents the cash generated *internally.* In contrast, investing and financing activities provide cash from *external* sources. Firms may use one of two methods prescribed by the Financial Accounting Standards Board (FASB) for calculating and presenting cash flow from operating activities: the direct method and the indirect method. The *direct method* shows cash collections from customers, interest and dividends collected, other operating cash receipts, cash paid to suppliers and employees, interest paid, taxes paid, and other operating cash payments. The *indirect method* starts with net income and adjusts for deferrals; accruals; noncash items, such as depreciation and amortization; and nonoperating items, such as gains and losses on asset sales. The direct and indirect methods yield identical figures for net cash flow from operating activities because the underlying accounting concepts are the same. According to *Accounting Trends and Techniques*, 594 firms out of 600 used the indirect method in 2007.[4] The *indirect method* is illustrated and explained for R.E.C. Inc. in the chapter and the *direct method* is illustrated in the appendix to this chapter.

Indirect Method

Exhibit 4.3 illustrates the steps necessary to convert net income to cash flow from operating activities. The steps shown in Exhibit 4.3 will be used to explain the calculation of cash flow from operating activities for R.E.C. Inc. using the indirect method. Exhibit 4.3 includes some adjustments not present for R.E.C. Inc.

R.E.C. Inc. Indirect Method

Net income	$ 9,394
Adjustments to reconcile net income to cash provided by operating activities:	
+ Depreciation and amortization expense	3,998
+ Increase in deferred tax liability	208
Cash provided (used) by current assets, liabilities	
− Increase in accounts receivables	(610)
− Increase in inventory	(10,272)
+ Decrease in prepaid expenses	247
+ Increase in accounts payable	6,703
+ Increase in accrued liabilities	356
Net cash flow from operating activities	$10,024

Depreciation and amortization are added back to net income because they reflect the recognition of a noncash expense. Remember that depreciation represents a cost allocation, not an outflow of cash. The acquisition of the capital asset was recognized as an investing cash outflow (unless it was exchanged for debt or stock) in the statement of cash flows for the period in which the asset was acquired. So depreciation itself does not require any outflow of cash in the year it

---

[4] American Institute of Certified Public Accountants, *Accounting Trends and Techniques*, 2007.

EXHIBIT 4.3

Net Cash Flow from Operating Activities—Indirect Method

Net income*

Noncash/Nonoperating revenue and expense included in income:

+ Depreciation, amortization, depletion expense for period

+ Increase in deferred tax liability
− Decrease in deferred tax liability

+ Decrease in deferred tax asset
− Increase in deferred tax asset

− Increase in investment account from equity income**
+ Decrease in investment account from equity income***

− Gain on sale of assets
+ Loss on sale of assets

Cash provided (used) by current assets and liabilities

+ Decrease in accounts receivable
− Increase in accounts receivable

+ Decrease in inventory
− Increase in inventory

+ Decrease in prepaid expenses
− Increase in prepaid expenses

+ Decrease in interest receivable
− Increase in interest receivable

+ Increase in accounts payable
− Decrease in accounts payable

+ Increase in accrued liabilities
− Decrease in accrued liabilities

+ Increase in deferred revenue
− Decrease in deferred revenue

Net cash flow from operating activities

*Before extraordinary items, accounting changes, discontinued operations.
**Amount by which equity income exceeds cash dividends received.
***Amount by which cash dividends received exceed equity income recognized.

is recognized. Deducting depreciation expense in the current year's statement of cash flows would be double counting. Amortization is similar to depreciation—an expense that enters into the determination of net income but that does not require an outflow of cash. Depletion would be handled in the same manner as depreciation and amortization. The depreciation and amortization expense for R.E.C. Inc. in 2010 is equal to the change in the balance sheet accumulated depreciation and amortization account. If the firm had dispositions of capital assets during the accounting period, however, the balance sheet change would not equal the expense recognition for the period because some of the account change would have resulted from the elimination of accumulated depreciation for the asset that was removed. The appropriate figure to subtract would be depreciation and amortization expense from the earnings statement.

The *deferred tax liability* account, as discussed in Chapter 2, reconciles the difference between tax expense recognized in the calculation of net income and the tax expense actually paid. The increase in the liability account for R.E.C. Inc. is added back to net income because more tax expense was recognized in the calculation of net income than was actually paid for taxes.

The increase in *accounts receivable* is deducted because more sales revenue has been included in net income than has been collected in cash from customers.

The increase in *inventory* is subtracted because R.E.C. Inc. has purchased more inventory than has been included in cost of goods sold. Cost of goods sold used in calculating net income includes only the inventory actually sold.

The decrease in *prepaid expenses* is added back because the firm has recognized an expense in the current period for which cash was paid in an earlier period, on a net basis.

The increase in *accounts payable* is added because less has been paid to suppliers for purchases of inventory than was included in cost of goods sold.

The increase in *accrued liabilities* is an addition to net income because it reflects the recognition of expense, on a net basis, prior to the payment of cash.

There are other potential adjustments, not required for R.E.C. Inc., that enter into the net income adjustment for noncash expense and revenues. One such item is the recognition of investment income from unconsolidated subsidiaries by the equity method of accounting, discussed in Chapter 3. When a company uses the equity method, earnings can be recognized in the income statement in excess of cash actually received from dividends, or the reverse can occur, for example, in the case of a loss recorded by an investee. For a firm using the equity method, there would be a deduction from net income for the amount by which investment income recognized exceeded cash received. Other potential adjustment items include changes relating to deferred income, deferred expense, the amortization of bond discounts and premiums, extraordinary items, and gains or losses on sales of long-lived assets.

Although *gains and losses from asset sales* are included in the calculation of net income, they are not considered an operating activity. A gain should be deducted from net income, and a loss should be added to net income to determine cash flow from operating activities. The entire proceeds from sales of long-lived assets are included as cash inflows from investing.

CASH FLOW FROM INVESTING ACTIVITIES

Additions to *property, plant, and equipment* represent a net addition to R.E.C. Inc.'s buildings, leasehold improvements, and equipment, a cash outflow of

$14.1 million. Other investing activities for R.E.C. Inc. result from a decrease in the *other assets* account on the balance sheet, which represent holdings of investment properties. The sale of these assets has provided a cash inflow of $295 thousand.

CASH FLOW FROM FINANCING ACTIVITIES

As a result of the exercise of stock options, R.E.C. Inc. issued new shares of stock during 2010. The total cash generated from stock sales amounted to $256 thousand. Note that two accounts on the balance sheet—*common stock* and *additional paid-in capital*—combine to explain this change:

Common stock	$209	Inflow
Additional paid-in capital	47	Inflow
	$256	Total Inflow

The two accounts—notes payable to banks and current maturities of long-term debt (carried as a current liability because the principal is payable within a year)—jointly explain R.E.C. Inc.'s net reduction in short-term borrowings in 2010 of $30 thousand:

Notes payable—banks	($398)	Outflow
Current maturities of long-term debt	368	Inflow
	($ 30)	Net outflow

In preparing the statement of cash flows, long-term borrowings should be segregated into two components: additions to long-term borrowings and reductions of long-term borrowings. This information is provided in Note C, Long-Term Debt, to the R.E.C. Inc. financial statements, where detail on the various long-term notes is provided. The two figures—additions to long-term debt and reductions of long-term debt—on the R.E.C. Inc. statement of cash flows reconcile the change in the *long-term debt* account on the R.E.C. Inc. balance sheet:

Additions to long-term borrowings	$5,600	Inflow
Reductions of long-term borrowings	(1,516)	Outflow
Increase in long-term debt	$4,084	

The payment of cash dividends by R.E.C. Inc. in 2010 of $1,582 million is the final item in the financing activities section. The change in *retained earnings* results from the combination of net income recognition and the payment of cash dividends; this information is provided in the R.E.C. Inc. Statement of Stockholders' Equity:

Net income	$9,394	Inflow
Dividends paid	(1,582)	Outflow
Change in retained earnings	$7,812	

It should be noted that the *payment* of cash dividends is the financing outflow; the *declaration* of a cash dividend would not affect cash.

CHANGE IN CASH

To summarize the cash inflows and outflows for 2010 for R.E.C. Inc., the net cash provided by operating activities, less the net cash used by investing activities, plus the net cash provided by financing activities produced a net decrease in *cash* and *marketable securities* for the period:

Net cash provided by operating activities	$10,024
Net cash used by investing activities	(13,805)
Net cash provided by financing activities	2,728
Decrease in cash and marketable securities	(1,053)

The statement for 2009 and 2008 would be prepared using the same process that was illustrated for 2010. The cash flows provided (used) by operating, investing, and financing activities vary considerably depending on the company, its performance for the year, its ability to generate cash, its financing and investment strategies, and its success in implementing these strategies. Figure 4.2 illustrates this for two companies in different industries.

FIGURE 4.2 Comparison of Cash Flows.

(In thousands of dollars)	Avnet, Inc.	Active Power, Inc.
For the year ended	June 30, 2007	December 31, 2007
Net cash provided (used) by:		
Operating activities	$724,639	$(10,423)
Investing activities	(485,794)	5,414
Financing activities	33,867	13,054
Net increase in cash and cash equivalents	$280,637*	$ 7,852*

Avnet, Inc., a distributor of electronic components and link in the technology supply chain, generated enough cash from operations to easily cover the company's investing activities, while also increasing the cash account. Active Power, Inc., an energy company that provides products for the majority of power disturbances, also increased its cash account overall, but not from generating operating cash flows. Instead, Active Power, Inc., generated cash from investing and financing activities to cover the deficit in operations while increasing the cash balance.

* Net increase in cash and cash equivalents was also impacted by cash flows from the effect of exchange rate changes of $7,925 for Avnet, Inc. and ($193) for Active Power, Inc.

ANALYZING THE STATEMENT OF CASH FLOWS

The statement of cash flows is an important analytical tool for creditors, investors, and other users of financial statement data that helps determine the following about a business firm:

- Its ability to generate cash flows in the future
- Its capacity to meet obligations for cash
- Its future external financing needs
- Its success in productively managing investing activities
- Its effectiveness in implementing financing and investing strategies

To begin the analysis of a statement of cash flows, it is essential to understand the importance of cash flow from operations, the first category on the statement.

Cash Flow from Operations

It is possible for a firm to be highly profitable and not be able to pay dividends or invest in new equipment. It is possible for a firm to be highly profitable and not be able to service debt. It is also possible for a firm to be highly profitable and go bankrupt. W. T. Grant is one of the classic examples.[5] How? The problem is cash. Consider the following questions:

1. You are a banker evaluating a loan request from a prospective customer. What is your primary concern when making a decision regarding approval or denial of the loan request?
2. You are a wholesaler of goods and have been asked to sell your products on credit to a potential buyer. What is the major determining factor regarding approval or denial of the credit sale?
3. You are an investor in a firm and rely on the receipt of regular cash dividends as part of your return on investment. What must the firm generate in order to pay dividends?

In each case, the answer is *cash*. The banker must decide whether the prospective borrower will have the cash to meet interest and principal payments on the debt. The wholesaler will sell goods on credit only to those customers who can satisfy their accounts. A company can pay cash dividends only by producing cash.

The ongoing operation of any business depends on its success in generating cash from operations. It is cash that a firm needs to satisfy creditors and investors. Temporary shortfalls of cash can be satisfied by borrowing or other

---

[5] J. A. Largay and C. P. Stickney, "Cash Flows, Ratio Analysis, and the W. T. Grant Bankruptcy," *Financial Analysts Journal*, July–August 1980.

means, such as selling long-lived assets, but ultimately a company must gener-ate cash.

Cash flow from operations has become increasingly important as an analyti-cal tool to determine the financial health of a business enterprise. Periods of high interest rates and inflation contributed to the enhanced attention paid to cash flow by investors and creditors. When interest rates are high, the cost of borrowing to cover short-term cash can be out of reach for many firms seeking to cover tempo-rary cash shortages. Periods of inflation distort the meaningfulness of net income, through the understatement of depreciation and cost of goods sold expenses, making other measures of operating performance and financial success impor-tant. Even when interest rates and inflation are low, there are other factors that limit the usefulness of net income as a barometer of financial health. Consider the case of Nocash Corporation.

Nocash Corporation

The Nocash Corporation had sales of $100,000 in its second year of operations, up from $50,000 in the first year. Expenses, including taxes, amounted to $70,000 in year 2, compared with $40,000 in year 1. The comparative income statements for the two years indicate substantial growth, with year 2 earnings greatly improved over those reported in year 1.

Nocash Corporation Income Statement for Year 1 and Year 2

	Year 1	Year 2
Sales	$50,000	$100,000
Expenses	40,000	70,000
Net income	$10,000	$ 30,000

So far, so good—a tripling of profit for Nocash. There are some additional facts, however, that are relevant to Nocash's operations but that do not appear on the firm's income statement:

1. In order to improve sales in year 2, Nocash eased its credit policies and attracted customers of a substantially lower quality than in year 1.
2. Nocash purchased a new line of inventory near the end of year 1, and it be-came apparent during year 2 that the inventory could not be sold, except at substantial reductions below cost.
3. Rumors regarding Nocash's problems with regard to accounts receivable and inventory management prompted some suppliers to refuse the sale of goods on credit to Nocash.

The effect of these additional factors can be found on Nocash's balance sheet.

Nocash Corporation Balance Sheet at December 31

	Year 1	Year 2	$ Change
Cash	$ 2,000	$ 2,000	0
Accounts receivable	10,000	30,000	+20,000[1]
Inventories	10,000	25,000	+15,000[2]
Total assets	$22,000	$57,000	+35,000
Accounts payable	7,000	2,000	−5,000[3]
Notes payable—to banks	0	10,000	+10,000
Equity	15,000	45,000	+30,000
Total liabilities and equity	$22,000	$57,000	+35,000

[1]Accounts receivable increased at a faster pace than sales as a result of deterioration in customer quality.
[2]Ending inventory increased and included items that would ultimately be sold at a loss.
[3]Nocash's inability to purchase goods on credit caused a reduction in accounts payable.

If Nocash's net income is recalculated on a cash basis, the following adjustments would be made, using the account balance changes between year 1 and year 2:

Net income	$30,000
(1) Accounts receivable	(20,000)
(2) Inventories	(15,000)
(3) Accounts payable	(5,000)
Cash income	($10,000)

(1) The increase in accounts receivable is subtracted because more sales revenue was recognized in computing net income than was collected in cash.

Sales recognized in net income		$100,000
Sales collected		
Beginning accounts receivable	$ 10,000	
Plus: sales, year 2	100,000	
Less: ending accounts receivable	(30,000)	80,000
Difference between net income and cash flow		$ 20,000

(2) The increase in inventory is deducted, reflecting the cash outflow for inventory purchases in excess of the expense recognized through cost of goods sold.

Purchases for inventory*	$75,000
Less: cost of goods sold	(60,000)
Difference between net income and cash flow	$15,000

(3) The decrease in accounts payable is deducted because the cash payments to suppliers in year 2 were greater than the amount of expense recorded. (In essence, cash was paid for some year 1 accounts as well as year 2 accounts.)

Payments to suppliers**	$ 80,000
Less: purchases for inventory*	75,000
Difference between net income and cash flow	$ 5,000
*Ending inventory	$ 25,000
Plus: cost of goods sold	60,000
Less: beginning inventory	(10,000)
Purchases of inventory	$ 75,000
**Beginning accounts payable	$ 7,000
Plus: purchases	75,000
Less: ending accounts payable	(2,000)
Payments to suppliers	$ 80,000

How did Nocash cover its $10,000 cash shortfall? Note the appearance of a $10,000 note payable to banks on the year 2 balance sheet. The borrowing has enabled Nocash to continue to operate, but unless the company can begin to generate cash from operations, its problems will compound. Bankers sometimes refer to this problem as a company's "selling itself out of business." The higher the cost of borrowing, the more costly and difficult it will be for Nocash to continue to operate.

R.E.C. INC.: ANALYSIS OF THE STATEMENT OF CASH FLOWS

An analysis of the statement of cash flows should, at a minimum, cover the following areas:

- Analysis of cash flow from operating activities
- Analysis of cash inflows
- Analysis of cash outflows

An example of an analysis of a statement of cash flows is presented for R.E.C. Inc. in the following sections.

R.E.C. Inc. Analysis: Cash Flow from Operating Activities

The statement of cash flows provides the figure "net cash flow from operating activities." An excerpt from the Statement of Cash Flows for R.E.C. Inc. is shown in Exhibit 4.4. The analyst should be concerned with the following in reviewing this information:

- The success or failure of the firm in generating cash from operations
- The underlying causes of the positive or negative operating cash flow
- The magnitude of positive or negative operating cash flow
- Fluctuations in cash flow from operations over time

For R.E.C. Inc. the first point of significance is the negative cash flow from operations in 2009 ($3,767 thousand). It should be noted that the negative cash

EXHIBIT 4.4

R.E.C. Inc. Cash Flows from Operating Activities for the Years Ended December 31, 2010, 2009, and 2008 (in Thousands)

	2010	2009	2008
Cash Flow from Operating Activities			
Net income	$ 9,394	$ 5,910	$ 5,896
Adjustments to reconcile net income to cash provided (used) by operating activities:			
Depreciation and amortization	3,998	2,984	2,501
Deferred income taxes	208	136	118
Cash Provided by (used for) Current Assets and Liabilities			
Accounts receivable	(610)	(3,339)	(448)
Inventories	(10,272)	(7,006)	(2,331)
Prepaid expenses	247	295	(82)
Accounts payable	6,703	(1,051)	902
Accrued liabilities	356	(1,696)	(927)
Net cash provided (used) by operating activities	$ 10,024	($ 3,767)	$ 5,629

flow occurred for a year in which the company reported positive net income of $5,910 thousand. The cash flow crunch was apparently caused primarily by a substantial growth in accounts receivable and inventories. Those increases were partly the result of the firm's expansion policies, and it would also be important to evaluate the quality of receivables and inventory—that is, are they collectable and salable? R.E.C. Inc. was able to recover in 2010, returning to strongly positive cash generation of $10,024 thousand, in spite of the continuation of inventory growth to support the expansion. The company obtained good supplier credit in 2010 and controlled the growth in accounts receivable. It will be necessary to monitor R.E.C. Inc.'s cash flow from operations closely and, in particular, the management of inventories. Inventory growth is desirable when supporting an expansion of sales but undesirable when, like Nocash Corporation, the inventory is not selling or is selling only at discounted prices.

The calculation of cash flow from operations illustrated for R.E.C. Inc. can be made for any company from its balance sheet and income statement, using the procedures outlined in the examples. Cash flow from operations is especially important for those firms that are heavily invested in inventories and that use trade accounts receivables and payables as a major part of ordinary business operations. Such problems as sales growth that is too rapid, slow-moving or obsolete inventory, price discounting within the industry, a rise in accounts receivable of inferior quality, and the tightening of credit by suppliers can all impair the firm's ability to generate cash from operations and lead to serious financial problems, including bankruptcy.

Summary Analysis of the Statement of Cash Flows

Exhibit 4.5 is an excerpt from R.E.C. Inc.'s Statement of Cash Flows and will be used with Exhibits 4.1 and 4.4 to illustrate how to prepare a summary analysis of the statement of cash flows. The summary analysis is one way to common size the cash flow statement. The purpose of the summary table is to provide an approach to analyzing a statement of cash flows that can be used for any firm that provides comparative cash flow data. The information in the summary table underlines the importance of internal cash generation—from operations—and the implications for investing and financing activities when this does and does not occur.

Exhibit 4.6 presents the summary analysis table to facilitate the analysis of R.E.C. Inc.'s statement of cash flows, including cash flow from operating activities. The columns of the exhibit with dollar amounts show the inflows and outflows over the three-year period from 2008 to 2010 for R.E.C. Inc. The columns of Exhibit 4.6 with percentages show the cash inflows as a percentage of total inflows and the outflows as a percentage of total outflows.

First, consider the dollar amounts. It is apparent that the magnitude of R.E.C. Inc.'s activity has increased sharply over the three-year period, with total

EXHIBIT 4.5

R.E.C. Inc. Cash Flows from Investing and Financing Activities for the Years Ended December 31, 2010, 2009, and 2008 (in Thousands)

	2010	2009	2008
Cash Flows from Investing Activities			
Additions to property, plant, and equipment	(14,100)	(4,773)	(3,982)
Other investing activities	295	0	0
Net cash provided (used) by investing activities	($ 13,805)	($ 4,773)	($ 3,982)
Cash Flow from Financing Activities			
Sales of common stock	256	183	124
Increase (decrease) in short-term borrowings (includes current maturities of long-term debt)	(30)	1,854	1,326
Additions to long-term borrowings	5,600	7,882	629
Reductions of long-term borrowings	(1,516)	(1,593)	(127)
Dividends paid	(1,582)	(1,862)	(1,841)
Net cash provided (used) by financing activities	$ 2,728	$ 6,464	$ 111

EXHIBIT 4.6

R.E.C. Inc. Summary Analysis Statement of Cash Flows

	2010	%	2009	%	2008	%
Inflows (dollars in thousands)						
Operations	$10,024	62.0	$ 0	0.0	$5,629	73.0
Sales of other assets	295	1.8	0	0.0	0	0.0
Sales of common stock	256	1.6	183	1.8	124	1.6
Additions to short-term debt	0	0.0	1,854	18.7	1,326	17.2
Additions to long-term debt	5,600	34.6	7,882	79.5	629	8.2
Total	$16,175	100.0	$ 9,919	100.0	$7,708	100.0
Outflows (dollars in thousands)						
Operations	$ 0	0.0	$ 3,767	31.4	$ 0	0.0
Purchase of property, plant, and equipment	14,100	81.8	4,773	40.0	3,982	66.9
Reductions of short-term debt	30	0.2	0	0.0	0	0.0
Reductions of long-term debt	1,516	8.8	1,593	13.2	127	2.1
Dividends paid	$ 1,582	9.2	$ 1,862	15.4	$1,841	31.0
Total	$17,228	100.0	$11,995	100.0	$5,950	100.0
Change in cash and marketable securities	($ 1,053)		($ 2,076)		$1,758	

cash inflows increasing from $7.7 million to $16.2 million and cash outflows from $6.0 million to $17.2 million. Using the summary analysis, an evaluation of the cash inflows and outflows for R.E.C. Inc. is discussed next.

Analysis of Cash Inflows

In percentage terms, it is noteworthy that operations supplied 62% of needed cash in 2010 and 73% in 2008. As a result of negative cash from operations in 2009, the firm had to borrow heavily, with debt (short term and long term) accounting for 98% of 2009 inflows. R.E.C. Inc. also borrowed in 2010 and 2008 to obtain needed cash not supplied by operations. Generating cash from operations is the preferred method for obtaining excess cash to finance capital expenditures and expansion, repay debt, and pay dividends; however, most firms at one time or another will use external sources to generate cash. Using external sources to generate the majority of cash year after year should be investigated further.

Analysis of Cash Outflows

The major increase in cash outflows is capital asset expansion. Although it appears that the purchases of property, plant, and equipment decreased in 2009 (40.0% of cash outflows) compared to 2008 (66.9% of cash outflows), realize that the common denominator in the summary analysis is one particular year's cash outflows. Capital expenditures actually increased in dollars from $3,982 thousand to $4,773 thousand, but the percentages are skewed in 2009 because of the negative cash flow from operations. Also notice that dividends paid increased from 2008 to 2009, decreasing in 2010 (in dollars), yet the percentages decline each year because each year's total cash outflows vary.

When analyzing the cash outflows, the analyst should consider the necessity of the outflow and how the outflow was financed. R.E.C. Inc. was able to cover capital expenditures easily with excess cash generated by operations in 2008. Capital expenditures are usually a good investment for most firms as purchasing new equipment and expansion should result in future revenues and cash flows from operations. Because of the negative cash flow from operations in 2009, R.E.C. Inc. had to borrow to finance capital expenditures, repayment of debt, and dividend payments. In 2010, the company's strong generation of cash from operations supported most of the capital expenditures (82%) with only 35% external financing. It is favorable that R.E.C. Inc. has financed long-term assets (capital expenditures) with either internally generated cash or long-term debt. Generally, it is best for firms to finance short-term assets with short-term debt and long-term assets with long-term debt or issuance of stock. Financing acquisitions and capital expenditures with short-term debt is risky because the firm may not generate cash flow quickly enough to repay short-term debt.

Repayment of debt is a necessary outflow. If the firm has generated cash from debt in prior years a cash outflow in a subsequent year to repay debt will be required. The notes to the financial statements reveal future debt repayments and are useful in assessing how much cash will be needed in upcoming years to repay outstanding debt.

Dividends are paid at the discretion of the board of directors. In theory, firms should only pay dividends if the company has excess cash, not needed for (a) expansion, (b) property, plant, or equipment, or (c) repayment of debt. It appears that R.E.C. Inc. may have reduced the dividends in 2010 as a result of the lack of cash from operations in 2009.

Are We There Yet?

The journey through the maze of information has taken us through all the financial statements and many other items in the annual report, but no, we are not quite to the end of the maze. Unfortunately, just like the income statement, management has determined ways to manipulate the statement of cash flows. While the cash balances and the overall change in cash can be easily verified, it is possible to manipulate cash amounts through the timing of items such as when cash payments are made, when investments are made or sold, and when loans are taken out or repaid. Some companies have developed creative techniques for manipulating cash flow from operations by how they record certain cash outflows (see discussion in Chapter 5).

Self-Test

Solutions are provided in Appendix B.

_____ 1. The statement of cash flows segregates cash inflows and outflows by:
   (a) Operating and financing activities.
   (b) Financing and investing activities.
   (c) Operating and investing activities.
   (d) Operating, financing, and investing activities.

_____ 2. Which of the following statements is false?
   (a) Publicly held companies may choose to prepare either a statement of cash flows or a statement of changes in financial position.
   (b) The statement of cash flows was mandated by the FASB in the late 1980s.
   (c) Understanding how to prepare a statement of cash flows helps the analyst to better understand and analyze the cash flow statement.
   (d) The statement of cash flows is prepared by calculating changes in all balance sheet accounts.

_____ 3. How would revenue from sales of goods and services be classified?
   (a) Operating outflow.
   (b) Operating inflow.
   (c) Investing inflow.
   (d) Financing inflow.

_____ 4. How would payments for taxes be classified?
   (a) Operating outflow.
   (b) Operating inflow.
   (c) Investing outflow.
   (d) Financing outflow.

_____ 5. How would the sale of a building be classified?
   (a) Operating outflow.
   (b) Operating inflow.
   (c) Investing inflow.
   (d) Financing inflow.

_____ 6. How would the repayment of debt principal be classified?
   (a) Operating outflow.
   (b) Operating inflow.
   (c) Investing outflow.
   (d) Financing outflow.

_____ 7. What type of accounts are accounts receivable and inventory?
   (a) Cash accounts.
   (b) Operating accounts.
   (c) Financing accounts.
   (d) Investing accounts.

_____ 8. What type of accounts are notes payable and current maturities of long-term debt?
(a) Cash accounts.
(b) Operating accounts.
(c) Financing accounts.
(d) Investing accounts.

_____ 9. The change in retained earnings is affected by which of the following?
(a) Net income and common stock.
(b) Net income and paid-in capital.
(c) Net income and payment of dividends.
(d) Payment of dividends and common stock.

_____ 10. Which method of calculating cash flow from operations requires the adjustment of net income for deferrals, accruals, noncash, and non-operating expenses?
(a) The direct method.
(b) The indirect method.
(c) The inflow method.
(d) The outflow method.

_____ 11. An inflow of cash would result from which of the following?
(a) The increase in an asset account other than cash.
(b) The decrease in an asset account other than cash.
(c) The decrease in an equity account.
(d) The decrease in a liability account.

_____ 12. An outflow of cash would result from which of the following?
(a) The decrease in an asset account other than cash.
(b) The increase in a liability account.
(c) The decrease in a liability account.
(d) The increase in an equity account.

_____ 13. What are internal sources of cash?
(a) Cash inflows from operating activities.
(b) Cash inflows from investing activities.
(c) Cash inflows from financing activities.
(d) All of the above.

_____ 14. What are external sources of cash?
(a) Cash inflows from operating activities.
(b) Cash inflows from investing activities.
(c) Cash inflows from financing activities.
(d) Both (b) and (c).

_____ 15. Which of the following items is included in the adjustment of net income to obtain cash flow from operating activities?
(a) Depreciation expense for the period.
(b) The change in deferred taxes.
(c) The amount by which equity income recognized exceeds cash received.
(d) All of the above.

_____ **16.** Which statement is true for gains and losses from capital asset sales?
(a) They do not affect cash and are excluded from the statement of cash flows.
(b) They are included in cash flows from operating activities.
(c) They are included in cash flows from investing activities.
(d) They are included in cash flows from financing activities.

_____ **17.** Which of the following current assets is included in the adjustment of net income to obtain cash flow from operating activities?
(a) Accounts receivable.
(b) Inventory.
(c) Prepaid expenses.
(d) All of the above.

_____ **18.** Which of the following current liability accounts is included in the adjustment of expenses to obtain cash flow from operating activities?
(a) Accounts payable.
(b) Notes payable and current maturities of long-term debt.
(c) Accrued liabilities.
(d) Both (a) and (c).

_____ **19.** How is it possible for a firm to be profitable and still go bankrupt?
(a) Earnings have increased more rapidly than sales.
(b) The firm has positive net income but has failed to generate cash from operations.
(c) Net income has been adjusted for inflation.
(d) Sales have not improved even though credit policies have been eased.

_____ **20.** Why has cash flow from operations become increasingly important as an analytical tool?
(a) Inflation has distorted the meaningfulness of net income.
(b) High interest rates can put the cost of borrowing to cover short-term cash needs out of reach for many firms.
(c) Firms may have uncollected accounts receivable and unsalable inventory on the books.
(d) All of the above.

_____ **21.** Which of the following statements is false?
(a) A negative cash flow can occur in a year in which net income is positive.
(b) An increase in accounts receivable represents accounts not yet collected in cash.
(c) An increase in accounts payable represents accounts not yet collected in cash.
(d) To obtain cash flow from operations, the reported net income must be adjusted.

_____ 22. Which of the following could lead to cash flow problems?
  (a) Obsolete inventory, accounts receivable of inferior quality, easing of credit by suppliers.
  (b) Slow-moving inventory, accounts receivable of inferior quality, tightening of credit by suppliers.
  (c) Obsolete inventory, increasing notes payable, easing of credit by suppliers.
  (d) Obsolete inventory, improved quality of accounts receivable, easing of credit by suppliers.

The following information is available for Jacqui's Jewelry and Gift Store:

Net income	$ 5,000
Depreciation expense	2,500
Increase in deferred tax liabilities	500
Decrease in accounts receivable	2,000
Increase in inventories	9,000
Decrease in accounts payable	5,000
Increase in accrued liabilities	1,000
Increase in property and equipment	14,000
Increase in short-term notes payable	19,000
Decrease in long-term bonds payable	4,000

Use the indirect method to answer questions 23–26.

_____ 23. What is net cash flow from operating activities?
  (a) ($3,000)
  (b) ($1,000)
  (c) $5,000
  (d) $13,000

_____ 24. What is net cash flow from investing activities?
  (a) $14,000
  (b) ($14,000)
  (c) $21,000
  (d) ($16,000)

_____ 25. What is net cash flow from financing activities?
  (a) $15,000
  (b) ($15,000)
  (c) $17,000
  (d) ($14,000)

_____ 26. What is the change in cash?
  (a) ($3,000)
  (b) $3,000
  (c) $2,000
  (d) ($2,000)

Study Questions, Problems, and Cases

4.1 Why is the statement of cash flows a useful document?

4.2 Define the following terms as they relate to the statement of cash flows: cash, operating activities, investing activities, and financing activities.

4.3 How does the direct method differ from the indirect method?

4.4 What can creditors, investors, and other users learn from an analysis of the cash flow statement?

4.5 Identify the following as financing activities (F) or investing activities (I):
(a) Purchase of equipment.
(b) Purchase of treasury stock.
(c) Reduction of long-term debt.
(d) Sale of building.
(e) Resale of treasury stock.
(f) Increase in short-term debt.
(g) Issuance of common stock.
(h) Purchase of land.
(i) Purchase of common stock of another firm.
(j) Payment of cash dividends.
(k) Gain on sale of land.
(l) Repayment of debt principal.

4.6 Indicate which of the following current assets and current liabilities are operating accounts (O) and thus included in the adjustment of net income to cash flow from operating activities and which are cash (C), investing (I), or financing (F) accounts.

(a) Accounts payable.
(b) Accounts receivable.
(c) Notes payable (to bank).
(d) Marketable securities.
(e) Accrued expenses.
(f) Inventory.

(g) Prepaid expenses.
(h) Current portion of long-term debt.
(i) Dividends payable.
(j) Income taxes payable.
(k) Interest payable.
(l) Certificates of deposit.

4.7 Indicate whether each of the following items would result in net cash flow from operating activities being higher (H) or lower (L) than net income.
(a) Decrease in accounts payable.
(b) Depreciation expense.
(c) Decrease in inventory.
(d) Gain on sale of assets.
(e) Increase in accounts receivable.
(f) Increase in deferred tax liabilities.
(g) Decrease in accrued liabilities.
(h) Increase in prepaid expenses.
(i) Increase in deferred revenue.
(j) Decrease in interest receivable.

4.8 Indicate whether each of the following events would cause an inflow or an outflow of cash and whether it would impact the investing (I) or financing (F) activities on the statement of cash flows.

(a) Repayments of long-term debt.
(b) Sales of marketable securities.
(c) Repurchase of company's common stock.
(d) Sales of common stock to investors.
(e) Purchase of equipment.
(f) Payment of dividends.
(g) Purchase of marketable securities.
(h) Borrowing from bank.
(i) Sale of building.
(j) Acquisition of company.

4.9 Condensed financial statements for Dragoon Enterprises follow.

(a) Calculate the amount of dividends Dragoon paid using the information given.
(b) Prepare a statement of cash flows using the indirect method.

Dragoon Enterprises Comparative Balance Sheets
December 31, 2009 and 2008

	2009	2008
Cash	$ 1,200	$ 850
Accounts receivable	1,750	1,200
Inventory	1,250	1,360
Plant and equipment	4,600	3,900
Accumulated depreciation	(1,200)	(1,100)
Long-term investments	970	1,110
Total Assets	8,570	7,320
Accounts payable	1,100	800
Accrued wages payable	250	350
Interest payable	70	120
Income tax payable	200	50
Bonds payable	1,100	1,400
Capital stock	1,000	930
Paid-in capital	400	70
Retained earnings	4,450	3,600
Total Liabilities and Equity	$ 8,570	$ 7,320

Income Statement For Year Ended December 31, 2009

Sales	$ 9,500
Cost of goods sold	6,650
Gross profit	2,850
Other expenses	
Selling and administrative	1,200
Depreciation	100
Interest	150
Income tax	350
Net income	$ 1,050

4.10 The following income statement and balance sheet information are available for two firms, Firm A and Firm B.
   (a) Calculate the amount of dividends Firm A and Firm B paid using the information given.
   (b) Prepare a statement of cash flows for each firm using the indirect method.
   (c) Analyze the difference in the two firms.

Income Statement For Year Ended December 31, 2009

	Firm A	Firm B
Sales	$1,000,000	$1,000,000
Cost of goods sold	700,000	700,000
Gross profit	300,000	300,000
Other expenses		
Selling and administrative	120,000	115,000
Depreciation	10,000	30,000
Interest expense	20,000	5,000
Earnings before taxes	150,000	150,000
Income tax expense	75,000	75,000
Net Income	$ 75,000	$ 75,000

Changes in Balance Sheet Accounts December 31, 2008, to December 31, 2009

	Firm A	Firm B
Cash and cash equivalents	$ 0	$+10,000
Accounts receivable	+40,000	+5,000
Inventory	+40,000	−10,000
Property, plant, and equipment	+20,000	+70,000
Less accumulated depreciation	(+10,000)	(+30,000)
Total Assets	$+90,000	$+45,000
Accounts payable	$−20,000	$ −5,000
Notes payable (current)	+17,000	+2,000
Long-term debt	+20,000	−10,000
Deferred taxes (noncurrent)	+3,000	+18,000
Capital, Stock	—	—
Retained earnings	+70,000	+40,000
Total Liabilities and Equity	$+90,000	$+45,000

4.11 The following comparative balance sheets and income statement are available for Little Bit Inc. Prepare a statement of cash flows for 2009 using the indirect method and analyze the statement.

	December 31,	
	2009	2008
Cash	$ 40,000	$ 24,000
Accounts receivable (net)	48,000	41,500
Inventory	43,000	34,500
Prepaid expenses	19,000	15,000
Total Current Assets	$150,000	$115,000
Plant and equipment	$ 67,000	$ 61,000
Less accumulated depreciation	(41,000)	(23,000)
Plant and equipment (net)	$ 26,000	$ 38,000
Long-term investments	90,000	89,000
Total Assets	$266,000	$242,000
Accounts payable	$ 13,000	$ 11,000
Accrued liabilities	55,000	71,000
Total Current Liabilities	$ 68,000	$ 82,000
Long-term debt	25,000	8,000
Deferred taxes	4,000	3,500
Total Liabilities	$ 97,000	$ 93,500
Common stock ($1 par) and additional paid-in capital	112,000	97,000
Retained earnings	57,000	51,500
Total Liabilities and Equity	$266,000	$242,000

Income Statement for 2009		
Sales		$155,000
Cost of goods sold		83,000
Gross profit		$ 72,000
Selling and administrative	$45,700	
Depreciation	18,000	63,700
Operating Profit		$ 8,300
Interest expense		2,000
Earnings before tax		$ 6,300
Tax expense		800
Net income		$ 5,500

4.12 The following cash flows were reported by Techno Inc. in 2009 and 2008.

(In thousands)	2009	2008
Net income	$316,354	$242,329
Noncash charges (credits) to income		
Depreciation and amortization	68,156	62,591
Deferred taxes	15,394	22,814
	$399,904	$327,734
Cash Provided (Used) by Operating Assets and Liabilities:		
Receivables	(288,174)	(49,704)
Inventories	(159,419)	(145,554)
Other current assets	(1,470)	3,832
Accounts payable, accrued liabilities	73,684	41,079
Total Cash Provided by Operations	$ 24,525	$177,387
Investment activities		
Additions to plant and equipment	(94,176)	(93,136)
Other investment activities	14,408	(34,771)
Net investment activities	($ 79,768)	($127,907)
Financing activities		
Purchases of treasury stock	(45,854)	(39,267)
Dividends paid	(49,290)	(22,523)
Net changes in short-term borrowings	125,248	45,067
Additions to long-term borrowings	135,249	4,610
Repayments of long-term borrowings		(250,564)
Net financing activities	$ 165,353	($262,677)
Increase (decrease) in cash	$ 110,110	($213,197)
Beginning cash balance	78,114	291,311
Ending cash balance	$ 188,224	$ 78,114

(a) Explain the difference between net income and cash flow from operating activities for Techno in 2009.

(b) Analyze Techno Inc.'s cash flows for 2009 and 2008.

4.13 Writing Skills Problem

Write a short article (250 words) for a local business publication in which you explain why cash flow from operations is important information for small business owners.

4.14 Research Problem

Choose five companies from different industries and locate their statements of cash flows for the most recent year.

(a) Create a table to compare the dollars provided or used by operating, investing, and financing activities, as well as the overall increase or decrease in cash.

(b) Create a second table for each company comparing this same information for each of the three years presented in that company's statement of cash flows. Include an additional column that looks at the combined cash flows for all three years.

(c) Write a short analysis of the information gathered. Your discussion should address, among other things, whether cash flow from operating activities is large enough to cover investing and financing activities, and if not, how the company is financing its activities. Discuss differences and similarities between the companies you have chosen.

4.15 Internet Problem

In the mid-2000s, the liquidity of General Motors Corporation (GM) came into question. Research GM's liquidity issues and write a report detailing what issues GM has faced since 2005, what the company has done to address its liquidity issues, and the current status of GM with regard to liquidity.

Hint: Access GM's annual reports back to the year 2005 and specifically read the management discussion and analysis section on liquidity and the letter to stockholders. Look at cash flow statements through the period, and conduct an Internet search to locate articles about GM and its liquidity issues.

4.16 Intel Case

The 2007 Intel Annual Report can be found at the following Web site: www.prenhall.com/fraser.

(a) Prepare a summary analysis of the Statements of Cash Flows for all three years.

(b) Analyze the Consolidated Statements of Cash Flows for Intel for 2007, 2006, and 2005.

4.17 Eastman Kodak Comprehensive Analysis Case Using the Financial Statement Analysis Template

Each chapter in the textbook contains a continuation of this problem. The objective is to learn how to do a comprehensive financial statement analysis in steps as the content of each chapter is learned. Using the 2007 Eastman Kodak Annual Report and Form 10-K, which can be found at www.prenhall .com/fraser complete the following requirements:

(a) Open the financial statement analysis template that you saved from the Chapter 1 Eastman Kodak problem and input the data from the Eastman Kodak cash flow statement. All cash flows from discontinued operations should be combined and input on the line labeled as such toward the bottom of the statement. In 2005, add the loss from the cumulative effect of the accounting change to the loss from continuing operations and input in the first line "Income (loss) from continuing operations." When you have finished inputting the data, review the cash flow statement to make sure there are no red blocks indicating that your numbers do not match the cover sheet information you input from the Chapter 1 problem. Make any necessary corrections before printing out both your input and the common-size cash flow statement that the template automatically creates for you.

(b) Analyze the cash flow statement of Eastman Kodak. Write a summary that includes important points that an analyst would use in assessing the ability of Eastman Kodak to generate cash flows and the appropriateness of the use of cash flows.

4.18 Avnet, Inc. Case

Avnet, Inc. and subsidiaries is a leading distributor of electronic components, enterprise computer and storage products and embedded subsystems. The company is a vital link in the technology supply chain that connects over 300 of the world's leading technology manufacturers and software developers. Avnet distributes products received as is or adds value before distribution. In addition the company provides engineering design, materials management and logistics services, system integration and configuration, and supply chain advisory services.*

Required

1. Using the Consolidated Statements of Cash Flows on page 139, prepare a summary analysis for the years ended June 30, 2007, 2006, and 2005. Analyze the cash flows for Avnet, Inc. for all three years.
2. Evaluate the creditworthiness of Avnet, Inc. based on only the cash flow statements.
3. What information from the balance sheet would be useful to a creditor in determining whether to loan Avnet, Inc. money?

Source: Avnet, Inc. Form 10-K, June 30, 2007.

AVNET, Inc. and Subsidiaries Consolidated Statements of Cash Flows

	Year Ended June 30,		
	2007	2006	2005
		(Thousands)	
Cash flows from operating activities:			
Net income	$393,067	$204,547	$168,239
Noncash and other reconciling items:			
Depreciation and amortization	53,775	66,526	61,746
Deferred income taxes (Note 9)	99,604	52,169	63,734
Noncash restructuring and other charges (Note 17)	1,404	15,308	—
Stock-based compensation (Note 12)	24,250	18,096	1,135
Other, net (Note 15)	26,341	47,667	45,980
Changes in (net of effects from business acquisitions):			
Receivables	(129,351)	(254,691)	(168,892)
Inventories	53,678	(142,563)	144,004
Accounts payable	262,192	99,670	191,270
Accrued expenses and other, net	(60,321)	(125,843)	(45,380)
Net cash flows provided by (used for) operating activities	724,639	(19,114)	461,836
Cash flows from financing activities:			
Issuances of notes in public offerings, net of issuance costs (Note 7)	593,169	246,483	—
Repayment of notes (Note 7)	(505,035)	(369,965)	(89,589)
(Repayment of) proceeds from bank debt, net	(122,999)	89,511	(10,789)
Payment of other debt, net (Note 7)	(780)	(643)	(86)
Other, net (Note 15)	69,512	30,991	2,274
Net cash flows provided by (used for) financing activities	33,867	(3,623)	(98,190)
Cash flows from investing activities:			
Purchases of property, plant, and equipment	(58,782)	(51,803)	(31.338)
Cash proceeds from sales of property, plant, and equipment	2,774	4,368	7,271
Acquisitions and investments	(433,231)	(317,114)	(3,563)
Cash proceeds from divestitures, net (Note 2)	3,445	22,779	—
Net cash flows used for investing activities	(485,794)	(341,770)	(27,630)
Effect of exchange rate changes on cash and cash equivalents	7,925	3,353	(10,816)
Cash and cash equivalents:			
—increase (decrease)	280,637	(361,154)	325,200
—at beginning of year	276,713	637,867	312,667
—at end of year	$557,350	$276,713	$637,867
Additional cash flow information (Note 15)			

See notes to consolidated financial statements.

4.19 Agilysys, Inc. Case

Excerpts from the Agilysys, Inc.'s Form 10-K are on pages 140–143.

Required

1. Using the Consolidated Statements of Cash Flows, prepare a summary analysis for the years ended March 31, 2007, 2006, and 2005. Analyze the cash flows for Agilysys, Inc. for all three years.
2. Explain what information you gain from the statement of cash flows that cannot be found directly from the balance sheet or income statement.

Item 1. Business.

Reference herein to any particular year or quarter refers to periods within the company's fiscal year ended March 31. For example, 2007 refers to the fiscal year ended March 31, 2007.

Overview

Agilysys, Inc. (the "company" or "Agilysys") is a leading provider of innovative IT solutions to corporate and public-sector customers with special expertise in select vertical markets, including retail and hospitality. The company delivers tailored solutions consisting of suppliers' products and services, combined with propri-etary software and services, directly to commercial end users of technology. Agilysys employs professional services consultants and systems engineers, who are leading professionals in IT, to evaluate, develop and implement solutions. To assure Agilysys solutions make use of the best available, highest quality products and leading-edge technologies, the company partners with leading suppliers in the IT industry—including Cisco, EMC, HP, IBM, Oracle and Motorola.

The company has customers and experience in many different industries including manufacturing, finance, healthcare, education, government, trans-portation, retail and hospitality.

Agilysys has special expertise in select vertical markets, including retail and hospitality. In the retail industry, Agilysys is a leader in designing and implement-ing hardware, software and service solutions for the supermarket, chain drug and general retail marketplace. In the hospitality industry, the company provides pro-prietary software solutions to automate functions for customers including hotels, casinos, resorts, conference centers, condominiums, golf courses and spas.

Headquartered in Boca Raton, Florida, Agilysys operates extensively through-out North America, with additional sales offices in the United Kingdom and China.

History and Significant Events

Agilysys was organized as an Ohio corporation in 1963. While originally focused on electronic components distribution, the company grew to become a leading distributor in both electronic components and enterprise computer systems products and solutions.

As of the fiscal year ended March 31, 2002, the company was structured into two divisions, the Computer Systems Division (CSD), which focused on the distribution and reselling of enterprise computer systems products and solutions, and the Industrial Electronics Division (IED), which focused on the distribution of electronic components. Each division represented, on average, approximately one-half of the company's total revenues.

In 2002, the company conducted a review of strategic alternatives and developed a long-term strategic plan designed to increase the intrinsic value of the company. The company's strategic transformation began with its divestiture of its broad-line electronic components distribution business, IED, to focus solely on the computer systems business. The sale of the electronic components business meant that the company would be less dependent on the more cyclical markets in the components business. In addition, this would allow the company to invest more in the computer systems business, which offered greater potential for sustainable growth at higher levels of profitability. The remaining CSD business consisted of the KeyLink Systems Distribution Business and the IT Solutions Business. The KeyLink Systems Distribution Business operated as a distributor of enterprise computing products selling to resellers, which then sold directly to end-user customers. The IT Solutions Business operated as a reseller providing enterprise servers, software, storage and services and sold directly to end-user customers. Overall, the company was a leading distributor and reseller of enterprise computer systems, software, storage and services from HP, IBM, Intel, Enterasys, Hitachi Data Systems, Oracle and other leading manufacturers.

The proceeds from the sale of the electronic components distribution business, combined with cash generated from the company's ongoing operations, were used to retire long-term debt and accelerate the growth of the company, both organically and through a series of acquisitions. The growth of the company has been supported by a series of acquisitions that strategically expanded the company's range of solutions and markets served, including:

- The September 2003 acquisition of Kyrus Corporation, a leading provider of retail store solutions and services with a focus on the supermarket, chain drug and general retail segments of the retail industry.
- The February 2004 acquisition of Inter-American Data, Inc., a leading developer and provider of software and service solutions to the hotel casino and destination resort segments of the hospitality industry.
- The May 2005 acquisition of The CTS Corporations, a leading services organization specializing in IT storage solutions for large and medium-sized corporate and public-sector customers.
- The December 2005 acquisition of a competitor's operations in China. This provided Agilysys entry into the enterprise IT solutions market in Hong Kong and China serving large and medium-sized businesses in those growing markets.
- The January 2007 acquisition of Visual One Systems, which expanded the company's position as a leading software developer and services provider to the hospitality industry.

In March 2007 the company completed its transformation with the sale of the assets and operations of its KeyLink Systems Distribution Business. This final event completes the Agilysys multi-year transformation to move closer to the customer and higher up the IT value scale, effectively positioning it to focus on its higher-growth IT Solutions Business. As a result of the divestiture, the company is freed from the increasing channel conflict and marketplace restrictions that existed in the business.

Today, Agilysys is a growing, vibrant technology company. The company is a high-value provider of IT solutions with low working capital needs and significant financial flexibility to fund growth, both organically and through acquisition. As discussed under Note 18 to the consolidated financial statements, the company continued to accelerate its growth in the first quarter of 2008 through the acquisitions of Stack Computer, Innovative Systems Design, Inc. and InfoGenesis, Inc.

Agilysys, Inc. and Subsidiaries: Consolidated Statements of Cash Flows

(In thousands)	Year Ended March 31		
	2007	2006	2005
Operating activities			
Net income	$ 232,855	$ 28,114	$ 19,485
Less: Income from discontinued operations	(244,490)	(48,858)	(44,603)
Loss from continuing operations	(11,635)	(20,744)	(25,118)
Adjustments to reconcile loss from continuing operations to net cash provided by (used for) operating activities (net of effects from business acquisitions):			
Investment impairment	5,892	—	—
Gain on redemption of investment by affiliated company	—	(622)	—
Loss on redemption of Mandatorily Redeemable Convertible Trust Preferred Securities	—	4,811	—
Loss on disposal of property and equipment	1,501	302	93
Depreciation	1,565	1,822	2,084
Amortization	6,315	6,978	6,122
Deferred income taxes	1,478	(2,274)	7,122
Stock-based compensation	4,232	594	1,295
Excess tax benefit from exercise of stock options	(1,854)	—	—
Changes in working capital:			
Accounts receivable	(3,939)	(15,344)	25,651
Inventories	122	1,165	(5,180)
Accounts payable	30,136	(8,873)	16,970
Accrued liabilities	124,705	3,060	(1,919)
Other working capital	(1,316)	4,752	(3,925)
Other non-cash adjustments	(4,554)	(1,529)	2,497
Total adjustments	164,283	(5,158)	50,810
Net cash provided by (used for) operating activities	152,648	(25,902)	25,692

Investing activities
  Proceeds from sale of investment in affiliated

company	—	788	—
Purchase of marketable securities	—	(6,822)	—
Proceeds from sale of marketable securities	**1,147**	—	—
Proceeds from sale of business	**485,000**	—	—
Acquisition of business, net of cash acquired	**(10,613)**	(27,964)	—
Purchase of property and equipment	**(6,250)**	(3,252)	(1,213)
Proceeds from escrow settlement	**423**	—	—
Net cash provided by (used for) investing			
activities	**469,707**	(37,250)	(1,213)
Financing activities			
Redemption of Mandatorily Redeemable			
Convertible Trust Preferred Securities	—	(107,536)	—
Principal payment under long-term obligations	**(59,567)**	(286)	(375)
Issuance of common shares	**10,107**	5,442	4,007
Excess tax benefit from exercise of stock options	**1,854**	—	—
Dividends paid	**(3,675)**	(3,608)	(3,330)
Net cash (used for) provided by financing			
activities	**(51,281)**	(105,988)	302
Effect of exchange rate changes on cash	**(97)**	367	810
Cash flows provided by (used for) continuing			
operations	**570,977**	(168,773)	25,591
Cash flows of discontinued operations			
Operating cash flows	**(114,087)**	74,767	67,128
Investing cash flows	**(73)**	(24)	(742)
Net increase (decrease) in cash	**456,817**	(94,030)	91,977
Cash at beginning of period	**147,850**	241,880	149,903
Cash at end of period	**$ 604,667**	$ 147,850	$ 241,880
Supplemental disclosures of cash flow			
information:			
Cash payments for interest			
Distributions on Mandatorily Redeemable			
Convertible Trust Preferred Securities	$ —	$ 1,482	$ 8,463
Other	**3,135**	6,068	6,044
Cash payments for income taxes, net			
of refunds received	**22,978**	10,478	7,205
Change in value of available-for-sale			
securities, net of taxes	**86**	9	—

See accompanying notes to consolidated financial statements.

APPENDIX 4A
STATEMENT OF CASH FLOWS—
DIRECT METHOD

DIRECT METHOD

Exhibit 4A.1 illustrates the statement of cash flows prepared using the direct method, and Exhibit 4A.2 illustrates the calculation of net cash flow from operating activities by the direct method. This method translates each item on the accrual-based income statement to a cash revenue or expense item. The calculation of cash flow from operating activities in Exhibit 4A.2 represents an approximation of the *actual* receipts and payments of cash required by the direct method.

The steps shown in Exhibit 4A.2 will be used to explain the calculation of net cash flow from operating activities on the R.E.C. Inc. Statement of Cash Flows for 2010.

R.E.C. Inc. Direct Method		
Sales	$215,600	
Increase in accounts receivable	(610)	
Cash collections on sales		214,990
Cost of goods sold	129,364	
Increase in inventory	10,272	
Increase in accounts payable	(6,703)	
Cash payments for supplies		−132,933
Selling and administrative expenses		−45,722
Other operating expenses	21,271	
Depreciation and amortization	(3,998)	
Decrease in prepaid expense	(247)	
Increase in accrued liabilities	(356)	
Cash paid for other operating expense		−16,670
Interest revenue		+422
Interest expense		−2,585
Tax expense	7,686	
Increase in deferred tax liability	(208)	
Cash paid for taxes		−7,478
Net cash flow from operating activities		$ 10,024

The increase in accounts receivable is subtracted from sales revenue because more sales revenue was recognized in the income statement than was received in cash.

The increase in inventories is added to cost of goods sold because more cash was paid to purchase inventories than was included in cost of goods sold expense; that is, cash was used to purchase inventory that has not yet been sold.

EXHIBIT 4A.1

R.E.C. Inc. Consolidated Statements of Cash Flows for the Years Ended December 31, 2010, 2009, and 2008 (in Thousands)

	2010	2009	2008
Cash Flow from Operating Activities—Direct Method			
Cash received from customers	$214,990	$149,661	$140,252
Interest received	422	838	738
Cash paid to suppliers for inventory	(132,933)	(99,936)	(83,035)
Cash paid to employees (S&A Expenses)	(45,722)	(26,382)	(25,498)
Cash paid for other operating expenses	(16,670)	(21,350)	(20,848)
Interest paid	(2,585)	(2,277)	(1,274)
Taxes paid	(7,478)	(4,321)	(4,706)
Net cash provided (used) by operating activities	$ 10,024	($ 3,767)	$ 5,629
Cash Flow from Investing Activities			
Additions to property, plant, and equipment	(14,100)	(4,773)	(3,982)
Other investing activities	295	0	0
Net cash provided (used) by investing activities	($ 13,805)	($ 4,773)	($ 3,982)
Cash Flow from Financing Activities			
Sales of common stock	256	183	124
Increase (decrease) in short-term borrowings			
(includes current maturities of long-term debt)	(30)	1,854	1,326
Additions to long-term borrowings	5,600	7,882	629
Reductions of long-term borrowings	(1,516)	(1,593)	(127)
Dividends paid	(1,582)	(1,862)	(1,841)
Net cash provided (used) by financing activities	$ 2,728	$ 6,464	$ 111
Increase (decrease) in cash and marketable			
securities	($ 1,053)	($ 2,076)	$ 1,758
Supplementary Schedule			
Cash Flow from Operating Activities—Indirect Method			
Net income	$ 9,394	$ 5,910	$ 5,896
Noncash revenue and expense included in			
net income			
Depreciation and amortization	3,998	2,984	2,501
Deferred income taxes	208	136	118
Cash provided (used) by current assets and			
liabilities			
Accounts receivable	(610)	(3,339)	(448)
Inventories	(10,272)	(7,006)	(2,331)
Prepaid expenses	247	295	(82)
Accounts payable	6,703	(1,051)	902
Accrued liabilities	356	(1,696)	(927)
Net cash provided (used) by operations	$ 10,024	($ 3,767)	$ 5,629

The increase in accounts payable is subtracted from cost of goods sold because R.E.C. Inc. was able to defer some payments to suppliers for purchases of inventory; more cost of goods sold expense was recognized than was actually paid in cash.

Depreciation and amortization expense is subtracted from other operating expenses. Remember that depreciation represents a cost allocation, not an out-flow of cash. The acquisition of the capital asset was recognized as an investing cash outflow (unless it was exchanged for debt or stock) in the statement of cash flows for the period in which the asset was acquired. So depreciation itself does not require any outflow of cash in the year it is recognized. Deducting deprecia-tion expense in the current year's statement of cash flows would be double counting. Amortization is similar to depreciation—an expense that enters into the determination of net income but does not require an outflow of cash. Depletion would be handled in the same manner as depreciation and amortiza-tion. The depreciation and amortization expense for R.E.C. Inc. in 2010 is equal to the change in the balance sheet accumulated depreciation and amortization ac-count. If the firm had dispositions of capital assets during the accounting period, however, the balance sheet change would not equal the expense recognition for the period because some of the account change would have resulted from the elimination of accumulated depreciation for the asset that was removed. The ap-propriate figure to subtract would be depreciation and amortization expense from the earnings statement.

The decrease in prepaid expense is subtracted from other operating expenses because the firm is recognizing as expense in 2010 items for which cash was paid in the previous year; that is, the firm is utilizing on a net basis some of the prior years' prepayments.

The increase in accrued liabilities is subtracted from other operating expenses because R.E.C. Inc. has recognized more in expense on the income statement than has been paid in cash.

Finally, the increase in the deferred tax liability account is subtracted from tax expense to obtain cash payments for taxes. The deferred tax liability, ex-plained in Chapter 2, was created as a reconciliation between the amount of tax expense reported on the income statement and the cash actually paid or payable to the IRS. If a deferred tax liability increases from one year to the next, tax ex-pense deducted on the earnings statement to arrive at net income has exceeded cash actually paid for taxes. Thus, an increase in the deferred tax liability account is subtracted from tax expense to arrive at cash from operations. A decrease in deferred tax liabilities would be added. A change in deferred tax assets would be handled in the opposite way from the deferred tax liability.

Exhibit 4A.2 includes other possible adjustments, not present for R.E.C. Inc., that would be made to calculate net cash flow from operating activities by the direct method.

EXHIBIT 4A.2

R.E.C. Inc. Net Cash Flow from Operating Activities Direct Method		
Sales	− Increase in accounts receivable + Decrease in accounts receivable + Increase in deferred revenue − Decrease in deferred revenue	= Cash collections from customers
Cost of Goods Sold	+ Increase in inventory − Decrease in inventory − Increase in accounts payable + Decrease in accounts payable	= Cash paid to suppliers
Salary Expense	− Increase in accrued salaries payable + Decrease in accrued salaries payable	= Cash paid to employees
Other Operating Expenses	− Depreciation, amortization, depletion expense for period + Increase in prepaid expenses − Decrease in prepaid expenses − Increase in accrued operating expenses + Decrease in accrued operating expenses	= Cash paid for other operating expenses
Interest Revenue	− Increase in interest receivable + Decrease in interest receivable	= Cash revenue from interest
Interest Expense	− Increase in accrued interest payable + Decrease in accrued interest payable	= Cash paid for interest
Investment Income	− Increase in investment account from equity income* + Decrease in investment account from equity income**	= Cash revenue from dividends
Tax Expense	− Increase in deferred tax liability + Decrease in deferred tax liability − Decrease in deferred tax asset + Increase in deferred tax asset − Increase in accrued taxes payable + Decrease in accrued taxes payable − Decrease in prepaid tax + Increase in prepaid tax	= Cash paid for taxes
Net cash flow from operating activities		

*Amount by which equity income recognized exceeds cash dividends received.
**Amount by which cash dividends received exceed equity income recognized.

5

A Guide to Earnings and Financial Reporting Quality

Qual-i-ty (n). Synonyms: excellence, superiority, class, eminence, value.

Before delving into the analysis of financial statements in Chapter 6, this chapter considers the *quality* of reported financial information, which is a critical element in evaluating financial statement data. The earnings statement encompasses a number of areas that provide management with opportunities for influencing the outcome of reported earnings in ways that may not best represent economic reality or the future operating potential of a firm. These include:

- Accounting choices, estimates, and judgments.
- Changes in accounting methods and assumptions.
- Discretionary expenditures.
- Nonrecurring transactions.
- Nonoperating gains and losses.
- Revenue and expense recognitions that do not match cash flow.

In evaluating a business firm, it is essential that the financial statement analyst consider the qualitative as well as the quantitative components of earnings for an accounting period. The higher the quality of financial reporting, the more useful is the information for business decision making. The analyst should develop an earnings figure that reflects the future ongoing potential of the firm. This process requires a consideration of qualitative factors and necessitates, in some cases, an actual adjustment of the reported earnings figure.

In addition to earnings quality, the quality of the information on the balance sheet and statement of cash flows is equally important. Because these financial statements are interrelated, quality of financial reporting issues often affects more than one financial statement.

The primary focus of this chapter is to provide the financial statement user with a step-by-step guide that links the items on an earnings statement with the key areas in the financial statement data that affect earnings quality. Exhibit 5.1 is a checklist for earnings quality. Items that affect the quality of

EXHIBIT 5.1

A Checklist for Earnings Quality

I. Sales
    1. Premature revenue recognition
    2. Gross vs. net basis
    3. Allowance for doubtful accounts
    4. Price vs. volume changes
    5. Real vs. nominal growth

II. Cost of Goods Sold
    6. Cost flow assumption for inventory
    7. Base LIFO layer liquidations
    8. Loss recognitions on write-downs of inventories (also see item 11)

III. Operating Expenses
    9. Discretionary expenses
    10. Depreciation
    11. Asset impairment
    12. Reserves
    13. In-process research and development
    14. Pension accounting—interest rate assumptions

IV. Nonoperating Revenue and Expense
    15. Gains (losses) from sales of assets
    16. Interest income
    17. Equity income
    18. Income taxes
    19. Unusual items
    20. Discontinued operations
    21. Extraordinary items

V. Other Issues
    22. Material changes in number of shares outstanding
    23. Operating earnings, a.k.a. core earnings, pro forma earnings, or EBITDA

information on the balance sheet and statement of cash flows will be covered later in this chapter.

The list does not, by any means, include every item that affects earnings quality. Rather, the examples illustrate some of the qualitative issues that are most commonly encountered in financial statement data. Another purpose of the chapter is to provide the financial statement user with an approach to use in analyzing and interpreting the qualitative factors. The checklist represents an attempt to provide a framework for the analysis of earnings quality rather than a complete list of its components.

Although the examples in this book deal primarily with the financial reporting of wholesale, retail, and manufacturing firms, the concepts and techniques presented can also apply to other types of industries. For instance, there is a discussion in this chapter of the provision for doubtful accounts as it impacts earnings quality. The same principles, on a larger scale, would apply to the provision for loan loss reserves for financial institutions. Almost all of the items on the checklist—other than those directly related to cost of goods sold—would apply to most types of business firms, including service-oriented companies.

USING THE CHECKLIST

Each item on the checklist in Exhibit 5.1 will be discussed and illustrated with examples from publicly held corporations.

I. Sales or Revenues

1. PREMATURE REVENUE RECOGNITION.   According to generally accepted accounting principles (GAAP), revenue should not be recognized until there is evidence that a true sale has taken place; that is, delivery of products has occurred or title to those products has passed to the buyer, or services have been rendered, the price has been determined, and collection is expected. Unfortunately, many firms have violated this accounting principle by recording revenue before these conditions have been met. While financial statement users cannot readily determine premature revenue recognition policy, they can look for certain clues in the financial statement information. An important place to start is the firm's revenue recognition policy, which is discussed in financial statement notes, to determine whether any changes have been made to the policy and if so, to evaluate the reason for the change and its impact. Analyzing the relationship among sales, accounts receivable, and inventory can signal "red flags" if these accounts are not moving in comparable patterns. Fourth-quarter spikes in revenue may also indicate premature revenue recognition for companies that do not typically experience high seasonal fourth-quarter sales.

Bally's Fitness Centers boosted revenue from at least 1997 through 2003 by recording revenue prematurely for its initiation fees, prepaid dues, and reactivation fees. The SEC filed financial fraud charges against the company on February 28, 2008, alleging that Bally Total Fitness Holding Corporation had overstated year-end 2001 stockholders' equity by nearly $1.8 billion, or more than 340%. The complaint also alleged that Bally's understated its net losses in 2002 and 2003 by $92.4 million and $90.8 million, respectively.[1] Bally's agreed to a settlement offer, but the firm had already filed bankruptcy and was under new private ownership when this occurred.

Dell, Inc., in 2007, admitted to financial statement manipulations that included premature revenue recognition. As a result, financial statements for the years 2003 through 2006 were restated. Senior executives and other employees overstated revenues to meet quarterly performance goals. As a reseller of other companies' software products, Dell should have deferred revenue recognition, but chose instead to record the revenue prematurely. The restatement in fiscal 2005 caused a reduction in revenue for software sales in the amount of $105 million.[2]

Another scheme used to inflate revenues is to keep the accounting books open longer than the end of the quarter. Computer Associates used such a strategy prior to 2001, referred to as the "35-day month practice," to prematurely record $2.2 billion of revenue. Former chief executive Sanjay Kumar pleaded guilty to securities fraud charges and obstruction of justice and received a 12-year prison sentence and $8 million in fines as a result of this scheme.[3]

2. GROSS VERSUS NET BASIS.   Another tactic to boost revenues is to record sales at the gross rather than the net price. "Gross" refers to the total amount that the final customer pays for an item. "Net" refers to the gross amount less the cost of the sale, which equals the fee that is paid to the reseller of the item. Some companies act as an agent between the customer and seller of a product or service. Agents receive the "net" amount for their role. For example, Concert.com Company acts as an agent to sell concert tickets for a variety of venues in the United States. Concert.com receives a commission of $20 for each concert ticket it sells. A customer orders two tickets to a concert at the Star Theater costing $100 per person. Concert.com receives the order and credit card authorization, which it passes on to Star Theater. The tickets are sent to the customer by Star Theater. Because Concert.com does not take title to the tickets, it does not have ownership risk or responsibility for the tickets. GAAP requires that Concert.com use the net method for recording revenue, which means Concert.com will record $40 as revenue. Had Concert.com assumed the risks of ownership by taking title to the tickets, the gross method would have been used to record $200 of revenue and $160 of cost of sales, resulting in gross profit of $40.

---

[1] U.S. Securities and Exchange Commission, Litigation Release No. 20470, February 28, 2008.
[2] Christopher Lawton, "Dell Details Accounting Woes; Methods for Recognizing Revenue From Software, Warranties Led to Errors," *Wall Street Journal*, October 31, 2007.
[3] William M. Bulkeley, "CA Ex-CEO Kumar Receives 12-year Prison Term," *Wall Street Journal*, November 3, 2006.

Reading the notes to the financial statements to determine how revenue is recorded can enlighten users of financial statements that a firm is recording at gross prices. In the Yahoo! 2007 Form 10-K Annual Report, the company states:

> In addition to delivering search and display advertising on Yahoo! Properties, the Company also generates revenues from search and/or display advertising offerings on Affiliate sites. The Company pays Affiliates for the revenues generated from the display of these advertisements on the Affiliates' Websites. These payments are called traffic acquisition costs ("TAC"). In accordance with EITF Issue No. 99-19, "Reporting Revenue Gross as a Principal Versus Net as an Agent," the revenues derived from these arrangements that involve traffic supplied by Affiliates is reported gross of the payment to Affiliates. These revenues are reported gross due to the fact that the Company is the primary obligor to the advertisers who are the customers of the advertising service.[4]

SEC guidelines allow companies such as Yahoo! to record revenues at gross amounts when the company acts as a principal in the transaction.[5] The problem from a financial statement user's perspective is that, in reality, the company will receive only the net amount when the transaction is complete. Google, on the other hand, records some revenue at gross prices, but other revenue is recorded at net amounts as outlined in notes to its financial statements in the 2007 Google Form 10-K Annual Report:

> We recognize as revenues the fees charged advertisers each time a user clicks on one of the text-based ads that are displayed next to the search results pages on our site or on the search results pages or content pages of our Google Network members' web sites and, for those advertisers who use our cost-per impression pricing, the fees charged advertisers each time an ad is displayed on our members' sites. In addition, we recognize as revenues the fees charged advertisers when ads are published in the magazines or broadcasted by the radio stations (or each time a listener responds to that ad) of our Google Network members. We recognize these revenues as such because the services have been provided, and the other criteria set forth under Staff Accounting Bulletin Topic 13: *Revenue Recognition* have been met, namely, the fees we charge are fixed or determinable, we and our advertisers understand the specific nature and terms of the agreed-upon transactions and collectibility is reasonably assured. In accordance with Emerging Issues Task Force ("EITF") Issue No. 99-19, *Reporting Revenue Gross as a Principal Versus Net as an Agent* ("EITF 99-19"), we report our Google AdSense revenues on a gross basis principally because we are the primary obligor to our advertisers.

Although Google and Yahoo! have both followed GAAP, comparability issues occur for the financial statement user trying to compare revenues and gross

---

[4] Reproduced with permission of Yahoo! Inc. © 2008 Yahoo! Inc. YAHOO! and the YAHOO! logo are registered trademarks of Yahoo! Inc.

[5] "Revenue Recognition in Financial Statements," *Staff Accounting Bulletin No. 101,* Washington, DC, Securities and Exchange Commission, December 3, 1999.

profit margins of companies such as Yahoo! and Google. The net earnings amount will not be impacted so this is not an issue of earnings quality, but rather an issue of the quality of reported revenues. Revenues appear larger when recorded at gross amounts, but gross profit margins appear better for firms recording revenues net. The analyst must recognize that the net amount is the most realistic amount as that is what the firm will actually receive in cash as a result of the transaction.

3. ALLOWANCE FOR DOUBTFUL ACCOUNTS. Most companies sell products on credit. Revenue is recognized on the income statement when the sales are made, and accounts receivable are carried on the balance sheet until the cash is collected. Because some customer accounts are never satisfied, the balance sheet includes an allowance for doubtful accounts. A discussion of sales, accounts receivable, and the allowance for doubtful accounts is provided in Chapters 2 and 3.

The allowance account, which is deducted from the balance sheet accounts receivable account, should reflect the volume of credit sales, the firm's past experience with customers, the customer base, the firm's credit policies, the firm's collection practices, economic conditions, and changes in any of these factors. There should be a consistent relationship, all other things being equal, between the rate of change in sales, accounts receivable, and the allowance for doubtful accounts. If the amounts are changing at different rates or in different directions—for example, if sales and accounts receivable are increasing, but the allowance account is decreasing or is increasing at a much smaller rate—the analyst should be alert to the potential for manipulation through the allowance account. Of course, there could also be a plausible reason for such a change.

As discussed in Chapter 2, the allowance for doubtful accounts is a type of reserve account and can be manipulated by under- or overestimating bad debt expenses. Underestimating bad debt expense will boost net income. On the other hand, by overestimating the allowance account, firms can set themselves up for a later correction that will ultimately boost net income. By analyzing the allowance for doubtful accounts as illustrated in Chapter 2, an astute analyst can make an assessment about the likelihood of manipulation.[6]

Companies should offer clear explanations of their accounts receivable and allowance for doubtful accounts in their notes if there are significant and abnormal changes to the accounts. Seagate Technology, in notes to its 2007 Form 10-K, explains why the firm's allowance account increased, despite a decreasing accounts receivable balance.

Accounts Receivable

(In Millions)	June 29, 2007	June 30, 2006
Accounts receivable	$1,433	$1,482
Allowance for doubtful accounts	(50)	(37)
	$1,383	$1,445

---

[6] The underlying liquidity of accounts receivable is also extremely important in assessing earnings quality. This topic is covered in Chapters 4 and 6.

The Company terminated its distributor relationships with eSys and the Company ceased shipments of its products to eSys. eSys was the largest distributor of Seagate products (including Maxtor products) for the fiscal year ended June 30, 2006, representing approximately 5% of the Company's revenues.

The Company recorded $40 million of allowance for doubtful accounts in the three months ended September 29, 2006, due to the inherent uncertainties following the termination of the distribution relationships, eSys' continuing delinquency in payments and failure to pay amounts when promised, and eSys' failure to comply with the terms of its commercial agreements with the Company. The Company is pursuing collection of all amounts owed by eSys as promptly as possible. Any amounts recovered on these receivables will be recorded in the period received.

While the Company terminated its distributor relationships with eSys, the Company has and will continue to aggressively pursue any claims that may be assertable against eSys as a result of material breaches of the distribution agreements and any intentionally wrongful conduct that may have occurred. Specifically, the Company has commenced legal proceedings against eSys under a distribution agreement and a corporate guarantee, against its Chief Executive Officer on a personal guarantee, and the Company may initiate further legal proceedings under various distribution agreements to recover all amounts owed for purchased product.

Many times, however, companies offer no explanation of questionable changes. Logitech International S.A. offers no explanation for the volatility in charges to bad debt expense or write-offs of accounts receivable that can be observed in the valuation schedule in the company's 2008 Form 10-K.

Schedule II LOGITECH INTERNATIONAL S.A.
VALUATION AND QUALIFYING ACCOUNTS
For the Fiscal Years Ending March 31, 2008, 2007 and 2006 (in thousands)

Fiscal Year	Description	Balance at beginning of period	Charged to Income Statement	Write-offs charged to allowance	Balance at end of period
2008	Allowance for doubtful accounts	$3,322	$603	$(1,428)	$2,497
2007	Allowance for doubtful accounts	$2,988	$527	$ (193)	$3,322
2006	Allowance for doubtful accounts	$5,166	$ 9	$(2,187)	$2,988

In a few cases, no information about the allowance account can be found at all in the Form 10-K. Procter & Gamble Company no longer includes information on the balance sheet, in the notes, or in a valuation schedule to indicate the company even has an allowance for doubtful accounts. With over $6.6 billion of accounts receivable it seems unlikely that the firm has no bad debt. In a conversation one of the authors had with an SEC employee, it was discovered that the SEC could not explain the lack of disclosure either. The quality of reported earnings is impacted negatively by the lack of disclosure.

4. PRICE VERSUS VOLUME CHANGES.   If a company's sales are increasing (or decreasing), it is important to determine whether the change is a result of price, volume, or a combination of both factors. Are sales growing because the firm is increasing prices or because more units are being sold, or both? It would seem that, in general, higher-quality earnings would be the product of both volume and price increases (during inflation). The firm would want to sell more units and keep prices increasing at least in line with the growth rate of general inflation.

Information regarding the reasons for sales growth (or decline) is one of the areas covered in a firm's management discussion and analysis section of the annual or 10-K report, discussed in Chapter 1. To relate sales growth to reasons for sales growth, use sales data from the income statement and the volume/price discussion from the management discussion and analysis section.

Micron Technology, Inc.'s Consolidated Statements of Operations include the following:

	2007	2006
Net sales (in millions)	$5,688	$5,272

The following is an excerpt from the Micron Technology Management Discussion and Analysis of Financial Condition and Results of Operations:

> Total net sales for 2007 increased 8% as compared to 2006 primarily due to an 11% increase in Memory sales partially offset by an 8% decline in Imaging sales. Memory sales for 2007 reflect a 204% increase in megabits sold partially offset by a 64% decline in per megabit average selling prices from 2006. Memory sales were 88% of total net sales in 2007 compared to 86% in 2006 and 94% in 2005. Imaging sales for 2007 decreased 8% from 2006 reflecting industry softness in mobile handset sales and pricing pressure.

A determination can be made from this information that the sales growth in 2007 was the result of memory sales volume increases as prices were declining.

5. REAL VERSUS NOMINAL GROWTH.   A related issue is whether sales are growing in "real" (inflation-adjusted) as well as "nominal" (as reported) terms. The change in sales in nominal terms can be readily calculated from the figures reported on the income statement. An adjustment of the reported sales figure with the Consumer Price Index (CPI) (or some other measure of general inflation) will enable the analyst to make a comparison of the changes in real and nominal terms. To make the calculation to compare real with nominal sales, begin with the sales figures reported in the income statement, and adjust years prior to the current year with the CPI or some other price index. An example using information from the 2007 Annual Report of General Motors Corporation Automotive Division is shown here:

Sales (in millions)	2007	2006	Percentage Change
As reported (nominal)	$178,199	$171,179	4.10
Adjusted (real)	$178,199	$176,019	1.24

Using base period CPI (1982–1984 = 100)

(2007 CPI/2006 CPI) × 2006 Sales = Adjusted sales

(207.3/201.6) × $171,179 = $176,019

Sales, when adjusted for general inflation, grew at a rate of 1.24% which means that nominal sales growth has kept pace with the general rate of inflation. Another way to see this is to note that nominal sales increased 4.10% while the CPI increased from 201.6 to 207.3 or only 2.83%.

II. Cost of Goods Sold

6. COST FLOW ASSUMPTION FOR INVENTORY.   During periods of inflation, the last-in, first-out (LIFO) cost flow assumption for inventory accounting, described in Chapter 2, produces lower earnings than first-in, first-out (FIFO) or average cost. Just the reverse occurs if the firm operates in an industry with volatile or falling prices. But LIFO results in the matching of current costs with current revenues and therefore produces higher-quality earnings than either FIFO or average cost. The inventory accounting system used by the company is described in the note to the financial statements that details accounting policies or the note discussing inventory. The following excerpt from the 2006 Form 10-K report of Eastman Kodak illustrates an interesting example of inventory method choices:

> On January 1, 2006, the Company elected to change its method of costing its U.S. inventories to the average cost method, which approximates FIFO, whereas in all prior years most of the Company's inventory in the U.S. was costed using the LIFO method. As a result of this change, the cost of all the Company's inventories is determined by either the FIFO or average cost method. The new method of accounting for inventory in the U.S. is deemed preferable as the average cost method provides better matching of revenue and expenses given the rapid technological change in the Company's products. The average cost method also better reflects more current costs of inventory on the Company's Statement of Financial Position.

Components of the Company's Consolidated Statement of Operations affected by the change in costing methodology as originally reported under the LIFO method and as adjusted for the change in inventory costing methodology from the LIFO method to the average cost method are as follows (in millions, except per share data):

Year Ended December 31, 2005

	As Previously Reported	LIFO to Average Cost Change in Costing Methodology Adjustments (1)	As Adjusted
Cost of goods sold	$10,617	$ 33	$10,650
Gross profit	3,651	(33)	3,618
Loss from continuing operations before interest, other income (charges), net and income taxes	(599)	(33)	(632)
Loss from continuing operations before income taxes	(766)	(33)	(799)
Provision (benefit) for income taxes	689	(134)	555
(Loss) earnings from continuing operations	(1,455)	101	(1,354)
Net (loss) earnings	$ (1,362)	$101	$ (1,261)
Basic and diluted net (loss) earnings per share	$ (4.73)	$ .35	$ (4.38)
Continuing operations	$ (5.05)	$ .35	$ (4.70)

(1) The impact on the provision (benefit) for income taxes for the year ended December 31, 2005, is primarily the result of the reduction in the U.S. net deferred tax assets for which a valuation allowance was previously recognized in the third quarter of 2005, as disclosed in Note 15.

Management is correct that the value of inventory on the statement of financial position will better reflect the current cost using average cost, which approximates FIFO; however, they are incorrect that the method does a better job matching revenues and expenses because the first goods in do not necessarily reflect the current costs. The change in inventory methods is a good choice for Eastman Kodak because the firm has transitioned from an old-economy manufacturer of film, to a high-technology firm manufacturing such products as digital cameras. High-technology firms generally choose the FIFO method of inventory to reduce taxes because they tend to operate in deflationary environments. In a deflationary environment, the first goods reflect older, higher costs, whereas the last goods reflect current, lower costs.

7. BASE LIFO LAYER LIQUIDATIONS.   A base LIFO layer liquidation occurs with the use of LIFO in a situation in which the firm sells more goods than purchased during an accounting period. During inflation, this situation results in the lowest cost of goods sold expense from using LIFO because the older, less expensive items were sold. Usually, companies maintain a base layer of LIFO inventory that remains fairly constant. Goods are bought during the year and sales are made from the more recent purchases (for purposes of cost allocation). It is only when stocks of inventory are substantially reduced that the base layer is affected and LIFO earnings are higher. Base LIFO layer liquidations occur when companies are shrinking rather than increasing inventories. There is an actual reduction of inventory levels, but the earnings boost stems from the cost flow assumption: that the older and lower-priced products are those being sold. The effects of LIFO reductions, which are disclosed in notes to the financial statements, can be substantial. A base LIFO layer liquidation reduces the quality of earnings in the sense that there is an improvement in operating profit from what would generally be considered a negative occurrence: inventory reductions. In considering the future, ongoing potential of the company, it would be appropriate to exclude from earnings the effect of LIFO liquidations because a firm would not want to continue benefiting from inventory shrinkages. An example of a base LIFO layer liquidation occurred at Olin Corporation in 2006. The following excerpt is from the notes to the financial statements of Olin Corporation's 2006 annual report:

> During 2006, primarily as part of the Metals restructuring actions, which included the closure of the Waterbury and Seymour facilities, the reduction in LIFO inventory quantities resulted in LIFO inventory liquidation gains of $25.9 [millions].

8. LOSS RECOGNITIONS ON WRITE-DOWNS OF INVENTORIES. The principle of conservatism in accounting requires that firms carry inventory in the accounting records at the lower of cost (as determined by the cost flow assumption such as LIFO, FIFO, or average cost) or market. If the value of inventory falls below its original cost, the inventory is written down to market value. Market generally is determined by the cost to replace or reproduce the inventory but should not exceed the net realizable amount (selling price less completion and disposal costs) the company could generate from selling the item. The amount of the write-down will affect comparability, thus quality, of the profit margins from period to period.

When the write-down of inventory is included in cost of goods sold, the gross profit margin is affected in the year of the write-down. Significant write-downs of inventory are relatively infrequent; however, an example of an inventory write-down was announced by Ford Motor Company in January 2002. Due to the large drop in value of the metal palladium, used in auto manufacturing, the company announced they would record a $1 billion write-off. Ford had purchased this metal, once priced at less than $100 per ounce, for amounts over $1,000 per ounce. When prices fell, Ford revalued their palladium inventory to $440 per ounce.[7] In

---

[7] Gregory L. White, "How Ford's Big Batch of Rare Metal Led to $1 Billion Write-Off," *Wall Street Journal*, February 6, 2002.

comparing the gross profit margin between periods, the analyst should be aware of the impact on the margin that occurs from such write-downs.

Sometimes, companies may write down the value of inventories every year in the three-year reporting period; one example is LaBarge, Inc., a designer and manufacturer of specialized, custom electronic systems. The notes on inventory in LaBarge, Inc.'s 2007 Form 10-K reveal the following information:

> For the fiscal years ended July 1, 2007, July 2, 2006, and July 3, 2005, expense for obsolete or slow-moving inventory charged to income before income taxes was $1.3 million, $0.9 million, and $1.0 million, respectively.

In this case, the analyst may view these write-downs as a recurring part of the firm's business operations.

III. Operating Expenses

9. DISCRETIONARY EXPENSES. A company can increase earnings by reducing variable operating expenses in a number of areas such as the repair and maintenance of capital assets, research and development, and advertising and marketing. If such discretionary expenses are reduced primarily to benefit the current year's reported earnings, the long-run impact on the firm's operating profit may be detrimental and thus the quality lowered. The analyst should review the trends of these discretionary expenses and compare them with the firm's volume of activity and level of capital investment. Amounts of discretionary expenditures are disclosed in the financial statements and notes. Advertising expenses are usually detailed in the summary of significant accounting policies note, such as the following for Cognex Corporation:

> Advertising costs are expensed as incurred and totaled $1,770,000 in 2007, $2,144,000 in 2006, and $3,057,000 in 2005.

Product revenue declined from $214,938,000 in 2006 to $201,714,000 in 2007, and net income fell from $39,855,000 to $26,899,000. No explanation is provided in notes to the financial statements or Management's Discussion and Analysis to explain the significant reduction in advertising expense, but the analyst should question the effect on revenue and income. Cognex increased expenditures for research and development and for other selling, general, and administrative expense; it is possible that the firm reduced advertising costs to offset these increases, but with a possible negative impact on profitability.

10. DEPRECIATION. The amount of annual depreciation expense recognized for an accounting period, as discussed in Chapter 1, depends on the choice of depreciation method and estimates regarding the useful life and salvage value of the asset being depreciated. Most companies use the straight-line method rather than an accelerated method for reporting purposes because it produces a smoother earnings stream and higher earnings in the early years of the depreciation period. The straight-line method, however, is lower in quality in most cases because it does not reflect the economic reality of product usefulness in that most machinery and equipment do not wear evenly over the depreciation period.

There are additional issues that affect earnings quality with regard to the depreciation expense figure. Companies that misclassify operating expenses as capital expenditures have created poor quality of financial reporting not only on the income statement, but on all financial statements. Recording an amount that should be deducted in its entirety in one year as a capital expenditure results in the expense being depreciated over several years. This is exactly what WorldCom did in 2001 and 2002. The firm was able to increase profits by $11 billion. The cash flow effects of this are discussed later in this chapter. While it is nearly impossible to determine that a company has misclassified expenses by reading the annual report or Form 10-K, a thorough financial statement analysis would most likely raise red flags that something was amiss.[8]

Another issue affecting the area of depreciation is that comparing companies is difficult when each firm chooses not only different depreciation methods, but also different lives for their long-lived assets. Depreciation policy is explained in the notes to the financial statements, such as the two following excerpts from 2007 Form 10-K annual reports from competitors Mattel, Inc. and Hasbro, Inc.:

> Mattel, Inc.—Depreciation is computed using the straight-line method over estimated useful lives of 10 to 40 years for buildings, 3 to 10 years for machinery and equipment, and 10 to 20 years, not to exceed the lease term, for leasehold improvements. Tools, dies and molds are amortized using the straight-line method over 3 years.

> Hasbro, Inc.—Depreciation and amortization are computed using accelerated and straight-line methods to amortize the cost of property, plant and equipment over their estimated useful lives. The principal lives, in years, used in determining depreciation rates of various assets are: land improvements 15 to 19, buildings and improvements 15 to 25, and machinery and equipment 3 to 12. Tools, dies and molds are amortized over a three-year period or their useful lives, whichever is less, using an accelerated method.

11. ASSET IMPAIRMENT.   As was discussed in item 8, the write-down of asset values, following the principle of carrying assets at the lower of cost or market value, affects the comparability and thus the quality of financial data. The reasons for the write-downs would also be important in assessing the quality of the financial data. Information on asset write-downs is presented in notes to the financial statements. Firms also write down the carrying cost of property, plant, and equipment and intangible assets when there is a permanent impairment in value and certain investments in marketable equity securities are carried at market value. Miva,

---

[8] For additional reading about this issue, see Lyn Fraser and Aileen Ormiston, *Understanding the Corporate Annual Report: Nuts, Bolts and a Few Loose Screws,* Upper Saddle River, NJ: Prentice Hall, 2003.

Inc., an online media and advertising network company, reported significant asset impairment charges in its 2007 Form 10-K for 2007, 2006, and 2005. As a result of Miva's stock price declining in 2005, the market capitalization of the company fell below the recorded equity. An assessment of the company's goodwill and indefinite-lived intangible assets resulted in an impairment charge greater than $117 million for that year. In 2006 and 2007, Miva recorded impairment charges of more than $63 million and $20 million, respectively, to write down tangible and intangible long-lived assets. The impairment was caused by operating losses related to Miva Media US and reduced traffic generated by Miva's European distribution partners, slower-than-anticipated deployment of new services, and legal issues in Miva Media Europe.

The FASB has to a certain extent eliminated an earnings management opportunity resulting from asset impairment charges. If it is later deemed that too much was written off, FASB Statement No. 144, "Accounting for the Impairment or Disposal of Long-Lived Assets," does not allow a firm to write back up the value of the asset.

12. RESERVES.   Accrual accounting requires companies to estimate and accrue obligations for items that may be paid in future periods but should be accrued in the current period. The creation and use of these reserve accounts is required to properly match revenues and expenses; however, the abuse of reserve accounts has been an ongoing issue. Cookie-jar accounting, as the abuse is referred to, occurs when companies create or use reserve accounts for the purpose of setting aside funds in good years by overreserving (i.e., reducing net income) and then reducing charges or even reversing charges to the reserve accounts (i.e. increasing net income) in poor years. The net effect is to smooth out earnings from year to year. Examples of reserve accounts include the allowance for doubtful accounts (discussed in Chapter 2 and item 3 of this chapter), and reserve accounts for items such as product warranties, restructuring, sales returns, and environmental obligations. In 2007, Dell, Inc. admitted not only to recording revenue prematurely to manipulate financial statement information, but also to abusing its product warranty account by using it as a cookie jar.[9]

Companies will often take enormous write-offs in one period, referred to as "big bath" charges, to clean up their balance sheets. Generally, profits will improve in the subsequent period after the big bath has been taken. For the quarter ending April 28, 2001, Cisco Systems recognized restructuring costs and other special charges of $1.2 billion and inventory write-downs of $2.2 billion, contributing to a loss for the quarter of $2.7 billion. Cisco was able to announce a profit of $7 million for the following quarter, ending July 28, 2001. In 2007, many banks took the big bath in order to write off losses in the values of securities held by banks. If banks have overestimated losses, they could report higher profits in the future if the securities' values later rebound.[10]

---

[9] Christopher Lawton, "Dell Details Accounting Woes; Methods for Recognizing Revenue From Software, Warranties Led to Errors," *Wall Street Journal*, October 31, 2007.

[10] Cecilie Rohwedder, "Worries Shift To Overstating Summer Losses," *Wall Street Journal*, October 4, 2007.

13. IN-PROCESS RESEARCH AND DEVELOPMENT.   In-process research and development charges are one-time charges taken at the time of an acquisition. The charged amounts are part of the acquisition price that the acquiring company determines are not yet viable research and development because they are still in process. These charges can be written off immediately under current accounting rules. Any revenue gains from the research in the future will cause higher earnings that have not been matched to the expenses that created them.

Estimating the value of the research and development that is to be written off is difficult, and, as a result, users of financial statements are unlikely to be able to determine whether these charges are appropriate. From a user's perspective, this is a problematic area, as companies can write off significant amounts of research and development the year of an acquisition in order to boost earnings in later years. Amgen, Inc., a biotechnology company, made acquisitions for $700 million and $2,474 million, respectively, and immediately wrote off $590 million and $1,231 million, respectively, in 2007 and 2006 of in-process research and development. Though these amounts may be accurate, investors and creditors have no way to know for sure.

14. PENSION ACCOUNTING—INTEREST RATE ASSUMPTIONS.   Although a detailed explanation of pension accounting is beyond the scope of this book, it is important to be aware of some basic pension accounting principles as they impact earnings quality. The reader is referred to the discussion of disclosure requirements for postretirement benefits other than pensions in Chapter 2.

Pension accounting is based on expectations regarding the benefits that will be paid when employees retire and on the interest that pension assets will earn over time. The provisions for pension accounting are specified in Statement of Financial Accounting Standards (SFAS) No. 87, "Employers' Accounting for Pensions,"[11] as amended by Statement of Financial Accounting Standards (SFAS) No. 158, "Employers' Accounting for Defined Benefit Pension and Other Post Retirement Plans." SFAS 158 is intended to improve financial statement disclosure by requiring companies to recognize an asset for a plan's overfunded status or a liability for a plan's underfunded status on the balance sheet rather than in notes to the financial statements. The funded status is measured as the difference between a plan's assets and the plan's projected benefit obligations.

If a company changes, based on actuarial estimates, the interest rate assumptions used in pension accounting, this change then affects the amount of annual pension expense and the present value of the pension benefits. If the assumed rate of interest is increased, pension cost is reduced and earnings increased. For example, if you need $5,000 in 20 years, the amount you would have to invest today would be different if your investment earned 6% or 8%. At 6% you would have to invest $1,560 to accumulate to $5,000 at annual compound interest in 20 years; if the interest rate were increased to 8%, you would have to contribute only

---

[11] For a detailed discussion of FASB Statement 87, see L. Revsine, "Understanding Financial Accounting Standard 87," *Financial Analysts Journal*, January–February 1989.

$1,075.[12] Also, the present value of the benefits to be paid in the future is affected by increasing the interest rate. The present value of $5,000 to be paid in 20 years is $1,560 at a 6% discount rate and $1,075 at an 8% rate.

To summarize the effects of a change in the pension interest rate assumption, if the assumed interest rate is lowered, the annual pension cost will increase and the present value of the benefits will also increase; if the assumed interest rate is increased, pension cost and the present value of the benefits are reduced.

As an example, information from the 2007 Kennametal, Inc. Form 10-K will be used to illustrate disclosures related to pensions and postretirement benefits. Reference to the new FASB standard is made in the management's discussion and analysis section:

> In September 2006, the FASB issued SFAS 158. SFAS 158 requires an employer to recognize the overfunded or underfunded status of a defined benefit postretirement plan as an asset or liability in its statement of financial position and to recognize changes in that funded status through comprehensive income of a business entity in the year in which the changes occur. SFAS 158 also requires an employer to measure the funded status of a plan as of the date of its year-end statement of financial position. The funded status of each of our pension and other postretirement benefit plans is currently measured as of June 30. We adopted SFAS 158 effective June 30, 2007. The provisions of SFAS 158 are to be applied on a prospective basis; therefore, prior periods presented have not been restated. The adoption of SFAS 158 had the following impacts on our consolidated balance sheet: a $1.0 million reduction in intangible assets, a $0.3 million increase in long-term deferred tax assets, a $39.1 million reduction in other long-term assets, an $8.0 million increase in other current liabilities, a $9.5 million reduction in long-term deferred tax liabilities, a $5.1 million reduction in accrued postretirement benefits, a $2.6 million reduction in accrued pension benefits and a $30.6 million reduction in accumulated other comprehensive income.

Kennametal reports two liabilities on its balance sheet:

As of June 30	2007	2006
(in thousands)		
Accrued Post Retirement Benefits	$26,546	$31,738
Accrued Pension Benefits	105,214	113,030

---

[12] (5,000 × 0.312 = $1,560; $5,000 × 0.215 = $1,075) (factors for present value of single sum for 20 periods, 6% and 8%).

Tables from the footnote disclosures relating to employees' defined benefit plans from the 2007 Kennametal, Inc. Form 10-K are provided below:[13]

(In Thousands)	2007	2006	2005
Service cost	$ 9,934	$11,715	$ 9,445
Interest cost	37,920	34,259	34,245
Expected return on plan assets	(45,097)	(38,026)	(37,536)
Amortization of transition obligations	153	107	158
Amortization of prior service (credit) cost	(9)	853	707
Effect of divestiture	—	12	386
Recognition of actuarial losses	5,779	13,925	1,216
Net periodic pension cost	$ 8,680	$22,845	$ 8,621
Rates of return on plan assets:			
U.S. plans	8.3%	8.5%	8.5%
International plans	7.1%	6.7%	6.8%

There are two noteworthy items from this information. First, Kennametal recorded income from its pension plans in all three years as a result of the $45,097, $38,026, and $37,536 thousand of "expected" return on plan assets. Second, the expected returns were based on the expected rates of return on plan assets, which Kennametal estimated to be 8.3% in 2007and 8.5% in the United States in 2006 and 2005. Kennametal decreased its interest rate assumption in 2007, which is not surprising given the state of the economy and declining interest rates that were occurring. The next table allows the user to compare the expected return to the actual return on the plan assets:

(In Thousands)	2007	2006
Fair value of plan assets, beginning of year	$581,558	$483,659
Actual return on plan assets	74,825	43,324
Company contributions	5,244	80,990
Participant contributions	687	922
Benefits and expenses paid	(29,625)	(30,849)
Foreign currency translation adjustments	10,029	3,512
Fair value of plan assets, end of year	$642,718	$581,558

---

[13] The service cost represents the increase during the year in the discounted present value of payable benefits, resulting from employees' working an additional year; interest cost arises from the passage of time and increases interest expense; return on plan assets reduces pension expense; other components include net amortization and deferrals and are related to the choice of discount and interest rates. The same rate must be used to compute service cost and interest cost, but a different rate can be used to compute the expected rate of return on pension plan assets.

The fair value of the plan assets has increased from 2006 to 2007. In 2006 and 2007 the actual return on assets was greater than the expected return on plan assets shown in the first table. This confirms for the user that the rate of return being used by Kennametal to calculate the expected return on assets is not overly optimistic.

The funded status of Kennametal's pension plans is calculated as follows:

	2007	2006
Fair value of plan assets, end of year	$642,718	$581,558
Less: Benefit obligation, end of year	670,696	659,754
Funded status of plans	$ (27,978)	$ (78,196)

The following table reveals whether the pension plan is over- or underfunded:

(In Thousands)	2007	2006
Funded status of plans	$(27,978)	$(78,196)
Unrecognized transition obligation	—	2,287
Unrecognized prior service cost	—	2,607
Unrecognized actuarial losses	—	105,417
Net amount recognized	$(27,978)	$ 32,115
Amounts recognized in the balance sheet consist of:		
Long-term prepaid benefit	$82,505	$118,299
Short-term accrued benefit obligation	(5,269)	(208)
Accrued benefit obligation	(105,214)	(113,030)
Intangible assets	—	1,489
Accumulated other comprehensive income	—	25,565
Net amount recognized	$(27,978)	$ 32,115

Kennametal has an underfunded plan and, therefore, records an overall pension liability on the balance sheet. The accrued benefit obligation shown in the table above agrees with the line item on Kennametal's balance sheet for the long-term portion of the pension liability. The reconciliation of the funded status of the plan with the amounts shown on the balance sheet is a result of a combination of items. The FASB has included smoothing mechanisms that serve to reduce the volatility to the net income number when recording pension costs. In addition, the many estimates and assumptions used to calculate pension costs cause this amount to be different than the actual amount, and the firm must incorporate the correction of these errors in the amounts shown in the above table.

IV. Nonoperating Revenue and Expense

15. GAINS (LOSSES) FROM SALES OF ASSETS.   When a company sells a capital asset, such as property or equipment, the gain or loss is included in net income for the period. The sale of a major asset is sometimes made to increase earnings and/or to generate needed cash during a period when the firm is performing poorly. Such transactions are not part of the normal operations of the firm and should be excluded from net income when considering the future operating potential of the company.

The following table found in the Goodyear Tire & Rubber Company's 2007 Form 10-K illustrates nonoperating revenues and expenses:

Note 3. Other (Income) and Expense

(In Millions)	2007	Restated 2006	2005
Interest income	$(128)	$(86)	$(58)
Net (gains) losses on asset sales	(15)	(40)	36
Financing fees	106	40	109
General and product liability—discontinued products	15	26	9
Foreign currency exchange	31	(2)	21
Insurance settlements	—	(1)	(43)
Equity in earnings of affiliates	(9)	(10)	(11)
Royalty income	(15)	(8)	(6)
Fire loss expense	12	—	—
Miscellaneous	2	(6)	5
	$ (1)	$(87)	$ 62

The asset sales, fire loss expense, and insurance settlements would most likely be excluded when projecting future operating earnings.

16. INTEREST INCOME.   Interest income is also nonoperating in nature except for certain types of firms such as financial institutions. Interest income results primarily from short-term temporary investments in marketable securities to earn a return on cash not immediately needed in the business. These security investments were explained in Chapter 2. In the assessment of earnings quality, the analyst should be alert to the materiality and variability in the amount of interest income because it is not part of operating income. Interest income is disclosed on the face of the income statement or in notes to the financial statements.

Using the information given on interest income for Goodyear Tire & Rubber Company in the previous item (number 15) one can see that more interest income has been earned each year. Further investigation reveals that the increase of interest income was a result of higher levels of cash deposits in the United States. This information is important in analyzing earnings quality because the 2007 interest income may not be sustainable. Projecting future cash balances is important to determining future amounts of interest income.

17. EQUITY INCOME.   Use of the equity method to account for investments in un-consolidated subsidiaries, discussed and illustrated in Chapter 3, permits the investor to recognize as investment income the investor's percentage ownership share of the investee's reported income rather than recognizing income only to the extent of cash dividends actually received. The net effect is that the investor, in most cases, records more income than is received in cash. Using the information given on equity in earnings of affiliates for Goodyear Tire & Rubber Company in item 15, one can see that the equity investments Goodyear has made have not performed well. Goodyear is recording losses as a result of its investments; however, this does not negatively affect Goodyear's cash value because no cash has been paid out by Goodyear.

Cash flow from operations, discussed in Chapter 4, excludes the amount by which investment income recognized exceeds or is less than cash received. Goodyear Tire & Rubber Company received no dividends from these affiliated companies; therefore, it would be appropriate to eliminate this noncash portion of earnings for comparative purposes, by adding back equity losses or deducting equity earnings.

18. INCOME TAXES.   The provision for income tax expense on the income statement differs from the tax actually paid, as was discussed in Chapters 2 and 3. When assessing the net earnings number, it is important to differentiate between increases and decreases to net earnings caused by tax events. A significant change in the effective tax rate may be a one-time nonrecurring item. Included in the income tax notes to the financial statements is a reconciliation of the U.S. federal statutory tax rate to the company's effective tax rate, such as the following from the 2007 Applied Materials, Inc. Annual Report:

	2005	2006	2007
U.S. statutory tax rate	35.0%	35.0%	35.0%
Favorable resolutions from audits of prior years' income tax filings	(7.5)	(2.1)	(1.0)
Foreign earnings repatriation under the American Jobs Creation Act of 2004	2.0	—	—
Effect of foreign operations taxed at various rates	(1.2)	(0.8)	(1.6)
State income taxes, net of federal benefit	0.6	0.6	1.1
Research and other tax credits	(1.2)	(0.1)	(0.6)
Export sales/production benefit	(5.9)	(4.2)	(1.3)
Other	1.7	1.6	(1.7)
Effective Tax Rate	23.5%	30.0%	29.9%

In 2005, Applied Materials' effective tax rate of 23.5% is significantly lower than the statutory rate as well as the company's effective tax rate the next two years. The reasons are that Applied Materials received favorable resolutions from audits of prior years' income tax filings, as well as benefits from export sales and production. In subsequent years, these items did not provide as large a benefit. The analyst should take this into consideration when projecting future net earnings.

In addition, the income tax notes to the financial statements reveal year-to-year changes in deferred tax accounts.

19. UNUSUAL ITEMS.   Some companies will create a line item on the income statement for unusual items or special charges. The company wants the user of the financial statements to realize that these items are not recurring operating expenses. The analyst should always investigate these items by reading the notes and the management discussion and analysis to determine whether these items are non-operating and/or nonrecurring. The second quarter earnings release of Waste Management in 2001 revealed that the company included $1 million for the painting of trash trucks and $30 million in consulting fees as "unusual expenses."[14] When adjusting operating and net profit figures for comparison purposes, it would be appropriate to include these items as ordinary operating expenses.

20. DISCONTINUED OPERATIONS.   Discontinued operations should be excluded in considering future earnings. Two items are recorded if the discontinued operations have been sold: the gain or loss from operations of the division up to the time of sale, and the gain or loss as a result of the sale, both net of tax. The income statement disclosure for Avery Dennison Corporation, from its 2007 Form 10-K Annual Report, is as follows:

	(Dollars in Millions)		
Years Ended December 31,	**2007**	**2006**	**2005**
Income from continuing operations	$303.5	$358.5	$292.2
Income (loss) from discontinued operations, net of tax (including gain on disposal of $1.3 and tax benefit of $14.9 in 2006)	—	14.7	(65.4)
Net income	$303.5	$373.2	$226.8

It would be appropriate to deduct the income on discontinued operations in 2006 from earnings and add back the loss from discontinued operations in 2005 for comparative purposes.

21. EXTRAORDINARY ITEMS.   Extraordinary items are gains and losses that are both unusual and infrequent in nature. They are shown separately, net of tax, on the income statement. Because very few transactions meet the definition of extraordinary, it is rare to see such items on an earnings statement. For many years the FASB required gains and losses on debt extinguishments to be reported as extraordinary items; however, the issuance of FASB Statement No. 145, "Rescission of FASB

---

[14] Aaron Elstein, "'Unusual Expenses' Raise Concerns," *Wall Street Journal*, August 23, 2001.

Statements No. 4, 44, 64, Amendment of FASB Statement No. 13, and Technical Corrections," only allows this treatment if the gain or loss meets the criteria for an extraordinary item.

Huntsman Corporation reported an extraordinary loss of $6.5 million in 2007 and an extraordinary gain of $55.9 million in 2006 as a result of acquiring a business. The acquisition cost of the business was $158.2 million and the fair value of the net assets acquired was $207.6 million, resulting in negative goodwill of $49.4 million. The negative goodwill is recorded as extraordinary and in this case was recorded over a two-year period as explained in the notes to the financial statements:

> During 2006, we recorded an extraordinary gain on the acquisition of $55.9 million based on the preliminary purchase price allocation. During the six months ended June 30, 2007, we adjusted the preliminary purchase price allocation for, among other things, the finalization of restructuring plans, estimates of asset retirement obligations, the determination of related deferred taxes and finalization of the post-closing working capital adjustments, resulting in a reduction to the extraordinary gain of $6.5 million.

The gain or loss should be eliminated from earnings when evaluating a firm's future earnings potential.

V. Other Issues

22. MATERIAL CHANGES IN NUMBER OF SHARES OUTSTANDING. The number of common stock shares outstanding and thus the computation of earnings per share can change materially from one accounting period to the next. These changes result from such transactions as treasury stock purchases and the purchase and retirement of a firm's own common stock. The reasons for the repurchase of common stock should be determined if possible. Some firms use repurchase programs to obtain shares of stock to be used in employee stock option programs. Other firms offer no reason for their repurchase program. It is important to consider whether a firm is spending scarce resources to merely increase earnings per share (EPS). The effects of reducing outstanding shares of common stock result in an increase to EPS. Microsoft offers an interesting example.

In its 2004 annual report, Microsoft explains its repurchase program as follows:

> Our board of directors has approved a program to repurchase shares of our common stock to reduce the dilutive effect of our stock option and stock purchase plans.

However, in 2007, Microsoft no longer offers the same reason for repurchasing its own common stock. The notes to the financial statements explain the repurchase program as follows:

> On July 20, 2006, we announced the completion of the repurchase program initially approved by our Board of Directors on July 20, 2004, to buy back up to $30.00 billion in Microsoft common stock.

On July 20, 2006, we also announced that our Board of Directors authorized two new share repurchase programs: a $20.00 billion tender offer, which was completed on August 17, 2006; and authorization for up to an additional $20.00 billion ongoing share repurchase program with an expiration of June 30, 2011. Under the tender offer, we repurchased approximately 155 million shares of common stock, or 1.5% of our common shares outstanding, for approximately $3.84 billion at a price per share of $24.75. On August 18, 2006, we announced that the authorization for the $20.00 billion ongoing share repurchase program had been increased by approximately $16.16 billion. As a result, we are authorized to repurchase additional shares in an amount up to $36.16 billion through June 30, 2011. As of June 30, 2007, approximately $15.14 billion remained of the $36.16 billion approved repurchase amount.

Other information in the 2007 Microsoft annual report reveals that Microsoft repurchased 971, 754, and 312 million shares, respectively, in 2007, 2006, and 2005 while only issuing 289, 106, and 160 million shares in those same years. The financial statements of Microsoft reveal that retained earnings was a positive number at the beginning of 2005, but became an accumulated deficit in 2006 with a much larger negative balance by the end of 2007. This change is a direct result of the large dividends paid in 2005, combined with the stock repurchase program. Microsoft still has a significant amount of cash and marketable securities; however, the balances in these accounts have dropped from $27 billion in 2006 to $17 billion in 2007. The cash flow statement shows that cash flow from operating activities was not nearly enough to cover the stock repurchases, let alone the cash dividends paid. Looking at the common stock prices for the years 2006 and 2007 does indicate that perhaps the repurchase program has helped increase the value of the stock as it has risen from a low of $21.46 per share in 2006 to a high of $31.48 per share in 2007.

23. OPERATING EARNINGS, A.K.A. CORE EARNINGS, PRO FORMA EARNINGS, OR EBITDA. Operating earnings or profit (discussed in Chapter 3) is an important figure for assessing the ongoing potential of a firm. Some companies have created their own operating profit numbers and tried to convince users that these figures are the ones to focus on instead of the GAAP-based amounts. These "company created" numbers go by a variety of names such as core earnings, pro forma earnings, or EBITDA. EBITDA, for example, refers to operating earnings before interest, tax, depreciation, and amortization expenses are deducted. Those who support focusing on EBITDA argue that depreciation and amortization charges are not cash items and should be ignored. In essence, they are asking that users ignore the fact that companies make long-term investments. Depreciation and amortization expenses are the allocation of an original cash amount spent for items such as equipment. In January 2003, the SEC adopted a new rule requiring companies that report pro forma financial information to present this information in a manner that is not misleading and also to reconcile the pro forma financial information with GAAP.

WHAT ARE THE REAL EARNINGS?

Each individual user of financial statements should adjust the earnings figure to reflect what that particular user believes is relevant to the decision at hand. Based on the checklist, Exhibit 5.2 shows the items that should be considered as adjustments to earnings.

QUALITY OF FINANCIAL REPORTING—THE BALANCE SHEET

Many items discussed in the earnings quality section also impact balance sheet quality, such as the value attached to accounts receivable, inventory, and long-term assets. When evaluating balance sheet information, several items should also be assessed. The type of debt used to finance assets should generally be matched; that is, short-term debt should be used to finance current assets, and long-term debt (or equity) should be used to finance long-term assets. A mismatching of debt to assets could be an indication that the firm may be having trouble finding financing sources. The accounting fraud that led to the bankruptcy of Parmalat, the Italian dairy company, revolved around debt issues at the firm. Despite supposedly large cash balances (later found to be nonexistent), Parmalat went to the markets continuously and issued bonds to raise more funding. This inconsistency should have raised red flags well before the scandal unfolded.

As discussed in Chapter 2, the "Commitments and Contingencies" disclosures in the notes to the financial statements should be evaluated carefully.

EXHIBIT 5.2

Adjustments to Earnings

Start with net income, then consider the following adjustments:

a. add or deduct amounts for questionable items charged to bad debt expense (item 3)

b. deduct base LIFO layer liquidations (item 7)

c. add back loss recognized on write-downs of assets (items 8 and 11)

d. deduct amounts for discretionary expenses that firm may have delayed (item 9)

e. add or deduct amounts recorded as charges or credits to reserve accounts that are nonrecurring such as restructuring costs (item 12)

f. add back charges for in-process research and development (item 13)

g. add or deduct losses and gains from sales of assets (item 15)

h. deduct nonrecurring amounts of interest income (item 16)

i. add or deduct equity losses or income (item 17)

j. add or deduct nonrecurring amounts of income tax expense (item 18)

k. add back unusual expenses that are nonrecurring (item 19)

l. add or deduct losses or gains attributable to discontinued operations and extraordinary items (items 20 and 21)

These disclosures are often presented in the section where information on off–balance-sheet financing and other complex financing arrangements can be found. Despite the seeming surprise of Enron's downfall, many clues could have been found by tracking the complexities of the references to commitments and contingencies for several years preceding its bankruptcy.

The eight pages of notes to the financial statements related to the commitments and contingencies of Pfizer Inc. in 2007 may help the user of the financial statements understand the potential liabilities that may affect the firm in the future. Besides operating lease commitments, environmental matters, and guarantees, Pfizer is involved in many legal proceedings. Some of the lawsuits Pfizer is party to involve patents, product liability, consumer, commercial, securities, environmental and tax litigations and claims; and government investigations; among other legal proceedings. Though most of the information in the notes cannot be quantified on a financial statement, the notes do allow readers to determine for themselves the significance of the lawsuits.

Also included in the commitments note is information on capital and operating leases. While capital leases are included on the balance sheet, the financial statement user should consider the effects on certain leverage ratios (discussed in Chapter 6) if operating leases are extensive. The firm is committed to make lease payments, and if these leases had been negotiated as capital leases, there would be a higher amount of debt on the balance sheet. For example, Walgreen Company, a drug retailer, has no long-term debt according to its 2007 balance sheet. Reading the note on leases, however, the analyst can see that the firm is committed to pay a minimum of $29,135.9 million for leases in the future. This amount is greater than Walgreen's total assets in 2007 of $19,313.6 million.

QUALITY OF FINANCIAL REPORTING—THE STATEMENT OF CASH FLOWS

Since the requirement of the statement of cash flows in the 1980s, many investors and creditors have focused on cash flow from operations (CFO) more heavily than the earnings numbers. Readers should be aware that the CFO figure, while highly useful, can also be manipulated. The demise of WorldCom in 2002 brought to the forefront one issue of manipulating CFO.

WorldCom recorded as capital expenditures billions of dollars that should have been recorded as operating expenses. For the cash flow statement, these outflows appear as investing activities rather than as a direct reduction of cash flow from operations. (The expense portion of a capital expense is depreciation, which is added back to net income in determining cash flow from operating activities.) The effects of recording operating expenses as capital expenditures are illustrated by the following example:

A company records $100 million in operating expenses as a capital expenditure to be depreciated over 10 years with no salvage value.
—Net income is overstated by $90 million. (Only the $10 million in depreciation expense has been included as an expense.)

—Cash flow from operations is overstated by $100 million. On the statement of cash flows, depreciation expense of $10 million is added back to net income in determining cash flow from operations.

—Investing activity outflows are overstated by $100 million.

Other techniques exist for companies to inflate the CFO figure. Through the management of current asset and liability accounts, companies can cause increases to CFO. For example, by selling accounts receivable, a firm receives cash immediately, and this is recorded as a decrease in accounts receivable and an increase to CFO. Delaying cash payment on accounts payable also has the effect of increasing CFO. Significant changes in current asset and current liability accounts should be scrutinized in the assessment of CFO.

The SEC's concerns about how companies accounted for vendor financing transactions in their cash flow statements led to restatements in 2004 of prior cash flow numbers at companies such as General Motors, Ford Motor Company, General Electric, and Caterpillar. The SEC has made it clear that vendor financing is a result of operating activities and, as such, should be included as part of CFO, not cash from investing activities as the above-mentioned companies were reporting these amounts. Caterpillar's CFO, positive before the restatement, declined $6.3 billion in 2002 and $7.7 billion in 2003 after the restatement, causing CFO to be negative both years.[15]

CFO should also be adjusted for any other items that are deemed nonrecurring or nonoperating. Cash flows from items such as discontinued operations or nonrecurring expenses or income should be removed for analytical purposes.

Self-Test

Solutions are provided in Appendix B.

_____ 1. When should revenue be recognized, assuming generally accepted accounting principles are followed?
   (a) Revenue should be recognized when cash is collected from the customer.
   (b) Revenue should be recognized based on the company's individual policy.
   (c) Revenue should be recognized when delivery of products or title to those products has passed to the buyer or services have been rendered and the price has been determined with the expectation of collection.
   (d) Revenue should be recognized when a contract has been signed that details the date and time that the product will be delivered or the services rendered and the price has been determined.

---

[15] Michael Rapoport, "'Cash Flow' Isn't What It Used to Be," *Wall Street Journal*, March 24, 2005.

_____ 2. Which of the following is a technique for boosting revenues?
   (a) Follow the "35-day month practice" in which the books are kept open longer than the month end in order to record extra sales.
   (b) Record transactions at the net amount.
   (c) Delay shipment of goods.
   (d) Increase the allowance for doubtful accounts.

_____ 3. Why is it important to analyze the relationship among sales, accounts receivable, and the allowance for doubtful accounts?
   (a) Comparing the three accounts' growth rates is the only way to determine whether the firm is using vendor financing.
   (b) The allowance for doubtful accounts is a reserve account that can be used to manipulate the earnings number.
   (c) Price and volume changes will cause the relationship among the three accounts to be volatile.
   (d) It is important to determine whether the three accounts are changing with the inflation rate.

_____ 4. Where can information about sales price and volume changes be found?
   (a) On the face of the income statement.
   (b) In the notes to the financial statements.
   (c) On the balance sheet.
   (d) In the management's discussion and analysis.

_____ 5. Which method of inventory is generally thought to produce the highest quality of earnings?
   (a) FIFO.
   (b) LIFO.
   (c) Average cost.
   (d) All of the above.

_____ 6. When does a base LIFO layer liquidation occur?
   (a) A base LIFO layer liquidation occurs during a deflationary environment.
   (b) A base LIFO layer liquidation occurs when companies are shrinking rather than increasing inventories after a period of inflation.
   (c) A base LIFO layer liquidation occurs when a company switches from the FIFO to the LIFO method of inventory valuation.
   (d) A base LIFO layer liquidation occurs when a firm increases inventories after a period of inflation.

_____ 7. How should the effects of a base LIFO layer liquidation (assuming inflation) be handled for purposes of considering the future, ongoing potential of a company?
   (a) The effects of a base LIFO layer liquidation should be added back to net income.
   (b) The effects of a base LIFO layer liquidation should be deducted from cost of goods sold.
   (c) The effects of a base LIFO layer liquidation should be excluded from the reported earnings.
   (d) The effects of a base LIFO layer liquidation are irrelevant and should be ignored.

_____ **8.** If a firm has written down the value of their inventory, what should be of concern to the analyst?

(a) The analyst should consider removing the effects of the write-down from the profit margins to better compare changes from one period to the next.

(b) The analyst should deduct the loss from the write-down from the net earnings amount.

(c) The analyst does not need to do anything because write-downs of inventory are so frequent.

(d) The analyst cannot determine the effect of the write-down and, therefore, is unable to make any adjustments.

_____ **9.** Which of the following expenses is (are) usually considered to be discretionary?

(a) Research and development.

(b) Advertising.

(c) Depreciation.

(d) Both (a) and (b).

_____ **10.** Which of the following statements is false?

(a) The straight-line method of depreciation is lower in quality than other methods, in most cases, because it does not reflect the economic reality of product usefulness.

(b) Poor quality of financial reporting results when firms misclassify operating expenses as capital expenditures.

(c) Firms must follow the schedule prescribed by the FASB for determining the lives of long-lived assets.

(d) Analysts can learn about the depreciation policy of a firm by reading the notes to the financial statements.

_____ **11.** What is meant by the term "cookie-jar accounting"?

(a) The abuse that occurs when companies create reserve accounts for the purpose of setting aside funds in good years and then shifting the reserve amounts to the income statement in poor years.

(b) The abuse that occurs when companies use operational funds for nonoperational items such as parties, doughnuts, cookies, and personal travel expenses.

(c) The abuse that occurs when firms acquire another company and then write down the cost of in-process research and development.

(d) The abuse that occurs when firms charge ordinary business expenses as restructuring charges.

_____ **12.** Which of the following statements is true?

(a) The quality issues of pension accounting have been largely eliminated by the issuance of FASB Statement No. 87.

(b) If the assumed pension interest rate assumption is lowered, the annual pension cost will increase.

(c) If the assumed pension interest rate assumption is increased, the annual pension cost will increase.

(d) Due to the accounting rules for pension plans, most companies have underfunded pension plans.

_____ **13.** Which of the following is not classified as a nonoperating revenue or expense?

(a) Interest income.

(b) Equity income or loss.

(c) Gains or losses on the sales of assets.

(d) Salaries expense.

_____ **14.** What information cannot be found in the notes to the financial statements regarding income taxes?

(a) A reconciliation of the U.S. federal statutory tax rate to the company's effective tax rate.

(b) Year-to-year changes in deferred tax accounts.

(c) A reconciliation of any foreign statutory tax rate to the company's effective tax rate.

(d) None of the above.

_____ **15.** If discontinued operations have been sold, what must be recorded on the income statement?

(a) The gain or loss from operations of the division up to the time of sale, net of tax.

(b) The amount that the buyer paid for the discontinued operations.

(c) The gain or loss from the sale of the discontinued operations, net of tax.

(d) Both (a) and (c).

_____ **16.** What must be true for an item to be classified as an extraordinary item?

(a) The item must be both unusual and infrequent in nature.

(b) The item must be either unusual or infrequent in nature.

(c) The item must be registered as extraordinary with the FASB.

(d) The item must be approved as extraordinary by the SEC.

_____ **17.** Why would a firm repurchase its own common stock?

(a) The firm believes its stock is undervalued and purchases it as an investment.

(b) The firm purchases stock to be used in employee stock option programs.

(c) The firm is trying to reduce the number of shares outstanding in order to boost the earnings per share amount.

(d) All of the above.

_____ **18.** Which of the following statements is false?

(a) If a firm uses operating leases extensively, the analyst should investigate the impact of those leases on leverage ratios.

(b) The analyst should read the "Commitments and Contingencies" disclosures to learn of any off–balance-sheet financing or other complex financing arrangements.

(c) The analyst should assess whether the right type of debt is used to finance assets (i.e., short-term debt is used to finance long-term assets and long-term debt is used to finance current assets).

(d) The analyst should determine the significance of any legal proceedings.

_____ **19.** How have companies been able to manipulate the information on the statement of cash flows?

(a) Companies cannot manipulate cash flow information.

(b) Some companies recorded vendor financing transactions as investing, rather than operating activities.

(c) Some companies recorded increases to accounts receivable as decreases to cash flow from operations.

(d) Some companies borrowed money to increase the cash flow from financing activities.

_____ **20.** Which earnings number is the most relevant for decision-making purposes?

(a) An earnings number adjusted for items that are not relevant for the decision at hand.

(b) Pro forma earnings.

(c) EBITDA.

(d) Core earnings.

Study Questions, Problems, and Cases

5.1 Discuss the qualitative issues related to reported revenue.

5.2 Explain the importance of understanding inventory valuation methods in determining the quality of the profit numbers.

5.3 How is it possible for a firm to benefit from the write-down of an asset?

5.4 Should restructuring charges be classified as an operating expense or as a nonoperating expense?

5.5 When is it appropriate for a firm to repurchase its own common stock? When would it be considered a poor decision?

5.6 For the past three years DMR, Inc. did not write off numerous accounts of customers who were in default and unlikely to pay their bills. DMR management, who had earlier refused to approve any write-offs, told the accounting area to write off $500 million of accounts receivable. Wall Street analysts viewed this write-off as a one-time nonrecurring event. Explain the significance of this transaction to an analyst.

5.7 The following calculations have been made using Metro Tech's income statement:

Sales growth, current year	20%
Gross profit margin, current year	64%
Gross profit margin, last year	52%

Discuss all the reasons you can think of to explain the 12% change in gross profit margin. Which reasons would be considered a quality issue by an analyst?

5.8 The following information from a *BusinessWeek* article, "The Costco Way," in the April 12, 2004, issue, reveals key differences between Costco's and Wal-Mart's wage strategies. Explain how this information relates to the discussion in this chapter of discretionary expenses.

	Costco	Wal-Mart's Sam's Club
Average hourly wage	$ 15.97	$ 11.52*
Annual health costs per worker	$ 5,735	$ 3,500
Covered by health plan	82%	47%
Annual retirement costs per worker	$ 1,330	$ 747
Covered by retirement plans	91%**	64%
Employee turnover	6% a year	21% a year
Labor and overhead costs	9.8% of sales	17% of sales***
Sales per square foot	$ 795	$ 516
Profits per employee	$13,647	$11,039
Yearly operating-income growth****	10.1%	9.8%

*Excludes 25% of workforce that is lower-paid part-timers.
**Those on the job for less than a year aren't covered.
***For all of Wal-Mart.
****Over the past five years in the United States.

5.9 Writing Skills Problem

Even though firms follow the accounting rules (GAAP) when presenting their financial statements it is still possible for conflicts of interest to exist between what management wants investors and creditors to see and the economic reality of transactions. Write a short essay explaining how this can occur.

5.10 Research Problem

Locate a firm that has been involved in an investigation of its accounting practices by the SEC. Discuss the quality issues in the case and how they relate to the material learned in this chapter.

5.11 Internet Problem

Look up the SEC home page on the Internet at the following address: www.sec.gov/. Research and locate links related to accounting issues. Write a short summary of the types of items related to accounting that can be found on the SEC's Web site.

5.12 Intel Case

The 2007 Intel report can be found at the following Web site: www.prenhall .com/fraser. Review the quality of financial reporting for Intel. Write a summary explaining whether the quality is good or poor.

5.13 Eastman Kodak Comprehensive Analysis Case Using the Financial Statement Analysis Template

The 2007 Eastman Kodak Annual Report and Form 10-K can be found at the following Web site: www.prenhall.com/fraser.

(a) Using the checklist and the quality of financial reporting sections of Chapter 5, discuss the quality of Eastman Kodak's annual report and Form 10-K.

(b) Adjust the 2007 net earnings figure for Eastman Kodak, for purposes of comparing this amount to future earnings.

Note: The CPI for 2007 is 207.3 and for 2006 is 201.6.

6

The Analysis of
Financial Statements

Ratios are tools, and their value is limited when used alone. The more tools used,
the better the analysis. For example, you can't use the same golf club for every shot and
expect to be a good golfer. The more you practice with each club, however, the better able
you will be to gauge which club to use on one shot. So too, we need to be skilled
with the financial tools we use.

—DIANNE MORRISON

Chief Executive Officer, R.E.C. Inc.

The preceding chapters have covered in detail the form and content of the four basic financial statements found in the annual reports of U.S. firms: the balance sheet, the income statement, the statement of stockholders' equity, and the statement of cash flows; and Chapter 5 presented an in-depth approach to evaluating the quality of reported financial statement information. This chapter will develop tools and techniques for the interpretation of financial statement information.

OBJECTIVES OF ANALYSIS

Before beginning the analysis of any firm's financial statements, it is necessary to specify the objectives of the analysis. The objectives will vary depending on the perspective of the financial statement user and the specific questions that are addressed by the analysis of the financial statement data.

A *creditor* is ultimately concerned with the ability of an existing or prospective borrower to make interest and principal payments on borrowed funds. The questions raised in a credit analysis should include:

- What is the *borrowing cause*? What do the financial statements reveal about the reason a firm has requested a loan or the purchase of goods on credit?
- What is the firm's *capital structure*? How much debt is currently outstanding? How well has debt been serviced in the past?
- What will be the *source of debt repayment*? How well does the company manage working capital? Is the firm generating cash from operations?

The credit analyst will use the historical record of the company, as presented in the financial statements, to answer such questions and to predict the potential of the firm to satisfy future demands for cash, including debt service.

The *investor* attempts to arrive at an estimation of a company's future earnings stream in order to attach a value to the securities being considered for purchase or liquidation. The investment analyst poses such questions as:

- What is the company's *performance record*, and what are the *future expectations*? What is its record with regard to growth and stability of earnings? Of cash flow from operations?
- How much *risk* is inherent in the firm's existing capital structure? What are the *expected returns*, given the firm's current condition and future outlook?
- How successfully does the firm compete in its industry, and how well positioned is the company to hold or improve its *competitive position*?

The investment analyst also uses historical financial statement data to forecast the future. In the case of the investor, the ultimate objective is to determine whether the investment is sound.

Financial statement analysis from the standpoint of management relates to all of the questions raised by creditors and investors because these user groups must be satisfied for the firm to obtain capital as needed. Management must also consider its employees, the general public, regulators, and the financial press. Management looks to financial statement data to determine:

- How *well* has the firm performed and *why*? What *operating areas* have contributed to success and which have not?
- What are the *strengths and weaknesses* of the company's financial position?
- What *changes* should be implemented to improve future performance?

Financial statements provide insight into the company's current status and lead to the development of policies and strategies for the future. It should be pointed out, however, that management also has responsibility for preparing the financial statements. The analyst should be alert to the potential for management to influence the outcome of financial statement reporting in order to appeal to creditors, investors, and other users. It is important that any analysis of financial statements includes a careful reading of the notes to the financial statements, and it may be helpful to supplement the analysis with other material in the annual report and with other sources of information apart from the annual report.

SOURCES OF INFORMATION

The financial statement user has access to a wide range of data sources in the analysis of financial statements. The objective of the analysis will dictate to a considerable degree not only the approach taken in the analysis but also the particular resources that should be consulted in a given circumstance. The beginning point, however, should always be the financial statements themselves and the notes to the financial statements. In addition, the analyst will want to consider the following resources.

Proxy Statement

The proxy statement, discussed in Chapter 1, contains useful information about the board of directors, director and executive compensation, option grants, audit-related matters, related party transactions, and proposals to be voted on by shareholders.

Auditor's Report

The report of the independent auditor contains the expression of opinion as to the fairness of the financial statement presentation. Most auditor's reports are *unqualified,* which means that in the opinion of the auditor the financial statements present fairly the financial position, the results of operations, and the cash flows for the periods covered by the financial statements. A *qualified* report, an adverse opinion, or a disclaimer of opinion, is rare and therefore suggests that a careful evaluation of the firm be made. An unqualified opinion with explanatory language should be reviewed carefully by the analyst. In addition, the analyst should read the report and certification regarding the effectiveness of the internal controls over financial reporting.

Management Discussion and Analysis

The Management Discussion and Analysis of the Financial Condition and Results of Operations, discussed in Chapter 1, is a section of the annual report that is required and monitored by the Securities and Exchange Commission (SEC). In this section, management presents a detailed coverage of the firm's liquidity, capital resources, and operations. The material can be especially helpful to the financial analyst because it includes facts and estimates not found elsewhere in the annual report. For example, this report is expected to cover forward-looking information such as projections of capital expenditures and how such investments will be financed. There is detail about the mix of price relative to volume increases for products sold. Management must disclose any favorable or unfavorable trends and any significant events or uncertainties that relate to the firm's historical or prospective financial condition and operations.

Supplementary Schedules

Certain supplementary schedules are required for inclusion in an annual report and are frequently helpful to the analysis. For example, companies that operate in several unrelated lines of business provide a breakdown of key financial figures by operating segment.

Form 10-K and Form 10-Q

Form 10-K is an annual document filed with the SEC by companies that sell securities to the public and contains much of the same information as the annual report issued to shareholders. It also shows additional detail that may be of interest to the financial analyst, such as schedules listing information about management, a description of material litigation and governmental actions, and elaborations of some financial statement disclosures. Form 10-Q, a less extensive document, provides quarterly financial information. Both reports, as well as other SEC forms filed by companies, are available through the SEC Electronic Data Gathering, Analysis, and Retrieval (EDGAR) database.

Other Sources

There is a considerable body of material outside of the corporate annual report that can contribute to an analysis of financial statements. Most academic libraries and many public libraries have available computerized search systems and computerized databases that can greatly facilitate financial analysis.[1] Although not a replacement for the techniques that are discussed in this chapter, these research materials supplement and enhance the analytical process as well as provide time-saving features. Computerized financial statement analysis packages are also available that perform some of the ratio calculations and other analytical tools described in this chapter. (See the financial statement analysis template available at www.prenhall.com/fraser.)

Other general resources useful as aids in the analysis of financial statements can be found in the general reference section of public and university libraries. The following sources provide comparative statistical ratios to help determine a company's relative position within its industry:

1. Dun & Bradstreet Information Services, *Industry Norms and Key Business Ratios*. Murray Hill, NJ.
2. The Risk Management Association, *Annual Statement Studies*. Philadelphia, PA.
3. Gale Research Inc., *Manufacturing U.S.A. Industry Analyses*. Detroit, MI.

When analyzing a company it is also important to review the annual reports of suppliers, customers, and competitors of that company. The bankruptcy of a supplier could affect the firm's supply of raw materials, whereas the bankruptcy of a customer could negatively impact the collection of accounts receivable and

---

[1] One resource that is commonly available in both public and academic libraries is the Infotrak—General Business Index. This CD-ROM database provides indexing to approximately 800 business, trade, and management journals; it has company profiles, investment analyst reports, and a wide range of business news. To learn about the availability and use of this system or other search systems and databases, consult the library's reference librarian or the business reference librarian.

future sales. Knowing how one company compares financially to its competitors and understanding other factors such as innovation and customer service provided by the competition allows for a better analysis to predict the future prospects of the firm.

Additional resources for comparative and other information about companies can be found on the following free Internet sites:[2]

1. Yahoo!, http://finance.yahoo.com/
2. Market Watch, www.marketwatch.com
3. Reuters, www.investor.reuters.com

Many other Internet sites charge subscription fees to access information, but public and university libraries often subscribe, making this information free to the public. Libraries are currently in the process of converting information from hard copy format to online databases; the following useful references may be available at a local library:

1. Moody's Investor Service, *Mergent Manuals* and *Mergent Handbook*. New York, NY. (Formerly *Moody's Manuals and Handbook*. The online version is *Mergent FIS Online and Mergent Industry Surveys Disc*.)
2. Standard & Poor's Corporation, *Corporation Records, The Outlook, Stock Reports,* and *Stock Guide*. New York, NY. (The online version is *Standard and Poor's Net Advantage*.)
3. Value Line, Inc., *The Value Line Investment Survey*. New York, NY (www.valueline.com).
4. Zack's Investment Research Inc., *Earnings Forecaster*. Chicago, IL (www.zacks.com).
5. Gale Research Inc., *Market Share Reporter*. Detroit, MI (www.gale.cengage.com).
6. McGraw-Hill, *The Financial Analyst's Handbook*. Homewood, IL.
7. For mutual funds: Morningstar, *Morningstar Mutual Funds*. Chicago, IL (www.morningstar.com).

The following Web sites contain useful investment and financial information including company profile and stock prices; some sites charge fees for certain information:

1. SEC EDGAR Database, www.sec.gov/edgar.shtml
2. Hoover's Corporate Directory, www.hoovers.com/
3. Dun & Bradstreet, www.dnb.com/
4. Standard & Poor's Ratings Services, www2.standardandpoor.com/
5. CNN Financial Network, money.cnn.com/

Articles from current periodicals such as *BusinessWeek, Forbes, Fortune,* and the *Wall Street Journal* can add insight into the management and operations of individual firms as well as provide perspective on general economic and industry trends. The financial analysis described in this chapter should be used in the

---

[2] Internet sites are constantly changing; therefore, the content and Web addresses may change after publication of this book.

context of the economic and political environment in which the company operates. Reading about the economy regularly in business publications allows the analyst to assess the impact of unemployment, inflation, interest rates, gross domestic product, productivity, and other economic indicators on the future potential of particular firms and industries.

TOOLS AND TECHNIQUES

Various tools and techniques are used by the financial statement analyst to convert financial statement data into formats that facilitate the evaluation of a firm's financial condition and performance, both over time and in comparison with industry competitors. These include common-size financial statements, which express each account on the balance sheet as a percentage of total assets and each account on the income statement as a percentage of net sales; financial ratios, which standardize financial data in terms of mathematical relationships expressed in the form of percentages or times; trend analysis, which requires the evaluation of financial data over several accounting periods; structural analysis, which looks at the internal structure of a business enterprise; industry comparisons, which relate one firm with averages compiled for the industry in which it operates; and most important of all, common sense and judgment. These tools and techniques will be illustrated by walking through a financial statement analysis of R.E.C. Inc. This first part will cover number crunching—the calculation of key financial ratios. The second part will provide the integration of these numbers with other information—such as the statement of cash flows from Chapter 4 and background on the economy and the environment in which the firm operates—to help analyze R.E.C. Inc.'s performance over a five-year period and to assess the firm's strengths, weaknesses, and future prospects.

Common-Size Financial Statements

Common-size financial statements were covered in Chapters 2 and 3. Exhibits 2.2 (p. 39) and 3.3 (p. 82) present the common-size balance sheet and common-size income statement, respectively, for R.E.C. Inc. The information from these statements presented in prior chapters is summarized again, and will be used in the comprehensive analysis illustrated in this chapter.

From the common-size balance sheet in Exhibit 2.2, it can be seen that inventories have become more dominant over the five-year period in the firm's total asset structure and in 2010 comprised almost half (49.4%) of total assets. Holdings of cash and marketable securities have decreased from a 20% combined level in 2006 and 2007 to about 10% in 2010. The company has elected to make this shift to accommodate the inventory requirements of new store openings. The firm has opened 43 new stores in the past two years, and the effect of this market strategy is also reflected in the overall asset structure. Buildings, leasehold improvements, equipment, and accumulated depreciation and amortization have increased as a percentage of total assets. On the liability side, the proportion of debt required to finance investments in assets has risen, primarily from long-term borrowing.

The common-size income statement shown in Exhibit 3.3 reveals the trends of expenses and profit margins. Cost of goods sold has increased slightly in percentage terms, resulting in a small decline in the gross profit percentage. To improve this margin, the firm will either have to raise its own retail prices, change the product mix, or devise ways to reduce costs on goods purchased for resale. In the area of operating expenses, depreciation and amortization have increased relative to sales, again reflecting costs associated with new store openings. Selling and administrative expenses rose in 2008, but the company controlled these costs more effectively in 2009 and 2010 relative to overall sales. Operating and net profit percentages will be discussed more extensively in connection with the five-year trends of financial ratios later in the chapter. It can be seen from the common-size income statements that both profit percentages deteriorated through 2009 and rebounded in the most recent year as R.E.C. Inc. enjoyed the benefits of an economic recovery and profits from expansion.

Key Financial Ratios

The R.E.C. Inc. financial statements will be used to compute a set of key financial ratios for the years 2010 and 2009. Later in the chapter, these ratios will be evaluated in the context of R.E.C. Inc.'s five-year historical record and in comparison with industry competitors. The five categories of ratios to be covered are (1) liquidity ratios, which measure a firm's ability to meet cash needs as they arise; (2) activity ratios, which measure the liquidity of specific assets and the efficiency of managing assets; (3) leverage ratios, which measure the extent of a firm's financing with debt relative to equity and its ability to cover interest and other fixed charges; (4) profitability ratios, which measure the overall performance of a firm and its efficiency in managing assets, liabilities, and equity; and (5) market ratios, which measure returns to stockholders and the value the marketplace puts on a company's stock.

Before delving into the R.E.C. Inc. financial ratios, it is important to introduce a word of caution in the use of financial ratios generally. Although extremely valuable as analytical tools, financial ratios also have limitations. They can serve as screening devices, indicate areas of potential strength or weakness, and reveal matters that need further investigation. But financial ratios do not provide answers in and of themselves, and they are not predictive. Financial ratios should be used with caution and common sense, and they should be used in combination with other elements of financial analysis. It should also be noted that there is no one definitive set of key financial ratios, there is no uniform definition for all ratios, and there is no standard that should be met for each ratio. Finally, there are no "rules of thumb" that apply to the interpretation of financial ratios. Each situation should be evaluated within the context of the particular firm, industry, and economic environment.[3]

Figures from the R.E.C. Inc. Consolidated Balance Sheets, Statements of Earnings, and Statements of Cash Flows, Exhibits 6.1 (pp. 187–188) and 6.2 (p. 208),

---

[3] Analysts sometimes use an average number in the denominator of ratios that have a balance sheet account in the denominator. This is preferable when the company's balance sheet accounts vary significantly from one year to the next. The illustrations in this chapter do not use an average number in the denominator.

EXHIBIT 6.1

R.E.C. Inc. Consolidated Balance Sheets at December 31, 2010 and 2009 (in Thousands)

	2010	2009
Assets		
Current Assets		
Cash	$ 4,061	$ 2,382
Marketable securities (Note A)	5,272	8,004
Accounts receivable, less allowance for doubtful accounts of $448 in 2010 and $417 in 2009	8,960	8,350
Inventories (Note A)	47,041	36,769
Prepaid expenses	512	759
Total current assets	65,846	56,264
Property, Plant, and Equipment (Notes A, C, and E)		
Land	811	811
Buildings and leasehold improvements	18,273	11,928
Equipment	21,523	13,768
	40,607	26,507
Less accumulated depreciation and amortization	11,528	7,530
Net property, plant, and equipment	29,079	18,977
Other Assets (Note A)	373	668
Total Assets	$95,298	$75,909
Liabilities and Stockholders' Equity		
Current Liabilities		
Accounts Payable	$14,294	$ 7,591
Notes payable—banks (Note B)	5,614	6,012
Current maturities of long-term debt (Note C)	1,884	1,516
Accrued liabilities	5,669	5,313
Total current liabilities	27,461	20,432
Deferred Federal Income Taxes (Notes A and D)	843	635
Long-Term Debt (Note C)	21,059	16,975
Commitments (Note E)		
Total liabilities	49,363	38,042
Stockholders' Equity		
Common stock, par value $1, authorized, 10,000,000 shares; issued, 4,803,000 shares in 2010 and 4,594,000 shares in 2009 (Note F)	4,803	4,594
Additional paid-in capital	957	910
Retained Earnings	40,175	32,363
Total stockholders' equity	45,935	37,867
Total Liabilities and Stockholders' Equity	$95,298	$75,909

The accompanying notes are an integral part of these statements.

EXHIBIT 6.1 (Continued)

	2010	2009	2008
Net sales	$215,600	$153,000	$140,700
Cost of goods sold (Note A)	129,364	91,879	81,606
Gross profit	86,236	61,121	59,094
Selling and administrative expenses (Notes A and E)	45,722	33,493	32,765
Advertising	14,258	10,792	9,541
Depreciation and amortization (Note A)	3,998	2,984	2,501
Repairs and maintenance	3,015	2,046	3,031
Operating profit	19,243	11,806	11,256
Other income (expense)			
Interest income	422	838	738
Interest expense	(2,585)	(2,277)	(1,274)
Earnings before income taxes	17,080	10,367	10,720
Income taxes (Notes A and D)	7,686	4,457	4,824
Net earnings	$ 9,394	$ 5,910	$ 5,896
Basic earnings per common share (Note G)	$ 1.96	$ 1.29	$ 1.33
Diluted earnings per common share (Note G)	$ 1.92	$ 1.26	$ 1.31

are used to illustrate the calculation of financial ratios for 2010 and 2009, and these financial ratios will subsequently be incorporated into a five-year analysis of the firm.

Liquidity Ratios: Short-Term Solvency

Current Ratio

	2010	2009
$\dfrac{\text{Current assets}}{\text{Current liabilities}}$	$\dfrac{65,846}{27,461} = 2.40 \text{ times}$	$\dfrac{56,264}{20,432} = 2.75 \text{ times}$

The current ratio is a commonly used measure of short-run solvency, the ability of a firm to meet its debt requirements as they come due. Current liabilities are used as the denominator of the ratio because they are considered to represent the most urgent debts, requiring retirement within one year or one operating cycle. The available cash resources to satisfy these obligations must come primarily from cash or the conversion to cash of other current assets. Some analysts eliminate prepaid expenses from the numerator because they are not a potential source of cash but, rather, represent future obligations that have already been satisfied. The current ratio for R.E.C. Inc. indicates that, at year-end 2010, current assets covered current liabilities 2.4 times, down from 2009. To interpret the significance of this ratio, it will be necessary to evaluate the trend of liquidity over a longer period and to compare R.E.C. Inc.'s coverage with industry competitors. It is also essential to assess the composition of the components that comprise the ratio.

As a barometer of short-term liquidity, the current ratio is limited by the nature of its components. Remember that the balance sheet is prepared as of a particular date, and the actual amount of liquid assets may vary considerably from the date on which the balance sheet is prepared. Further, accounts receivable and inventory may not be truly liquid. A firm could have a relatively high current ratio but not be able to meet demands for cash because the accounts receivable are of inferior quality or the inventory is salable only at discounted prices. It is necessary to use other measures of liquidity, including cash flow from operations and other financial ratios that rate the liquidity of specific assets, to supplement the current ratio.

Quick or Acid-Test Ratio

	2010	2009
$\dfrac{\text{Current assets} - \text{Inventory}}{\text{Current liabilities}}$	$\dfrac{65,846 - 47,041}{27,461} = 0.68$ times	$\dfrac{56,264 - 36,769}{20,432} = 0.95$ times

The quick or acid-test ratio is a more rigorous test of short-run solvency than the current ratio because the numerator eliminates inventory, considered the least liquid current asset and the most likely source of losses. Like the current ratio and other ratios, there are alternative ways to calculate the quick ratio. Some analysts eliminate prepaid expenses and supplies (if carried as a separate item) from the numerator. The quick ratio for R.E.C. Inc. indicates some deterioration between 2009 and 2010; this ratio must also be examined in relation to the firm's own trends and to other firms operating in the same industry.

Cash Flow Liquidity Ratio

	2010	2009
$\dfrac{\text{Cash} + \text{Marketable securities} + \text{CFO*}}{\text{Current liabilities}}$	$\dfrac{4,061 + 5,272 + 10,024}{27,461} = 0.70$ times	$\dfrac{2,382 + 8,004 + (3,767)}{20,432} = 0.32$ times

*Cash flow from operating activities.

Another approach to measuring short-term solvency is the cash flow liquidity ratio,[4] which considers cash flow from operating activities (from the statement

---

[4] For additional reading about this ratio and its applications, see Lyn Fraser, "Cash Flow from Operations and Liquidity Analysis, A New Financial Ratio for Commercial Lending Decisions," *Cash Flow*, Robert Morris Associates, Philadelphia, PA. For other cash flow ratios, see C. Carslaw and J. Mills, "Developing Ratios for Effective Cash Flow Statement Analysis," *Journal of Accountancy*, November 1991; D. E. Giacomino and D. E. Mielke, "Cash Flows: Another Approach to Ratio Analysis," *Journal of Accountancy*, March 1993; and John R. Mills and Jeanne H. Yamamura, "The Power of Cash Flow Ratios," *Journal of Accountancy*, October 1998.

of cash flows). The cash flow liquidity ratio uses in the numerator, as an approximation of cash resources, cash and marketable securities, which are truly liquid current assets, and cash flow from operating activities, which represents the amount of cash generated from the firm's operations, such as the ability to sell inventory and collect the cash.

Note that both the current ratio and the quick ratio decreased between 2009 and 2010, which could be interpreted as a deterioration of liquidity. But the cash flow ratio increased, indicating an improvement in short-run solvency. Which is the correct assessment? With any ratio, the analyst must explore the underlying components. One major reason for the decreases in the current and quick ratios was the 88% growth in accounts payable in 2010, which could actually be a plus if it means that R.E.C. Inc. strengthened its ability to obtain supplier credit. Also, the firm turned around from negative to positive its generation of cash from operations in 2010, explaining the improvement in the cash flow liquidity ratio and indicating stronger short-term solvency.

Average Collection Period

	2010	2009
$\dfrac{\text{Net accounts receivable}}{\text{Average daily sales}}$	$\dfrac{8{,}960}{215{,}600/365} = 15 \text{ days}$	$\dfrac{8{,}350}{153{,}000/365} = 20 \text{ days}$

The average collection period of accounts receivable is the average number of days required to convert receivables into cash. The ratio is calculated as the relationship between net accounts receivable (net of the allowance for doubtful accounts) and average daily sales (sales/365 days). Where available, the figure for credit sales can be substituted for net sales because credit sales produce the receivables. The ratio for R.E.C. Inc. indicates that during 2010 the firm collected its accounts in 15 days on average, which is an improvement over the 20-day collection period in 2009.

The average collection period helps gauge the liquidity of accounts receivable, the ability of the firm to collect from customers. It may also provide information about a company's credit policies. For example, if the average collection period is increasing over time or is higher than the industry average, the firm's credit policies could be too lenient and accounts receivables not sufficiently liquid. The loosening of credit could be necessary at times to boost sales, but at an increasing cost to the firm. On the other hand, if credit policies are too restrictive, as reflected in an average collection period that is shortening and less than industry competitors, the firm may be losing qualified customers.

The average collection period should be compared with the firm's stated credit policies. If the policy calls for collection within 30 days and the average collection period is 60 days, the implication is that the company is not stringent in collection efforts. There could be other explanations, however, such as temporary problems due to a depressed economy. The analyst should attempt to determine the cause of a ratio that is too long or too short.

Another factor for consideration is the strength of the firm within its industry. There are circumstances that would enable a company in a relatively strong financial position within its industry to extend credit for longer periods than weaker competitors.

Days Inventory Held

	2010	2009
$\dfrac{\text{Inventory}}{\text{Average daily cost of sales}}$	$\dfrac{47,041}{129,364/365} = 133$ days	$\dfrac{36,769}{91,879/365} = 146$ days

The days inventory held is the average number of days it takes to sell inventory to customers. This ratio measures the efficiency of the firm in managing its inventory. Generally, a low number of days inventory held is a sign of efficient management; the faster inventory sells, the fewer funds tied up in inventory. On the other hand, too low a number could indicate understocking and lost orders, a decrease in prices, a shortage of materials, or more sales than planned. A high number of days inventory held could be the result of carrying too much inventory or stocking inventory that is obsolete, slow-moving, or inferior; however, there may be legitimate reasons to stockpile inventory, such as increased demand, expansion and opening of new retail stores, or an expected strike. R.E.C. Inc.'s days inventory held has decreased from 2009, an improvement over 2010.

The type of industry is important in assessing days inventory held. It is expected that florists and produce retailers would have a relatively low days inventory held because they deal in perishable products, whereas retailers of jewelry or farm equipment would have higher days inventory held, but higher profit margins. When making comparisons among firms, it is essential to check the cost flow assumption, discussed in Chapter 2, used to value inventory and cost of goods sold.

Days Payable Outstanding

	2010	2009
$\dfrac{\text{Accounts payable}}{\text{Average daily cost of sales}}$	$\dfrac{14,294}{129,364/365} = 41$ days	$\dfrac{7,591}{91,879/365} = 31$ days

The days payable outstanding is the average number of days it takes to pay payables in cash. This ratio offers insight into a firm's pattern of payments to suppliers. Delaying payment of payables as long as possible, but still making payment by the due date, is desirable. R.E.C. Inc. is taking longer to pay suppliers in 2010 compared to 2009.

Cash Conversion Cycle or Net Trade Cycle

The cash conversion cycle or net trade cycle is the normal operating cycle of a firm that consists of buying or manufacturing inventory, with some purchases on credit and the creation of accounts payable; selling inventory, with some sales on credit and the creation of accounts receivable; and collecting the cash. The cash conversion cycle measures this process in number of days and is calculated as follows for R.E.C. Inc.:

	2010	2009
Average collection period	5 days	20 days
plus		
Days inventory held	133 days	146 days
minus		
Days payable outstanding	(41 days)	(33 days)
equals		
Cash conversion or net trade cycle	107 days	133 days

The cash conversion cycle helps the analyst understand why cash flow generation has improved or deteriorated by analyzing the key balance sheet accounts—accounts receivable, inventory, and accounts payable—that affect cash flow from operating activities. R.E.C. Inc. has improved its cash conversion cycle by improving collection of accounts receivable, moving inventory faster, and taking longer to pay accounts payable. Despite this improvement, the firm has a mismatching of cash inflows and outflows since it takes 148 days to sell inventory and collect the cash, yet R.E.C. Inc.'s suppliers are being paid in 41 days. As mentioned previously, the company opened 43 new stores, and that is most likely the cause of the high level of inventory. In the future, R.E.C. Inc. should be able to improve further the days inventory held and the cash conversion cycle.

Activity Ratios: Asset Liquidity, Asset Management Efficiency

Accounts Receivable Turnover

	2010	2009
$\dfrac{\text{Net Sales}}{\text{Net accounts receivable}}$	$\dfrac{215,600}{8,960} = 24.06 \text{ times}$	$\dfrac{153,000}{8,350} = 18.32 \text{ times}$

Inventory Turnover

	2010	2009
$\dfrac{\text{Cost of goods sold}}{\text{Inventory}}$	$\dfrac{129,364}{47,041} = 2.75 \text{ times}$	$\dfrac{91,879}{36,769} = 2.50 \text{ times}$

Accounts Payable Turnover

	2010	**2009**
$\dfrac{\text{Cost of goods sold}}{\text{Accounts payable}}$	$\dfrac{129,364}{14,294} = 9.05 \text{ times}$	$\dfrac{91,879}{7,591} = 12.10 \text{ times}$

The accounts receivable, inventory, and payables turnover ratios measure how many times, on average, accounts receivable are collected in cash, inventory is sold, and payables are paid during the year. These three measures are mathematical complements to the ratios that make up the cash conversion cycle, and therefore, measure exactly what the average collection period, days inventory held, and days payable outstanding measure for a firm; they are merely an alternative way to look at the same information.

R.E.C. Inc. converted accounts receivable into cash 24 times in 2010, up from 18 times in 2009. Inventory turned over 2.75 times in 2010 compared to 2.5 times in 2009, meaning that inventory was selling slightly faster. The lower payables turnover indicates that the firm is taking longer to repay payables.

Fixed Asset Turnover

	2010	**2009**
$\dfrac{\text{Net sales}}{\text{Net property, plant, equipment}}$	$\dfrac{215,600}{29,079} = 7.41 \text{ times}$	$\dfrac{153,000}{18,977} = 8.06 \text{ times}$

Total Asset Turnover

	2010	**2009**
$\dfrac{\text{Net sales}}{\text{Total assets}}$	$\dfrac{215,600}{95,298} = 2.26 \text{ times}$	$\dfrac{153,000}{75,909} = 2.02 \text{ times}$

The fixed asset turnover and total asset turnover ratios are two approaches to assessing management's effectiveness in generating sales from investments in assets. The fixed asset turnover considers only the firm's investment in property, plant, and equipment and is extremely important for a capital-intensive firm, such as a manufacturer with heavy investments in long-lived assets. The total asset turnover measures the efficiency of managing all of a firm's assets. Generally, the higher these ratios, the smaller is the investment required to generate sales and thus the more profitable is the firm. When the asset turnover ratios are low relative to the industry or the firm's historical record, either the investment in assets is too heavy and/or sales are sluggish. There may, however, be plausible explanations; for example, the firm may have undertaken an extensive plant modernization or placed assets in service at year-end, which will generate positive results in the long-term. Large amounts of cash, cash equivalents, marketable securities, and long-term investments unrelated to the core operations of the firm will cause the total asset turnover to be lower as the return on these items is recorded in nonoperating revenue accounts, not sales.

For R.E.C. Inc., the fixed asset turnover has slipped slightly, but the total asset turnover has improved. The firm's investment in fixed assets has grown at a faster rate (53%) than sales (41%), and this occurrence should be examined within the framework of the overall analysis of R.E.C. Inc. The increase in total asset turnover is the result of improvements in inventory and accounts receivable turnover.

Leverage Ratios: Debt Financing and Coverage

Debt Ratio

	2010	2009
$\dfrac{\text{Total liabilities}}{\text{Total assets}}$	$\dfrac{49{,}363}{95{,}298} = 51.8\%$	$\dfrac{38{,}042}{75{,}909} = 50.1\%$

Long-Term Debt to Total Capitalization

	2010	2009
$\dfrac{\text{Long-term debt}}{\text{Long-term debt + Stockholders' equity}}$	$\dfrac{21{,}059}{21{,}059 + 45{,}935} = 31.4\%$	$\dfrac{16{,}975}{16{,}975 + 37{,}867} = 31.0\%$

Debt to Equity

	2010	2009
$\dfrac{\text{Total liabilities}}{\text{Stockholders' equity}}$	$\dfrac{49{,}363}{45{,}935} = 1.07 \text{ times}$	$\dfrac{38{,}042}{37{,}867} = 1.00 \text{ times}$

Each of the three debt ratios measures the extent of the firm's financing with debt. The amount and proportion of debt in a company's capital structure is extremely important to the financial analyst because of the trade-off between risk and return. Use of debt involves risk because debt carries a fixed commitment in the form of interest charges and principal repayment. Failure to satisfy the fixed charges associated with debt will ultimately result in bankruptcy. A lesser risk is that a firm with too much debt has difficulty obtaining additional debt financing when needed or finds that credit is available only at extremely high rates of interest. Although debt implies risk, it also introduces the potential for increased benefits to the firm's owners. When debt is used successfully—if operating earnings are more than sufficient to cover the fixed charges associated with debt—the returns to shareholders are magnified through financial leverage, a concept that is explained and illustrated later in this chapter.

The debt ratio considers the proportion of all assets that are financed with debt. The ratio of long-term debt to total capitalization reveals the extent to which long-term debt is used for the firm's permanent financing (both long-term debt and equity). The debt-to-equity ratio measures the riskiness of the firm's capital structure in terms of the relationship between the funds supplied by creditors (debt) and investors (equity). The higher the proportion of debt, the greater is the degree of risk because creditors must be satisfied before owners in the event of bankruptcy. The equity base provides, in effect, a cushion of protection for the suppliers of debt. Each of the three ratios has increased somewhat for R.E.C. Inc. between 2010 and 2009, implying a slightly riskier capital structure.

The analyst should be aware that the debt ratios do not present the whole picture with regard to risk. There are fixed commitments, such as lease payments, that are similar to debt but are not included in debt. The fixed charge coverage ratio, illustrated later, considers such obligations. Off–balance-sheet financing arrangements, discussed in Chapter 1, also have the characteristics of debt and must be disclosed in notes to the financial statements according to the provisions of FASB Statement No. 105. These arrangements should be included in an evaluation of a firm's overall capital structure.

Times Interest Earned

	2010	2009
Operating profit / Interest expense	$\dfrac{19{,}243}{2{,}585} = 7.4$ times	$\dfrac{11{,}806}{2{,}277} = 5.2$ times

Cash Interest Coverage

	2010	2009
CFO + interest paid + taxes paid[5] / Interest paid	$\dfrac{10{,}024 + 2{,}585 + 7{,}478}{2{,}585}$	$\dfrac{(3{,}767) + 2{,}277 + 4{,}321}{2{,}277}$
	= 7.77 times	= 1.24 times

For a firm to benefit from debt financing, the fixed interest payments that accompany debt must be more than satisfied from operating earnings.[6] The higher the times interest earned ratio the better; however, if a company is generating high profits, but no cash flow from operations, this ratio is misleading. It takes cash to make interest payments! The cash interest coverage ratio measures how many times interest payments can be covered by cash flow from operations before interest and taxes. Although R.E.C. Inc. increased its use of debt in 2010, the company also improved its ability to cover interest payments from operating

---

[5] The amounts for interest and taxes paid are found in the supplemental disclosures on the statement of cash flows.
[6] The operating return, operating profit divided by assets, must exceed the cost of debt and interest expense divided by liabilities.

profits and cash from operations. Note that in 2009, the firm could cover interest payments only 1.24 times due to the poor cash generated from operations before interest and taxes. The times interest earned ratio in 2009 is somewhat misleading in this instance.

Fixed Charge Coverage

	2010	2009
$\dfrac{\text{Operating profit} + \text{Rent expense*}}{\text{Interest expense} + \text{Rent expense*}}$	$\dfrac{19{,}243 + 13{,}058}{2{,}585 + 13{,}058} = 2.1 \text{ times}$	$\dfrac{11{,}806 + 7{,}111}{2{,}277 + 7{,}111} = 2.0 \text{ times}$

*Rent expense = operating lease payments (see Exhibit 1.2, Note E in Chapter 1).

The fixed charge coverage ratio is a broader measure of coverage capability than the times interest earned ratio because it includes the fixed payments associated with leasing. Operating lease payments, generally referred to as rent expense in annual reports, are added back in the numerator because they were deducted as an operating expense to calculate operating profit. Operating lease payments are similar in nature to interest expense in that they both represent obligations that must be met on an annual basis. The fixed charge coverage ratio is important for firms that operate extensively with operating leases. R.E.C. Inc. experienced a significant increase in the amount of annual lease payments in 2010 but was still able to improve its fixed charge coverage slightly.

Cash Flow Adequacy

	2010	2009
$\dfrac{\text{Cash flow from operating activities}}{\substack{\text{Capital expenditures} + \text{debt repayments} \\ + \text{ dividends paid}}}$	$\dfrac{10{,}024}{\substack{14{,}100 + 30 + 1{,}516 \\ + 1{,}582}} = 0.58 \text{ times}$	$\dfrac{(3{,}767)}{\substack{4{,}773 + 1{,}593 \\ + 1{,}862}} = (0.46) \text{ times}$

Credit rating agencies often use cash flow adequacy ratios to evaluate how well a company can cover annual payments of items such as debt, capital expenditures, and dividends from operating cash flow. Cash flow adequacy is generally defined differently by analysts; therefore, it is important to understand what is actually being measured. Cash flow adequacy is being used here to measure a firm's ability to cover capital expenditures, debt maturities, and dividend payments each year. Companies over the long run should generate enough cash flow from operations to cover investing and financing activities of the firm. If purchases of fixed assets are financed with debt, the company should be able to cover the principal payments with cash generated by the company. A larger ratio would be expected if the company pays dividends annually because cash used for dividends should be generated internally by the company, rather than by borrowing. As indicated in Chapter 4, companies must generate cash to be successful.

Borrowing each year to pay dividends and repay debt is a questionable cycle for a company to be in over the long run.

In 2010, R.E.C. Inc. had a cash flow adequacy ratio of 0.58 times, an improvement over 2009 when the firm failed to generate cash from operations.

Profitability Ratios: Overall Efficiency and Performance

Gross Profit Margin

	2010	2009
$\dfrac{\text{Gross profit}}{\text{Net sales}}$	$\dfrac{86,236}{215,600} = 40.0\%$	$\dfrac{61,121}{153,000} = 39.9\%$

Operating Profit Margin

	2010	2009
$\dfrac{\text{Operating profit}}{\text{Net sales}}$	$\dfrac{19,243}{215,600} = 8.9\%$	$\dfrac{11,806}{153,000} = 7.7\%$

Net Profit Margin

	2010	2009
$\dfrac{\text{Net earnings}}{\text{Net sales}}$	$\dfrac{9,394}{215,600} = 4.4\%$	$\dfrac{5,910}{153,000} = 3.9\%$

Gross profit margin, operating profit margin, and net profit margin represent the firm's ability to translate sales dollars into profits at different stages of measurement. The gross profit margin, which shows the relationship between sales and the cost of products sold, measures the ability of a company both to control costs of inventories or manufacturing of products and to pass along price increases through sales to customers. The operating profit margin, a measure of overall operating efficiency, incorporates all of the expenses associated with ordinary business activities. The net profit margin measures profitability after consideration of all revenue and expense, including interest, taxes, and nonoperating items.

There was little change in the R.E.C. Inc. gross profit margin, but the company improved its operating margin. Apparently, the firm was able to control the growth of operating expenses while sharply increasing sales. There was also a slight increase in net profit margin, a flow-through from operating margin, but it will be necessary to look at these ratios over a longer term and in conjunction with other parts of the analysis to explain the changes.

Cash Flow Margin

	2010	2009
$\dfrac{\text{Cash flow from operating activities}}{\text{Net sales}}$	$\dfrac{10{,}024}{215{,}600} = 4.6\%$	$\dfrac{(3{,}767)}{153{,}000} = (2.5\%)$

Another important perspective on operating performance is the relationship between cash generated from operations and sales. As pointed out in Chapter 4, it is cash, not accrual-measured earnings, that a firm needs to service debt, pay dividends, and invest in new capital assets. The cash flow margin measures the ability of the firm to translate sales into cash.

In 2010, R.E.C. Inc. had a cash flow margin that was greater than its net profit margin, the result of a strongly positive generation of cash. The performance in 2010 represents a solid improvement over 2009 when the firm failed to generate cash from operations and had a negative cash flow margin.

Return on Total Assets (ROA) or Return on Investment (ROI)

	2010	2009
$\dfrac{\text{Net earnings}}{\text{Total assets}}$	$\dfrac{9{,}394}{95{,}298} = 9.9\%$	$\dfrac{5{,}910}{75{,}909} = 7.8\%$

Return on Equity (ROE)

	2010	2009
$\dfrac{\text{Net earnings}}{\text{Stockholders' equity}}$	$\dfrac{9{,}394}{45{,}935} = 20.5\%$	$\dfrac{5{,}910}{37{,}867} = 15.6\%$

Return on investment and return on equity are two ratios that measure the overall efficiency of the firm in managing its total investment in assets and in generating return to shareholders. Return on investment or return on assets indicates the amount of profit earned relative to the level of investment in total assets. Return on equity measures the return to common shareholders; this ratio is also calculated as return on common equity if a firm has preferred stock outstanding. R.E.C. Inc. registered a solid improvement in 2010 of both return ratios.

Cash Return on Assets

	2010	2009
$\dfrac{\text{Cash flow from operating activities}}{\text{Total assets}}$	$\dfrac{10{,}024}{95{,}298} = 10.5\%$	$\dfrac{(3{,}767)}{75{,}909} = (5.0\%)$

The cash return on assets offers a useful comparison to return on investment. Again, the relationship between cash generated from operations and an accrual-based number allows the analyst to measure the firm's cash-generating ability of assets. Cash will be required for future investments.

Market Ratios

Four market ratios of particular interest to the investor are earnings per common share, the price-to-earnings ratio, the dividend payout ratio, and dividend yield. Despite the accounting scandals, including Enron and WorldCom, which illustrated the flaws in the earnings numbers presented to the public, investors continue to accept and rely on the earnings per share and price-to-earnings ratios. A discussion of these ratios is included because the reporting of these numbers does, in fact, have a significant impact on stock price changes in the marketplace. The authors hope, however, that readers of this book understand that a thorough analysis of the company, its environment, and its financial information offers a much better gauge of the future prospects of the company than looking exclusively at earnings per share and price-to-earnings ratios. These two ratios are based on an earnings number that can be misleading at times given the many accounting choices and techniques used to calculate it.

Earnings per common share is net income for the period divided by the weighted average number of common shares outstanding. One million dollars in earnings will look different to the investor if there are 1 million shares of stock outstanding or 100,000 shares. The earnings per share ratio provides the investor with a common denominator to gauge investment returns.

The basic earnings per share computations for R.E.C. Inc. are made as follows:

	2010	2009	2008
$\dfrac{\text{Net earnings}}{\text{Average shares outstanding}}$	$\dfrac{9,394,000}{4,792,857} = 1.96$	$\dfrac{5,910,000}{4,581,395} = 1.29$	$\dfrac{5,896,000}{4,433,083} = 1.33$

Earnings per share figures must be disclosed on the face of the income statement for publicly held companies.

The price-to-earnings ratio (P/E ratio) relates earnings per common share to the market price at which the stock trades, expressing the "multiple" that the stock market places on a firm's earnings. For instance, if two competing firms had annual earnings of $2.00 per share, and Company 1 shares sold for $10.00 each and Company 2 shares were selling at $20.00 each, the market is placing a different value on the same $2.00 earnings: a multiple of 5 for Company 1 and 10 for Company 2. The P/E ratio is the function of a myriad of factors, which include the quality of earnings, future earnings potential, and the performance history of the company.[7]

---

[7] Using diluted earnings per share in market ratios offers a worst-case scenario figure that analysts may find useful.

The P/E ratio for R.E.C. Inc. would be determined as follows:

	2010	2009	2008
$\dfrac{\text{Market price of common stock}}{\text{Earnings per share}}$	$\dfrac{30.00}{1.96} = 15.3$	$\dfrac{17.00}{1.29} = 13.2$	$\dfrac{25.00}{1.33} = 18.8$

The P/E ratio is higher in 2010 than 2009 but below the 2008 level. This could be due to developments in the market generally and/or because the market is reacting cautiously to the firm's good year. Another factor could be the reduction of cash dividend payments.

The dividend payout ratio is determined by the formula cash dividends per share divided by earnings per share:

	2010	2009	2008
$\dfrac{\text{Dividends per share}}{\text{Earnings per share}}$	$\dfrac{0.33}{1.96} = 16.8\%$	$\dfrac{0.41}{1.29} = 31.8\%$	$\dfrac{0.41}{1.33} = 30.8\%$

R.E.C. Inc. reduced its cash dividend payment in 2010. It is unusual for a company to reduce cash dividends because this decision can be read as a negative signal regarding the future outlook. It is particularly uncommon for a firm to reduce dividends during a good year. The explanation provided by management is that the firm has adopted a new policy that will result in lower dividend payments in order to increase the availability of internal funds for expansion; management expects the overall long-term impact to be extremely favorable to shareholders and has committed to maintaining the $0.33 per share annual cash dividend.

The dividend yield shows the relationship between cash dividends and market price:

	2007	2006	2005
$\dfrac{\text{Dividends per share}}{\text{Market price of common stock}}$	$\dfrac{0.33}{30.00} = 1.1\%$	$\dfrac{0.41}{17.00} = 2.4\%$	$\dfrac{0.41}{25.00} = 1.6\%$

The R.E.C. Inc. shares are yielding a 1.1% return based on the market price at year-end 2010; an investor would likely choose R.E.C. Inc. as an investment more for its long-term capital appreciation than for its dividend yield.

Figure 6.1 shows in summary form the use of key financial ratios discussed in the chapter.

ANALYZING THE DATA

Would you as a bank loan officer extend $1.5 million in new credit to R.E.C. Inc.? Would you as an investor purchase R.E.C. Inc. common shares at the current market price of $30 per share? Would you as a wholesaler of running shoes sell

FIGURE 6.1   Summary of Financial Ratios

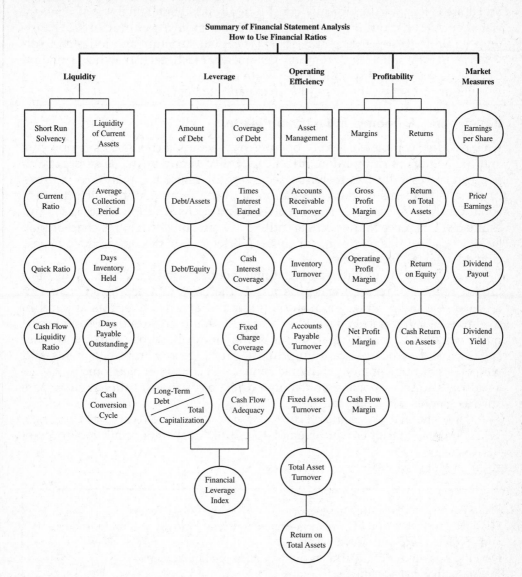

your products on credit to R.E.C. Inc.? Would you as a recent college graduate accept a position as manager-trainee with R.E.C. Inc.? Would you as the chief financial officer of R.E.C. Inc. authorize the opening of 25 new retail stores during the next two years?

　　To answer such questions, it is necessary to complete the analysis of R.E.C. Inc.'s financial statements, utilizing the common-size financial statements and key financial ratios as well as other information presented throughout the book. Ordinarily, the analysis would deal with only one of the above questions, and the perspective of the financial statement user would determine the focus of the analysis. Because the purpose of this chapter is to present a general approach to financial statement analysis, however, the evaluation will cover each of five broad areas that would typically constitute a fundamental analysis of financial statements: (1) background on firm, industry, economy, and outlook; (2) short-term liquidity; (3) operating efficiency; (4) capital structure and long-term solvency; and (5) profitability. From this general approach, each analytical situation can be tailored to meet specific user objectives.

Figure 6.2 shows the steps of a financial statement analysis.

Background: Economy, Industry, and Firm

An individual company does not operate in a vacuum. Economic developments and the actions of competitors affect the ability of any business enterprise to perform successfully. It is therefore necessary to preface the analysis of a firm's financial statements with an evaluation of the environment in which the firm conducts business. This process involves blending hard facts with guesses and estimates. Reference to the section entitled "Other Sources" in this chapter may be beneficial for this part of the analysis. A brief section discussing the business climate of R.E.C. Inc. follows.[8]

Recreational Equipment and Clothing Incorporated (R.E.C. Inc.) is the third largest retailer of recreational products in the United States. The firm offers a broad line of sporting goods and equipment and active sports apparel in medium-to-higher price ranges. R.E.C. Inc. sells equipment used in running, aerobics, walking, basketball, golf, tennis, skiing, football, scuba diving, and other sports; merchandise for camping, hiking, fishing, and hunting; men's and women's sporting apparel; gift items; games; and consumer electronic products. The firm also sells sporting goods on a direct basis to institutional customers such as schools and athletic teams.

The general and executive offices of the company are located in Dime Box, Texas, and these facilities were expanded in 2010. Most of the retail stores occupy

FIGURE 6.2   Steps of a Financial Statement Analysis

---

1. Establish objectives of the analysis.
2. Study the industry in which firm operates and relate industry climate to current and projected economic developments.
3. Develop knowledge of the firm and the quality of management.
4. Evaluate financial statements.
   - Tools: Common-size financial statements, key financial ratios, trend analysis, structural analysis, and comparison with industry competitors.
   - Major Areas: Short-term liquidity, operating efficiency, capital structure and long-term solvency, profitability, market ratios, and quality of financial reporting.
5. Summarize findings based on analysis and reach conclusions about firm relevant to the established objectives.

---

[8] The background section of R.E.C. Inc. is based on an unpublished paper by Kimberly Ann Davis, "A Financial Analysis of Oshman's Sporting Goods, Inc."

leased spaces and are located in major regional or suburban shopping districts throughout the southwestern United States. Eighteen new retail outlets were added in late 2009, and 25 new stores were opened in 2010. The firm owns distribution center warehouses located in Arizona, California, Colorado, Utah, and Texas.

The recreational products industry is affected by current trends in consumer preferences, a cyclical sales demand, and weather conditions. The running boom has shifted to walking and aerobics; golf, once on the downswing, is increasing in popularity. Recreational product retailers also rely heavily on sales of sportswear for their profits, because the markup on sportswear is generally higher than on sports equipment, and these products are also affected by consumer preference shifts. With regard to seasonality, most retail sales occur in November, December, May, and June. Sales to institutions are highest in August and September. Weather conditions also influence sales volume, especially of winter sports equipment—come on, Rocky Mountain snow!

Competition within the recreational products industry is based on price, quality, and variety of goods offered as well as the location of outlets and the quality of services offered. R.E.C. Inc.'s two major competitors are also full-line sporting goods companies. One operates in the northwest and the other primarily in the eastern and southeastern United States, reducing direct competition among the three firms.

The current outlook for the sporting goods industry is promising, following a recessionary year in 2009.[9] Americans have become increasingly aware of the importance of physical fitness and have become more actively involved in recreational activities. The 25-to-44 age group is the most athletically active and is projected to be the largest age group in the United States during the next decade. The southwestern United States is expected to provide a rapidly expanding market because of its population growth and excellent weather conditions for year-round recreational participation.

Short-Term Liquidity

Short-term liquidity analysis is especially important to creditors, suppliers, management, and others who are concerned with the ability of a firm to meet near-term demands for cash. The evaluation of R.E.C. Inc.'s short-term liquidity position began with the preparation and interpretation of the firm's common-size balance sheet earlier in the chapter. From that assessment, it was evident that inventories have increased relative to cash and marketable securities in the current asset section, and there has been an increase in the proportion of debt, both short and long term. These developments were traced primarily to policies and financing needs related to new store openings. Additional evidence useful to short-term liquidity analysis is provided by a five-year trend of selected financial ratios and a comparison with industry averages. Sources of comparative industry ratios include Dun & Bradstreet, *Industry Norms and Key Business Ratios*, New York, NY; The Risk Management Association, *Annual Statement Studies*,

---

[9] The recession is assumed for purposes of writing this book and does not represent the authors' forecast.

Philadelphia, PA; and Standard & Poor's Corporation, *Industry Surveys*, New York, NY. As a source of industry comparative ratios, the analyst may prefer to develop a set of financial ratios for one or more major competitors.

R.E.C. Inc.	2010	2009	2008	2007	2006	Industry Average 2010
Current ratio	2.40	2.75	2.26	2.18	2.83	2.53
Quick ratio	0.68	0.95	0.87	1.22	1.20	0.97
Cash flow liquidity	0.70	0.32	0.85	0.78	0.68	*
Average collection period	15 days	20 days	13 days	11 days	10 days	17 days
Days inventory held	133 days	146 days	134 days	122 days	114 days	117 days
Days payable outstanding	41 days	33 days	37 days	34 days	35 days	32 days
Cash conversion cycle	107 days	133 days	110 days	99 days	89 days	102 days
Cash flow from operating activities ($ thousands)	10,024	(3,767)	5,629	4,925	3,430	*

*Not available

Liquidity analysis predicts the future ability of the firm to meet prospective needs for cash. This prediction is made from the historical record of the firm, and no one financial ratio or set of financial ratios or other financial data can serve as a proxy for future developments. For R.E.C. Inc., the financial ratios are somewhat contradictory.

The current and quick ratios have trended downward over the five-year period, indicating a deterioration of short-term liquidity. On the other hand, the cash flow liquidity ratio improved strongly in 2010 after a year of negative cash generation in 2009. The average collection period for accounts receivable and the days inventory held ratio—after worsening between 2006 and 2009—also improved in 2010. These ratios measure the quality or liquidity of accounts receivable and inventory. The average collection period increased to a high of 20 days in 2009, which was a recessionary year in the economy, then decreased to a more acceptable 15-day level in 2010. Days payable outstanding has varied each year, but has increased overall from 2006 to 2010. As long as the company is not late paying bills, this should not be a significant problem. The cash conversion cycle worsened from 2006 to 2009 due to an increasing collection period and longer number of days inventory was held. In 2010, a significant improvement in management of current assets and liabilities has caused the cash conversion cycle to drop by 26 days from the high of 133 days in 2009. It is now much closer to the industry average.

The common-size balance sheet for R.E.C. Inc. revealed that inventories now comprise about half of the firm's total assets. The growth in inventories has been necessary to satisfy the requirements associated with the opening of new retail outlets but has been accomplished by reducing holdings of cash and cash equivalents. This represents a trade-off of highly liquid assets for potentially less liquid assets. The efficient management of inventories is a critical ingredient for the firm's ongoing liquidity. In 2010, days inventory held improved in spite of the buildups necessary to stock new stores. Sales demand in 2010 was more than adequate to absorb the 28% increase in inventories recorded for the year.

The major question in the outlook for liquidity is the ability of the firm to produce cash from operations. Problems in 2009 resulted partly from the depressed state of the economy and poor ski conditions, which reduced sales growth. The easing of sales demand hit the company in a year that marked the beginning of a major market expansion. Inventories and receivables increased too fast for the limited sales growth of a recessionary year, and R.E.C. also experienced some reduction of credit availability from suppliers that felt the economic pinch. The consequence was a cash crunch and negative cash flow from operations.

In 2010, R.E.C. Inc. enjoyed considerable improvement, generating more than $10 million in cash from operations and progress in managing inventories and receivables. There appears to be no major problem with the firm's short-term liquidity position at the present time. Another poor year, however, might well cause problems similar to those experienced in 2009. The timing of further expansion of retail outlets will be of critical importance to the ongoing success of the firm.

Operating Efficiency

R.E.C. Inc.	2010	2009	2008	2007	2006	Industry Average 2010
Accounts receivable turnover	24.06	18.32	28.08	33.18	36.50	21.47
Inventory turnover	2.75	2.50	2.74	2.99	3.20	3.12
Accounts payable turnover	9.05	12.10	9.90	10.74	10.43	11.40
Fixed asset turnover	7.41	8.06	8.19	10.01	10.11	8.72
Total asset turnover	2.26	2.02	2.13	2.87	2.95	2.43

The turnover ratios measure the operating efficiency of the firm. The efficiency in managing the company's accounts receivable, inventory, and accounts payable was discussed in the short-term liquidity analysis. R.E.C. Inc.'s fixed asset turnover has decreased over the past five years and is now below the industry average. As noted earlier, R.E.C. Inc. has increased its investment in fixed assets as a result of home office and store expansion. The asset turnover ratios reveal a downward trend in the efficiency with which the firm is generating sales from investments in fixed and total assets. The total asset turnover rose in 2010, progress traceable to improved management of inventories and receivables. The fixed asset turnover ratio is still declining, a result of expanding offices and retail outlets, but should improve if the expansion is successful.

Capital Structure and Long-Term Solvency

The analytical process includes an evaluation of the amount and proportion of debt in a firm's capital structure as well as the ability to service debt. Debt implies risk because debt involves the satisfaction of fixed financial obligations. The disadvantage of debt financing is that the fixed commitments must be met for the firm to continue operations. The major advantage of debt financing is that, when used successfully, shareholder returns are magnified through financial leverage. The concept of financial leverage can best be illustrated with an example (Figure 6.3).

R.E.C. Inc.	2010	2009	2008	2007	2006	Industry Average 2010
Debt to total assets	51.8%	50.1%	49.2%	40.8%	39.7%	48.7%
Long-term debt to total capitalization	31.4%	31.0%	24.1%	19.6%	19.8%	30.4%
Debt to equity	1.07	1.00	0.96	0.68	0.66	0.98

The debt ratios for R.E.C. Inc. reveal a steady increase in the use of borrowed funds. Total debt has risen relative to total assets, long-term debt has increased as a proportion of the firm's permanent financing, and external or debt financing has increased relative to internal financing. Given the greater degree of risk implied by borrowing, it is important to determine (1) why debt has increased; (2) whether the firm is employing debt successfully; and (3) how well the firm is covering its fixed charges.

Why has debt increased? The Summary Statement of Cash Flows, discussed in Chapter 4 and repeated here as Exhibit 6.2, provides an explanation of borrowing cause. Exhibit 6.2 shows the inflows and outflows of cash both in dollar amounts and percentages.

Exhibit 6.2 shows that R.E.C. Inc. has substantially increased its investment in capital assets, particularly in 2010 when additions to property, plant, and equipment accounted for 82% of the total cash outflows. These investments have been financed largely by borrowing, especially in 2009 when the firm had a sluggish operating performance and no internal cash generation. Operations supplied 73% of R.E.C. Inc.'s cash in 2008 and 62% in 2010, but the firm had to borrow heavily in 2009 (98% of cash inflows). The impact of this borrowing is seen in the firm's debt ratios.

How effectively is R.E.C. Inc. using financial leverage? The answer is determined by calculating the financial leverage index (FLI), as follows:

$$\frac{\text{Return on equity}}{\text{Adjusted return on assets}} = \text{Financial leverage index}$$

The adjusted return on assets in the denominator of this ratio is calculated as follows:

$$\frac{\text{Net earnings} + \text{interest expense} (1 - \text{tax rate})^{10}}{\text{Total assets}}$$

---

[10] The effective tax rate to be used in this ratio was calculated in Chapter 3.

FIGURE 6.3   Example of Financial Leverage

Sockee Sock Company has $100,000 in total assets, and the firm's capital structure consists of 50% debt and 50% equity:

Debt	$ 50.000
Equity	50.000
Total assets	$100.000

Cost of debt = 10%
Average tax rate = 40%

If Sockee has $20,000 in operating earnings, the return to shareholders as measured by the return on equity ratio would be 18%:

Operating earnings	$20.000
Interest expense	5.000
Earnings before tax	15.000
Tax expense	6.000
Net earnings	$ 9.000

Return on equity: 9,000/50,000 = 18%

If Sockee is able to double operating earnings from $20,000 to $40,000, the return on equity will more than double, increasing from 18% to 42%:

Operating earnings	$40.000
Interest expense	5.000
Earnings before tax	35.000
Tax expense	14.000
Net earnings	$21.000

Return on equity: 21.000/50.000 = 42%

The magnified return on equity results from financial leverage. Unfortunately, leverage has a double edge. If operating earnings are cut in half from $20,000 to $10,000, the return on equity is more than halved, declining from 18% to 6%:

Operating earnings	$10.000
Interest expense	5.000
Earnings before tax	5.000
Tax expense	2.000
Net earnings	$ 3.000

Return on equity: 3.000/50.000 = 6%

The amount of interest expense is fixed, regardless of the level of operating earnings. When operating earnings rise or fall, financial leverage produces positive or negative effects on shareholder returns. In evaluating a firm's capital structure and solvency, the analyst must constantly weigh the potential benefits of debt against the risks inherent in its use.

EXHIBIT 6.2

R.E.C. Inc. Summary Analysis Statement of Cash Flows (in Thousands)

	2010	%	2009	%	2008	%
Inflows (thousands)						
Operations	$10,024	62.0	$ 0	0.0	$5,629	73.0
Sales of other assets	295	1.8	0	0.0	0	0.0
Sales of common stock	256	1.6	183	1.8	124	1.6
Additions of short-term debt	0	0.0	1,854	18.7	1,326	17.2
Additions of long-term debt	5,600	34.6	7,882	79.5	629	8.2
Total	$16,175	100.0	$ 9,919	100.0	$7,708	100.0
Outflows (thousands)						
Operations	$ 0	0.0	$ 3,767	31.4	$ 0	0.0
Purchase of property, plant, and equipment	14,100	81.8	4,773	40.0	3,982	66.9
Reductions of short-term debt	30	0.2	0	0.0	0	0.0
Reductions of long-term debt	1,516	8.8	1,593	13.2	127	2.1
Dividends paid	1,582	9.2	1,862	15.4	1,841	31.0
Total	$17,228	100.0	$11,995	100.0	$5,950	100.0
Change in cash and marketable securities	($ 1,053)		($ 2,076)		$1,758	

When the FLI is greater than 1, which indicates that return on equity exceeds return on assets, the firm is employing debt beneficially. An FLI of less than 1 means the firm is not using debt successfully. For R.E.C. Inc., the adjusted return on assets and FLI are calculated as follows:

	2010	2009	2008
$\dfrac{\text{Net earnings} + \text{interest expense } (1 - \text{tax rate})}{\text{Total assets}}$	$\dfrac{9{,}394 + 2{,}585(1 - 0.45)}{95{,}298}$	$\dfrac{5{,}910 + 2{,}277(1 - 0.43)}{75{,}909}$	$\dfrac{5{,}896 + 1{,}274(1 - 0.45)}{66{,}146}$

	2010	2009	2008
$\dfrac{\text{Return on equity}}{\text{Adjusted return on assets}}$	$\dfrac{20.45}{11.35} = 1.8$	$\dfrac{15.61}{9.50} = 1.6$	$\dfrac{17.53}{9.97} = 1.8$

The FLI for R.E.C. Inc. of 1.8 in 2010, 1.6 in 2009, and 1.8 in 2008 indicates a successful use of financial leverage for the three-year period when borrowing has increased. The firm has generated sufficient operating returns to more than cover the interest payments on borrowed funds.

How well is R.E.C. Inc. covering fixed charges? The answer requires a review of the coverage ratios.

R.E.C. Inc.	2010	2009	2008	2007	2006	Industry Average 2010
Times interest earned	7.44	5.18	8.84	13.34	12.60	7.2
Cash interest coverage	7.77	1.24	9.11	11.21	11.90	*
Fixed charge coverage	2.09	2.01	2.27	2.98	3.07	2.5
Cash flow adequacy	0.58	(0.46)	0.95	1.03	1.24	*

* Not available

Given the increased level of borrowing, the times interest earned and cash interest coverage ratios have declined over the five-year period but times interest earned remains above the industry average. Cash interest coverage indicates that R.E.C. Inc. is generating enough cash to actually make the cash payments. R.E.C. Inc. leases the majority of its retail outlets so the fixed charge coverage ratio, which considers lease payments as well as interest expense, is a more relevant ratio than times interest earned. This ratio has also decreased, as a result of store expansion and higher payments for leases and interest. Although below the industry average, the firm is still covering all fixed charges by more than two times out of operating earnings, and coverage does not at this point appear to be a problem. The fixed charge coverage ratio is a ratio to be monitored closely in the future, however, particularly if R.E.C. Inc. continues to expand. The cash flow adequacy ratio has dropped below 1.0 in 2008, 2009, and 2010, indicating the company does not generate enough cash from operations to cover capital expenditures, debt repayments, and cash dividends. To improve this ratio, the firm needs to begin reducing accounts receivables and inventories, thereby increasing cash from operations. Once the expansion is complete this should occur; however, if the expansion continues, cash flow adequacy will likely remain below 1.0.

Profitability

The analysis now turns to a consideration of how well the firm has performed in terms of profitability, beginning with the evaluation of several key ratios.

R.E.C. Inc.	2010	2009	2008	2007	2006	Industry Average 2010
Gross profit margin	40.00%	39.95%	42.00%	41.80%	41.76%	37.25%
Operating profit margin	8.93%	7.72%	8.00%	10.98%	11.63%	7.07%
Net profit margin	4.36%	3.86%	4.19%	5.00%	5.20%	3.74%
Cash flow margin	4.65%	(2.46)%	4.00%	4.39%	3.92%	*

* Not available

Profitability—after a relatively poor year in 2009 due to economic recession, adverse ski conditions, and the costs of new store openings—now looks more promising. Management adopted a growth strategy reflected in aggressive marketing and the opening of 18 new stores in 2009 and 25 in 2010. With the exception of the cash flow margin, the profit margins are all below their 2006 and 2007 levels but have improved in 2010 and are above industry averages. The cash flow margin, as a result of strong cash generation from operations in 2010, was at its highest level of the five-year period.

The gross profit margin was stable, a positive sign in light of new store openings featuring many "sale" and discounted items to attract customers, and the firm managed to improve its operating profit margin in 2010. The increase in operating profit margin is especially noteworthy because it occurred during an expansionary period with sizable increases in operating expenses, especially lease payments required for new stores. The net profit margin also improved in spite of increased interest and tax expenses and a reduction in interest revenue from marketable security investments.

R.E.C. Inc.	2010	2009	2008	2007	2006	Industry Average 2010
Return on assets	9.86%	7.79%	8.91%	14.35%	15.34%	9.09%
Return on equity	20.45%	15.61%	17.53%	24.25%	25.46%	17.72%
Cash return on assets	10.52%	(4.96)%	8.64%	15.01%	15.98%	*

* Not available

After declining steadily through 2009, return on assets, return on equity, and cash return on assets rebounded strongly in 2010. The return on assets and return on equity ratios measure the overall success of the firm in generating profits, whereas the cash return on assets measures the firm's ability to generate cash from its investment and management strategies. It would appear that R.E.C. Inc. is well positioned for future growth. As discussed earlier, it will be important to monitor the firm's management of inventories, which account for half of total assets and have been problematic in the past. The expansion will necessitate a continuation of expenditures for advertising, at least at the current level, to attract customers to both new and old areas. R.E.C. Inc. has financed much of its expansion with debt, and thus far its shareholders have benefited from the use of debt through financial leverage.

R.E.C. Inc. experienced a negative cash flow from operations in 2009, another problem that bears watching in the future. The negative cash flow occurred in a year of only modest sales and earnings growth:

R.E.C. Inc.	2010	2009	2008	2007	2006
Sales growth	40.9%	8.7%	25.5%	21.6%	27.5%
Earnings growth	59.0%	0.2%	5.2%	16.9%	19.2%

Sales expanded rapidly in 2010 as the economy recovered and the expansion of retail outlets began to pay off. The outlook is for continued economic recovery.

Relating the Ratios—The Du Pont System

Having looked at individual financial ratios as well as groups of financial ratios measuring short-term liquidity, operating efficiency, capital structure and long-term solvency, and profitability, it is helpful to complete the evaluation of a firm by considering the interrelationship among the individual ratios. That is, how do the various pieces of financial measurement work together to produce an overall return? The Du Pont System helps the analyst see how the firm's decisions and activities over the course of an accounting period—which is what financial ratios are measuring—interact to produce an overall return to the firm's shareholders, the return on equity. The summary ratios used are the following:

(1) Net profit margin	×	(2) Total asset turnover	=	(3) Return on investment
$\dfrac{\text{Net income}}{\text{Net sales}}$	×	$\dfrac{\text{Net sales}}{\text{Total assets}}$	=	$\dfrac{\text{Net income}}{\text{Total assets}}$
(3) Return on investment	×	(4) Financial leverage	=	(5) Return on equity
$\dfrac{\text{Net income}}{\text{Total assets}}$	×	$\dfrac{\text{Total assets}}{\text{Stockholders' equity}}$	=	$\dfrac{\text{Net income}}{\text{Stockholders' equity}}$

By reviewing this series of relationships, the analyst can identify strengths and weaknesses as well as trace potential causes of any problems in the overall financial condition and performance of the firm.

The first three ratios reveal that the (3) return on investment (profit generated from the overall investment in assets) is a product of the (1) net profit margin (profit generated from sales) and the (2) total asset turnover (the firm's ability to produce sales from its assets). Extending the analysis, the remaining three ratios show how the (5) return on equity (overall return to shareholders, the firm's owners) is derived from the product of (3) return on investment and (4) financial leverage (proportion of debt in the capital structure). Using this system, the analyst can evaluate changes in the firm's condition and performance, whether they are indicative of improvement or deterioration or some combination. The evaluation can then focus on specific areas contributing to the changes.

Evaluating R.E.C. Inc. using the Du Pont System over the five-year period from 2006 to 2010 would show the following relationships:

Du Pont System applied to R.E.C. Inc.

	(1) NPM	×	(2) TAT	=	(3) ROI	×	(4) FL	=	(5) ROE
2006	5.20	×	2.95	=	15.34	×	1.66	=	25.46
2007	5.00	×	2.87	=	14.35	×	1.69	=	24.25
2008	4.19	×	2.13	=	8.92	×	1.97	=	17.57
2009	3.86	×	2.02	=	7.80	×	2.00	=	15.60
2010	4.36	×	2.26	=	9.85	×	2.07	=	20.39

As discussed earlier in the chapter, return on equity is below earlier year levels but has improved since its low point in 2009. The Du Pont System helps provide clues as to why these changes have occurred. Both the profit margin and the asset turnover are lower in 2010 than in 2006 and 2007. The combination of increased debt (financial leverage) and the improvement in profitability and asset utilization has produced an improved overall return in 2010 relative to the two previous years. Specifically, the firm has added debt to finance capital asset expansion and has used its debt effectively. Although debt carries risk and added cost in the form of interest expense, it also has the positive benefit of financial leverage when employed successfully, which is the case for R.E.C. Inc. The 2010 improvement in inventory management has impacted the firm favorably, showing up in the improved total asset turnover ratio. The firm's ability to control operating costs while increasing sales during expansion has improved the net profit margin. The overall return on investment is now improving as a result of these combined factors.

Projections and Pro Forma Statements

Some additional analytical tools and financial ratios are relevant to financial statement analysis, particularly for investment decisions and long-range planning. Although an in-depth discussion of these tools is beyond the scope of this chapter, we provide an introductory treatment of projections, pro forma financial statements, and several investment-related financial ratios.

The investment analyst, in valuing securities for investment decisions, must project the future earnings stream of a business enterprise. References that provide earnings forecasts are found in the "Other Sources" section earlier in the chapter.

Pro forma financial statements are projections of financial statements based on a set of assumptions regarding future revenues, expenses, level of investment in assets, financing methods and costs, and working capital management.

Pro forma financial statements are utilized primarily for long-range planning and long-term credit decisions. A bank considering the extension of $1.5 million in new credit to R.E.C. Inc. would want to look at the firm's pro forma statements, assuming the loan is granted, and determine—using different scenarios regarding the firm's performance—whether cash flow from operations would be sufficient to service the debt. R.E.C. Inc.'s CEO, who is making a decision about new store expansion, would develop pro forma statements based on varying estimates of performance outcomes and financing alternatives.

It is important that the above described pro forma financial statements not be confused with "pro forma" earnings or "pro forma" financial statements that many firms now report in their annual reports and financial press releases. Many companies in recent years have made up their own definition of *pro forma* in order to present more favorable financial information than the generally accepted accounting principles (GAAP)-based number required to be reported. By eliminating items such as depreciation, amortization, interest, and tax expense from earnings, for example, some firms have tried to convince users of their annual reports to focus on the "pro forma" amount that is usually a profit, instead of the GAAP-based amount that is usually a loss. (This topic was discussed in Chapter 5.)

Summary of Analysis

The analysis of any firm's financial statements consists of a mixture of steps and pieces that interrelate and affect each other. No one part of the analysis should be interpreted in isolation. Short-term liquidity impacts profitability; profitability begins with sales, which relate to the liquidity of assets. The efficiency of asset management influences the cost and availability of credit, which shapes the capital structure. Every aspect of a firm's financial condition, performance, and outlook affects the share price. The last step of financial statement analysis is to integrate the separate pieces into a whole, leading to conclusions about the business enterprise. The specific conclusions drawn will be affected by the original objectives established at the initiation of the analytical process.

The major findings from the analysis of R.E.C. Inc.'s financial statements can be summarized by the following strengths and weaknesses.

Strengths

1. Favorable economic and industry outlook; firm well-positioned geographically to benefit from expected economic and industry growth
2. Aggressive marketing and expansion strategies
3. Recent improvement in management of accounts receivable and inventory
4. Successful use of financial leverage and solid coverage of debt service requirements
5. Effective control of operating costs
6. Substantial sales growth, partially resulting from market expansion and reflective of future performance potential
7. Increased profitability in 2010 and strong, positive generation of cash flow from operations

Weaknesses

1. Highly sensitive to economic fluctuations and weather conditions
2. Negative cash flow from operating activities in 2009
3. Historical problems with inventory management and some weakness in overall asset management efficiency
4. Increased risk associated with debt financing

The answers to specific questions regarding R.E.C. Inc. are determined by the values placed on each of the strengths and weaknesses. In general, the outlook for the firm is promising. R.E.C. Inc. appears to be a sound credit risk with attractive investment potential. The management of inventories, a continuation of effective cost controls, and careful timing of further expansion will be critically important to the firm's future success.

This book began with the notion that financial statements should serve as a map to successful business decision making, even though the user of financial statement data would confront mazelike challenges in seeking to find and interpret the necessary information. The chapters have covered the enormous volume of material found in corporate financial reporting, the complexities and confusions created by accounting rules and choices, the potential for management manipulations of financial statement results, and the difficulty in finding necessary information. The exploration of financial statements has required a close examination of the form and content of each financial statement presented in corporate annual reporting as well as the development of tools and techniques for analyzing the data. It is the hope of the authors that readers of this book will find that financial statements are a map, leading to sound and profitable business decisions (Figure 6.4).

FIGURE 6.4 The Maze Becomes a Map

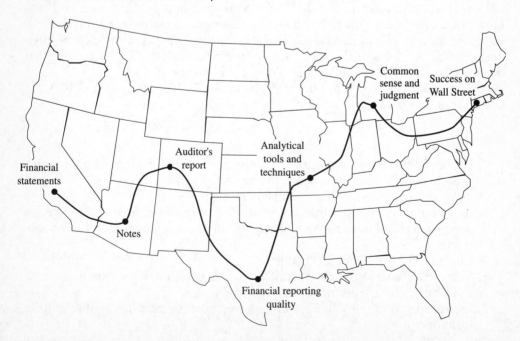

Self-Test

Solutions are provided in Appendix B.

_____ **1.** What is the first step in an analysis of financial statements?
(a) Check the auditor's report.
(b) Check references containing financial information.
(c) Specify the objectives of the analysis.
(d) Do a common-size analysis.

_____ **2.** What is a creditor's objective in performing an analysis of financial statements?
(a) To decide whether the borrower has the ability to repay interest and principal on borrowed funds.
(b) To determine if the firm would be a good place to obtain employment.
(c) To determine the company's taxes for the current year.
(d) To determine whether an investment is warranted by estimating a company's future earnings stream.

_____ **3.** What is an investor's objective in financial statement analysis?
(a) To decide whether the borrower has the ability to repay interest and principal on borrowed funds.
(b) To determine if the firm would be a good place to obtain employment.
(c) To determine the company's taxes for the current year.
(d) To determine whether an investment is warranted by estimating a company's future earnings stream.

_____ **4.** What information does the auditor's report contain?
(a) The results of operations.
(b) An unqualified opinion.
(c) An opinion as to the fairness of the financial statements.
(d) A detailed coverage of the firm's liquidity, capital resources, and operations.

_____ **5.** Which of the following would be helpful to an analyst evaluating the performance of a firm?
(a) Understanding the economic and political environment in which the company operates.
(b) Reviewing the annual reports of a company's suppliers, customers, and competitors.
(c) Preparing common-size financial statements and calculating key financial ratios for the company being evaluated.
(d) All of the above.

_____ **6.** Which of the following is not required to be discussed in the Management Discussion and Analysis of the Financial Condition and Results of Operations?
(a) Liquidity.
(b) Capital resources.
(c) Operations.
(d) Earnings projections.

_____ 7. What type of information found in supplementary schedules is required for inclusion in an annual report?
   (a) Segmental data.
   (b) Inflation data.
   (c) Material litigation and management photographs.
   (d) Management remuneration and segmental data.

_____ 8. What is Form 10-K?
   (a) A document filed with the American Institute of Certified Public Accountants (AICPA) containing supplementary schedules showing management remuneration and elaborations of financial statement disclosures.
   (b) A document filed with the SEC by companies selling securities to the public, containing much of the same information as the annual report as well as additional detail.
   (c) A document filed with the SEC containing key business ratios and forecasts of earnings.
   (d) A document filed with the SEC containing nonpublic information.

_____ 9. What information can be gained from sources such as Industry Norms and Key Business Ratios, Annual Statement Studies, Analyst's Handbook, and Industry Surveys?
   (a) The general economic condition.
   (b) Forecasts of earnings.
   (c) Elaborations of financial statement disclosures.
   (d) A company's relative position within its industry.

_____ 10. Which of the following is not a tool or technique used by a financial statement analyst?
   (a) Common-size financial statements.
   (b) Trend analysis.
   (c) Random sampling analysis.
   (d) Industry comparisons.

_____ 11. What do liquidity ratios measure?
   (a) A firm's ability to meet cash needs as they arise.
   (b) The liquidity of fixed assets.
   (c) The overall performance of a firm.
   (d) The extent of a firm's financing with debt relative to equity.

_____ 12. Which category of ratios is useful in assessing the capital structure and long-term solvency of a firm?
   (a) Liquidity ratios.
   (b) Activity ratios.
   (c) Leverage ratios.
   (d) Profitability ratios.

_____ 13. What is a serious limitation of financial ratios?
   (a) Ratios are screening devices.
   (b) Ratios can be used only by themselves.
   (c) Ratios indicate weaknesses only.
   (d) Ratios are not predictive.

_____ **14.** What is the most widely used liquidity ratio?
 (a) Quick ratio.
 (b) Current ratio.
 (c) Inventory turnover.
 (d) Debt ratio.

_____ **15.** What is a limitation common to both the current and the quick ratio?
 (a) Accounts receivable may not be truly liquid.
 (b) Inventories may not be truly liquid.
 (c) Marketable securities are not liquid.
 (d) Prepaid expenses are potential sources of cash.

_____ **16.** Why is the quick ratio a more rigorous test of short-run solvency than the current ratio?
 (a) The quick ratio considers only cash and marketable securities as current assets.
 (b) The quick ratio eliminates prepaid expenses for the numerator.
 (c) The quick ratio eliminates prepaid expenses for the denominator.
 (d) The quick ratio eliminates inventories from the numerator.

_____ **17.** What does an increasing collection period for accounts receivable suggest about a firm's credit policy?
 (a) The credit policy is too restrictive.
 (b) The firm is probably losing qualified customers.
 (c) The credit policy may be too lenient.
 (d) The collection period has no relationship to a firm's credit policy.

_____ **18.** Which of the following statements about inventory turnover is false?
 (a) Inventory turnover measures the efficiency of the firm in managing and selling inventory.
 (b) Inventory turnover is a gauge of the liquidity of a firm's inventory.
 (c) Inventory turnover is calculated with cost of goods sold in the numerator.
 (d) A low inventory turnover is generally a sign of efficient inventory management.

_____ **19.** Which of the following items would cause the cash conversion cycle to decrease?
 (a) Increasing days payable outstanding.
 (b) Increasing the average collection period.
 (c) Increasing the days inventory held.
 (d) None of the above.

_____ **20.** What do the asset turnover ratios measure?
 (a) The liquidity of the firm's current assets.
 (b) Management's effectiveness in generating sales from investments in assets.
 (c) The overall efficiency and profitability of the firm.
 (d) The distribution of assets in which funds are invested.

_____ **21.** Which of the following ratios would not be used to measure the extent of a firm's debt financing?
   (a) Debt ratio.
   (b) Debt to equity.
   (c) Times interest earned.
   (d) Long-term debt to total capitalization.

_____ **22.** Why is the amount of debt in a company's capital structure important to the financial analyst?
   (a) Debt implies risk.
   (b) Debt is less costly than equity.
   (c) Equity is riskier than debt.
   (d) Debt is equal to total assets.

_____ **23.** Why is the fixed charge coverage ratio a broader measure of a firm's coverage capabilities than the times interest earned ratio?
   (a) The fixed charge ratio indicates how many times the firm can cover interest payments.
   (b) The times interest earned ratio does not consider the possibility of higher interest rates.
   (c) The fixed charge ratio includes lease payments as well as interest payments.
   (d) The fixed charge ratio includes both operating and capital leases whereas the times interest earned ratio includes only operating leases.

_____ **24.** Which profit margin measures the overall operating efficiency of the firm?
   (a) Gross profit margin.
   (b) Operating profit margin.
   (c) Net profit margin.
   (d) Return on equity.

_____ **25.** Which ratio or ratios measure the overall efficiency of the firm in managing its investment in assets and in generating return to shareholders?
   (a) Gross profit margin and net profit margin.
   (b) Return on investment.
   (c) Total asset turnover and operating profit margin.
   (d) Return on investment and return on equity.

_____ **26.** What does a financial leverage index greater than one indicate about a firm?
   (a) The unsuccessful use of financial leverage.
   (b) Operating returns more than sufficient to cover interest payments on borrowed funds.
   (c) More debt financing than equity financing.
   (d) An increased level of borrowing.

_____ **27.** What does the price to earnings ratio measure?
   (a) The "multiple" that the stock market places on a firm's earnings.
   (b) The relationship between dividends and market prices.
   (c) The earnings for one common share of stock.
   (d) The percentage of dividends paid to net earnings of the firm.

Use the following data to answer questions 28 through 31:

JDL Corporation Selected Financial Data, December 31, 2009	
Current assets	$150,000
Current liabilities	100,000
Inventories	50,000
Accounts receivable	40,000
Net sales	900,000
Cost of goods sold	675,000

_____ **28.** JDL's current ratio is:
  (a) 1.0 to 1.
  (b) 0.7 to 1.
  (c) 1.5 to 1.
  (d) 2.4 to 1.

_____ **29.** JDL's quick ratio is:
  (a) 1.0 to 1.
  (b) 0.7 to 1.
  (c) 1.5 to 1.
  (d) 2.4 to 1.

_____ **30.** JDL's average collection period is:
  (a) 6 days.
  (b) 11 days.
  (c) 16 days.
  (d) 22 days.

_____ **31.** JDL's inventory turnover is:
  (a) 1.25 times.
  (b) 13.5 times.
  (c) 3.0 times.
  (d) 37.5 times.

Use the following data to answer questions 32 through 35:

RQM Corporation Selected Financial Data, December 31, 2009	
Net sales	$1,800,000
Cost of goods sold	1,080,000
Operating expenses	315,000
Net operating income	405,000
Net income	195,000
Total stockholders' equity	750,000
Total assets	1,000,000
Cash flow from operating activities	25,000

_____ **32.** RQM's gross profit margin, operating profit margin, and net profit margin, respectively, are:
  (a) 40.00%, 22.50%, 19.50%
  (b) 60.00%, 19.50%, 10.83%
  (c) 60.00%, 22.50%, 19.50%
  (d) 40.00%, 22.50%, 10.83%

_____ **33.** RQM's return on equity is:
- (a) 26%
- (b) 54%
- (c) 42%
- (d) 19%

_____ **34.** RQM's return on investment is:
- (a) 22.5%
- (b) 26.5%
- (c) 19.5%
- (d) 40.5%

_____ **35.** RQM's cash flow margin is:
- (a) 1.4%
- (b) 2.5%
- (c) 10.8%
- (d) 12.8%

Study Questions, Problems, and Cases

6.1 Explain how the credit analyst's focus will differ from the investment analyst's focus.

6.2 What are the limitations of financial ratios?

6.3 What do liquidity ratios measure? Activity ratios? Leverage ratios? Profitability ratios? Market ratios?

6.4 How is the Du Pont System helpful to the analyst?

6.5 Eleanor's Computers is a retailer of computer products. Using the financial data provided, complete the financial ratio calculations for 2010. Advise management of any ratios that indicate potential problems and provide an explanation of possible causes of the problems.

Financial Ratios	2008	2009	2010	Industry Averages 2010
Current ratio	1.71X	1.65X		1.70X
Quick ratio	0.92X	0.89X		0.95X
Average collection period	60 days	60 days		65 days
Inventory turnover	4.20X	3.90X		4.50X
Fixed asset turnover	3.20X	3.33X		3.00X
Total asset turnover	1.40X	1.35X		1.37X
Debt ratio	59.20%	61.00%		60.00%
Times interest earned	4.20X	3.70X		4.75X
Gross profit margin	25.00%	23.00%		22.50%
Operating profit margin	12.50%	12.70%		12.50%
Net profit margin	6.10%	6.00%		6.50%
Return on total assets	8.54%	8.10%		8.91%
Return on equity	20.93%	20.74%		22.28%

Income Statement for Year Ended 12/31/10		Balance Sheet at 12/31/10	
Sales	$1,500,000	Cash	$ 125,000
Cost of goods sold	1,200,000	Accounts receivable	275,000
Gross profit	$ 300,000	Inventory	325,000
Operating expenses	100,000	Current assets	$ 725,000
Operating profit	$ 200,000	Fixed assets (net)	$ 420,000
Interest expense	72,000	Total Assets	$1,145,000
Earnings before tax	128,000	Accounts payable	$ 150,000
Income tax (0.4)	51,200	Notes payable	225,000
Net Income	$ 76,800	Accrued liabilities	100,000
		Current liabilities	475,000
		Long-term debt	400,000
		Total liabilities	$ 875,000
		Equity	270,000
		Total liabilities and equity	$1,145,000

6.6 Luna Lighting, a retail firm, has experienced modest sales growth over the past three years but has had difficulty translating the expansion of sales into improved profitability. Using three years' financial statements, you have developed the following ratio calculations and industry comparisons. Based on this information, suggest possible reasons for Luna's profitability problems.

	2009	2008	2007	Industry Averages 2009
Current	2.3X	2.3X	2.2X	2.1X
Average collection period	45 days	46 days	47 days	50 days
Inventory turnover	8.3X	8.2X	8.1X	8.3X
Fixed asset turnover	2.7X	3.0X	3.3X	3.5X
Total asset turnover	1.1X	1.2X	1.3X	1.5X
Debt ratio	50%	50%	50%	54%
Times interest earned	8.1X	8.2X	8.1X	7.2X
Fixed charge coverage	4.0X	4.5X	5.5X	5.1X
Gross profit margin	43%	43%	43%	40%
Operating profit margin	6.3%	7.2%	8.0%	7.5%
Net profit margin	3.5%	4.0%	4.3%	4.2%
Return on assets	3.7%	5.0%	5.7%	6.4%
Return on equity	7.4%	9.9%	11.4%	11.8%

6.7 RareMetals, Inc. sells a rare metal found only in underdeveloped countries overseas. As a result of unstable governments in these countries and the rarity of the metal, the price fluctuates significantly. Financial information is given assuming the use of the first-in, first-out (FIFO) method of inventory valuation and also the last-in, first-out (LIFO) method of inventory valuation. Current assets other than inventory total $1,230 and current liabilities total $1,600. The ending inventory balances are $1,350 for FIFO and $525 for LIFO.

RareMetals, Inc. Income Statements (in Thousands)

	FIFO	LIFO
Net sales	$3,000	$3,000
Cost of goods sold	1,400	2,225
Gross profit	1,600	775
Selling, general and administrative	600	600
Operating profit	1,000	175
Interest expense	80	80
Earnings before taxes	920	95
Provision for income taxes	322	33
Net earnings	$ 598	$ 62

Required

(a) Calculate the following ratios assuming RareMetals, Inc. uses the FIFO method of inventory valuation: gross profit margin, operating profit margin, net profit margin, current ratio, and quick ratio.

(b) Calculate the ratios listed in (a) assuming RareMetals, Inc. uses the LIFO method of inventory valuation.

(c) Evaluate and explain the differences in the ratios calculated in (a) and (b).

(d) Will cash flow from operating activities differ depending on the inventory valuation method used? If so, estimate the difference and explain your answer.

6.8 ABC Company and XYZ Company are competitors in the manufacturing industry. The following ratios and financial information have been compiled for these two companies for the most recent year:

Financial ratios	ABC	XYZ
Liquidity		
Current (times)	0.92	1.51
Quick (times)	0.61	1.20
Cash flow liquidity (times)	0.35	0.85
Cash flow from operations (in millions of $)	995	2,520
Activity		
Accounts receivable turnover (times)	5.48	6.20
Inventory turnover (times)	4.75	4.00
Payables turnover (times)	2.82	3.55
Fixed asset turnover (times)	2.49	3.62
Total asset turnover (times)	1.10	1.10
Leverage		
Debt ratio (%)	76.02	51.21
Times interest earned (times)	12.31	17.28
Cash interest coverage (times)	9.89	30.19
Cash flow adequacy (times)	0.43	1.35
Profitability		
Gross profit margin (%)	43.08	43.11
Operating profit margin (%)	16.23	8.84
Net profit margin (%)	11.26	4.80
Cash flow margin (%)	6.98	12.59
Return on assets (%)	9.77	4.63
Return on equity (%)	40.86	10.23
Cash return on assets (%)	6.87	12.54
Earnings per share	4.59	1.19
Closing stock price	$41 per share	$35 per share

Required

(a) Compare and evaluate the strengths and weaknesses of ABC and XYZ Companies.

(b) Calculate the price-to-earnings (P/E) ratios for both firms. Explain what a P/E ratio tells an analyst. What could be the cause of the difference between ABC's and XYZ's P/E ratios?

6.9 Determine the effect on the current ratio, the quick ratio, net working capital (current assets less current liabilities), and the debt ratio (total liabilities to total assets) of each of the following transactions. Consider each transaction separately and assume that prior to each transaction the current ratio is 2X, the quick ratio is 1X, and the debt ratio is 50%. The company uses an allowance for doubtful accounts.

Use I for increase, D for decrease, and N for no change.

	Current Ratio	Quick Ratio	Net Working Capital	Debt Ratio
(a) Borrows $10,000 from bank on short-term note				
(b) Writes off a $5,000 customer account				
(c) Issues $25,000 in new common stock for cash				
(d) Purchases for cash $7,000 of new equipment				
(e) $5,000 inventory is destroyed by fire				
(f) Invests $3,000 in short-term marketable securities				
(g) Issues $10,000 long-term bonds				
(h) Sells equipment with book value of $6,000 for $7,000				
(i) Issues $10,000 stock in exchange for land				
(j) Purchases $3,000 inventory for cash				
(k) Purchases $5,000 inventory on credit				
(l) Pays $2,000 to supplier to reduce account payable				

6.10 Laurel Street, president of Uvalde Manufacturing Inc., is preparing a proposal to present to her board of directors regarding a planned plant expansion that will cost $10 million. At issue is whether the expansion should be financed with debt (a long-term note at First National Bank of Uvalde with an interest rate of 15%) or through the issuance of common stock (200,000 shares at $50 per share).

Uvalde Manufacturing currently has a capital structure of:

Debt (12% interest)	40,000,000
Equity	50,000,000

The firm's most recent income statement is presented next:

Sales	$100,000,000
Cost of goods sold	65,000,000
Gross profit	35,000,000
Operating expenses	20,000,000
Operating profit	15,000,000
Interest expense	4,800,000
Earnings before tax	10,200,000
Income tax expense (40%)	4,080,000
Net income	$ 6,120,000
Earnings per share (800,000 shares)	$ 7.65

Laurel Street is aware that financing the expansion with debt will increase risk but could also benefit shareholders through financial leverage. Estimates are that the plant expansion will increase operating profit by 20%. The tax rate is expected to stay at 40%. Assume a 100% dividend payout ratio.

Required

(a) Calculate the debt ratio, times interest earned, earnings per share, and the financial leverage index under each alternative, assuming the expected increase in operating profit is realized.

(b) Discuss the factors the board should consider in making a decision.

6.11 Using the ratios and information given for Wal-Mart, a retailer, analyze the short-term liquidity and operating efficiency of the firm as of January 31, 2008.

Financial ratios For the years ended January 31,	2008	2007
Liquidity		
Current (times)	0.81	0.90
Quick (times)	0.21	0.25
Cash flow liquidity (times)	0.44	0.53
Average collection period	4 days	3 days
Days inventory held	45 days	47 days
Days payable outstanding	39 days	39 days
Cash conversion cycle	10 days	11 days
Activity		
Fixed asset turnover (times)	3.90	3.94
Total asset turnover (times)	2.32	2.31
Other information		
Cash flow from operations (in millions of $)	20,354	19,997
Revenues (in millions of $)	378,799	348,650

6.12 The following ratios have been calculated for AMC Entertainment Inc., owner and operator of movie theaters. Analyze the capital structure, long-term solvency, and profitability of AMC.

Financial ratios	2007	2006
Leverage		
Debt ratio (%)	66.1	71.7
Long-term debt to total capital (%)	54.4	64.8
Times interest earned (times)	0.6	0.2
Cash interest coverage (times)	3.0	1.2
Fixed charge coverage (times)	0.9	0.8
Cash flow adequacy (times)	0.6	0.2
Profitability		
Gross profit margin (%)	62.0	61.7
Operating profit margin (%)	4.4	1.2
Net profit margin (%)	5.4	(11.3)
Cash flow margin (%)	17.0	1.4
Return on assets (%)	3.3	(4.3)
Return on equity (%)	9.6	(15.3)
Cash return on assets (%)	10.2	0.5

6.13 Writing Skills Problem

R.E.C. Inc.'s staff of accountants finished preparing the financial statements for 2010 and will meet next week with the company's CEO as well as the Director of Investor Relations and representatives from the marketing and art departments to design the current year's annual report.

Required

Write a paragraph in which you present the main idea(s) you think the company should present to shareholders in the annual report.

6.14 Research Problem

Using the articles referenced in footnote 4 in this chapter regarding cash flow ratios, create a list of cash flow ratios that you believe would be a good set of ratios to assess the cash flows of a firm. Choose an industry and locate four companies in that industry. Calculate the cash flow ratios for each company and then create an industry average of all four companies. Comment on how well you think your industry average would work as a guide when analyzing other firms in this industry.

6.15 Internet Problem

Choose an industry and find four companies in that industry. Using a financial Internet database such as www.marketwatch.com, calculate or locate the four market ratios discussed in the chapter for each of the four companies. Write an analysis comparing the market ratios of the four companies.

6.16 Intel Case

The 2007 Intel Annual Report can be found at the following Web site: www.prenhall.com/fraser.

(a) Using the Intel Annual Report, calculate key financial ratios for all years presented.

(b) Using the library, find industry averages to compare to the calculations in (a).

(c) Write a report to the management of Intel. Your report should include an evaluation of short-term liquidity, operating efficiency, capital structure and long-term solvency, profitability, market measures, and a discussion of any quality of financial reporting issues. In addition, strengths and weaknesses should be identified, and your opinion of the investment potential and the creditworthiness of the firm should be conveyed to management.

Hint: Use the information from the Intel Problems at the end of Chapters 1 through 5 to complete this problem.

6.17 Eastman Kodak Comprehensive Analysis Case Using the Financial Statement Analysis Template

Each chapter in the textbook contains a continuation of this problem. The objective is to learn how to do a comprehensive financial statement analysis in steps as the content of each chapter is learned. Using the 2007 Eastman Kodak Annual Report and Form 10-K, which can be found at www.prenhall .com/fraser, complete the following requirements:

(a) Open the financial statement analysis template that you have been using in the prior chapters. Link to the "Ratios" and the "Growth Rate Analysis" by clicking on the tabs at the bottom of the template. All of the ratios should be automatically calculated for you, assuming you have input all required data from prior chapters. Print these pages.

(b) Using all of your data and calculations for Eastman Kodak from prior chapters, write a comprehensive analysis of the company. Use Figure 6.2 as a guide.

6.18 Target Corporation Case

Target Corporation (Target) operates large general merchandise and food discount stores in all of the United States, with the exception of Alaska, Hawaii, and Vermont. The company also has its own credit card operations and operates a fully integrated online business, Target.com. Although the online portion of Target's business is small relative to the overall size of Target, sales are growing at a more rapid pace in the online business compared to the in-store sales. The company's philosophy is to offer their customers a delightful shopping experience and their team members a preferred place to work, and to invest in the communities in which Target conducts business to improve quality of life. Selected information from the 2007 Form 10-K of Target Corporation is on pages 228–237.*

Required

1. Analyze the firm's financial statements and supplementary information. Your analysis should include the preparation of common-size financial statements, key financial ratios, and an evaluation of short-term liquidity, operating efficiency, capital structure and long-term solvency, profitability, and market measures. (The financial statement analysis template can be accessed and used at www.prenhall.com/fraser.)
2. Identify the strengths and weaknesses of the company.
3. What is your opinion of the investment potential and the creditworthiness of Target Corporation?

Consolidated Statements of Operations

(millions, except per share data)	2007	2006	2005
Sales	$61,471	$57,878	$51,271
Credit card revenues	1,896	1,612	1,349
Total revenues	63,367	59,490	52,620
Cost of sales	41,895	39,399	34,927
Selling, general and administrative expenses	13,704	12,819	11,185
Credit card expenses	837	707	776
Depreciation and amortization	1,659	1,496	1,409
Earnings before interest expense and income taxes	5,272	5,069	4,323
Net interest expense	647	572	463
Earnings before income taxes	4,625	4,497	3,860
Provision for income taxes	1,776	1,710	1,452
Net earnings	$ 2,849	$ 2,787	$ 2,408
Basic earnings per share	3.37	$ 3.23	$ 2.73
Diluted earnings per share	$ 3.33	$ 3.21	$ 2.71
Weighted average common shares outstanding			
Basic	845.4	861.9	882.0
Diluted	850.8	868.6	889.2

See accompanying Notes to Consolidated Financial Statements.

*Source: Target Corporation 2007 Form 10-K.

Consolidated Statements of Financial Position

(millions, except footnotes)	February 2, 2008	February 3, 2007
Assets		
Cash and cash equivalents	$ 2,450	$ 813
Accounts receivable, net	8,054	6,194
Inventory	6,780	6,254
Other current assets	1,622	1,445
Total current assets	18,906	14,706
Property and equipment		
Land	5,522	4,934
Buildings and improvements	18,329	16,110
Fixtures and equipment	3,858	3,553
Computer hardware and software	2,421	2,188
Construction-in-progress	1,852	1,596
Accumulated depreciation	(7,887)	(6,950)
Property and equipment, net	24,095	21,431
Other noncurrent assets	1,559	1,212
Total assets	**$44,560**	**$37,349**
Liabilities and shareholders' investment		
Accounts payable	$ 6,721	$ 6,575
Accrued and other current liabilities	3,097	3,180
Current portion of long-term debt and notes payable	1,964	1,362
Total current liabilities	11,782	11,117
Long-term debt	15,126	8,675
Deferred income taxes	470	577
Other noncurrent liabilities	1,875	1,347
Shareholders' investment		
Common stock	68	72
Additional paid-in-capital	2,656	2,387
Retained earnings	12,761	13,417
Accumulated other comprehensive loss	(178)	(243)
Total shareholders' investment	15,307	15,633
Total liabilities and shareholders' investment	**$44,560**	**$37,349**

Common Stock Authorized 6,000,000,000 shares, $0.0833 par value; 818,737,715 shares issued and outstanding at February 2, 2008; 859,771,157 shares issued and outstanding at February 3, 2007
Preferred Stock Authorized 5,000,000 shares, $0.01 par value; no shares were issued or outstanding at February 2, 2008, or February 3, 2007
See accompanying Notes to Consolidated Financial Statements.

Consolidated Statements of Cash Flows

(millions)	2007	2006	2005
Operating activities			
Net earnings	**$2,849**	$2,787	$2,408
Reconciliation to cash flow			
Depreciation and amortization	**1,659**	1,496	1,409
Share-based compensation expense	**73**	99	93
Deferred income taxes	**(70)**	(201)	(122)
Bad debt provision	**481**	380	466
Loss on disposal of property and equipment, net	**28**	53	70
Other non-cash items affecting earnings	**52**	(35)	(50)
Changes in operating accounts providing/(requiring) cash:			
Accounts receivable originated at Target	**(602)**	(226)	(244)
Inventory	**(525)**	(431)	(454)
Other current assets	**(139)**	(30)	(28)
Other noncurrent assets	**101**	5	(24)
Accounts payable	**111**	435	489
Accrued and other current liabilities	**62**	430	421
Other noncurrent liabilities	**124**	100	2
Other	**(79)**	—	15
Cash flow provided by operations	**4,125**	4,862	4,451
Investing activities			
Expenditures for property and equipment	**(4,369)**	(3,928)	(3,388)
Proceeds from disposal of property and equipment	**95**	62	58
Change in accounts receivable originated at third parties	**(1,739)**	(683)	(819)
Other investments	**(182)**	(144)	—
Cash flow required for investing activities	**(6,195)**	(4,693)	(4,149)
Financing activities			
Additions to short-term notes payable	**1,000**	—	—
Reductions of short-term notes payable	**(500)**	—	—
Additions to long-term debt	**7,617**	1,256	913
Reductions of long-term debt	**(1,326)**	(1,155)	(527)
Dividends paid	**(442)**	(380)	(318)
Repurchase of stock	**(2,477)**	(901)	(1,197)
Premiums on call options	**(331)**	—	—
Stock option exercises and related tax benefit	**210**	181	231
Other	**(44)**	(5)	(1)
Cash flow provided by/(required for) financing activities	**3,707**	(1,004)	(899)
Net increase/(decrease) in cash and cash equivalents	**1,637**	(835)	(597)
Cash and cash equivalents at beginning of year	**813**	1,648	2,245
Cash and cash equivalents at end of year	**$2,450**	$ 813	$1,648

Amounts presented herein are on a cash basis and therefore may differ from those shown in other sections of this Annual Report. Consistent with the provisions of Statement of Financial Accounting Standards (SFAS) No. 95, "Statement of Cash Flows," cash flows related to accounts receivable are classified as either an operating activity or an investing activity, depending on their origin.

Cash paid for income taxes was $1,734, $1,823 and $1,448 during 2007, 2006 and 2005, respectively. Cash paid for interest (net of interest capitalized) was $633, $584 and $468 during 2007, 2006 and 2005, respectively.

See accompanying Notes to Consolidated Financial Statements.

Dividends declared per share were $.54, $.46 and $.38 in 2007, 2006 and 2005, respectively.

Liquidity and Capital Resources

Our year-end gross receivables were $8,624 million compared with $6,711 million in 2006, an increase of 28.5 percent. This growth was driven by many factors, including a product change from proprietary Target Cards to higher-limit Target Visa cards for a group of higher credit-quality Target Card Guests and the impact of an industry-wide decline in payment rates. Average receivables in 2007 increased 18.1 percent. Given the significant rate of growth of receivables in 2007, we expect that our average receivables balance during the first half of 2008 will be significantly greater than that in 2007. Additionally, absent product changes for additional Target Card holders in 2008, we expect that our year-end 2008 receivable balance will rise only modestly.

Year-end inventory levels increased $525 million, or 8.4 percent, reflecting the natural increase required to support additional square footage and comparable-store sales growth. This growth was partially funded by an increase in accounts payable over the same period.

Notes to Consolidated Financial Statements

1. Summary of Accounting Policies

Fiscal year Our fiscal year ends on the Saturday nearest January 31. Unless otherwise stated, references to years in this report relate to fiscal years, rather than to calendar years. Fiscal year 2007 (2007) ended February 2, 2008, and consisted of 52 weeks. Fiscal year 2006 (2006) ended February 3, 2007, and consisted of 53 weeks. Fiscal year 2005 (2005) ended January 28, 2006, and consisted of 52 weeks.

2. Revenues

Our retail stores generally record revenue at the point of sale. Sales from our online business include shipping revenue and are recorded upon delivery to the guest. Total revenues do not include sales tax as we consider ourselves a pass through conduit for collecting and remitting sales taxes. Generally, guests may return merchandise within 90 days of purchase. Revenues are recognized net of expected returns, which we estimate using historical return patterns. Commissions earned on sales generated by leased departments are included within sales and were $16 million in 2007, $15 million in 2006 and $14 million in 2005.

Revenue from gift card sales is recognized upon redemption of the gift card. Our gift cards do not have expiration dates. Based on historical redemption rates, a small and relatively stable percentage of gift cards will never be redeemed, referred to as "breakage." Estimated breakage revenue is recognized over a period of time in proportion to actual gift card redemptions and was immaterial in 2007, 2006 and 2005.

Credit card revenues are recognized according to the contractual provisions of each applicable credit card agreement. When accounts are written off, uncollected finance charges and late fees are recorded as a reduction of credit card revenues. Target retail store sales charged to our credit cards totaled $4,105 million, $3,961 million and $3,655 million in 2007, 2006 and 2005, respectively. We offer new account discounts and rewards programs on our REDcard products, the Target Visa, Target Card and Target Check Card. These discounts are redeemable only on purchases made at Target. The discounts associated with our REDcard products are included as reductions in sales in our Consolidated Statements of Operations and were $108 million, $104 million and $97 million in 2007, 2006 and 2005, respectively.

4. **Consideration Received from Vendors**

We receive consideration for a variety of vendor-sponsored programs, such as volume rebates, markdown allowances, promotions and advertising and for our compliance programs, referred to as "vendor income." Vendor income reduces either our inventory costs or selling, general and administrative expenses based on the provisions of the arrangement. Promotional and advertising allowances are intended to offset our costs of promoting and selling merchandise in our stores. Under our compliance programs, vendors are charged for merchandise shipments that do not meet our requirements ("violations"), such as late or incomplete shipments. These allowances are recorded when violations occur. Substantially all consideration received is recorded as a reduction of cost of sales.

We establish a receivable for vendor income that is earned but not yet received. Based on provisions of the agreements in place, this receivable is computed by estimating when we have completed our performance and the amount earned. We perform detailed analyses to determine the appropriate level of the receivable in the aggregate. The majority of year-end receivables associated with these activities are collected within the following fiscal quarter.

5. **Advertising Costs**

Advertising costs are expensed at first showing or distribution of the advertisement and were $1,195 million, $1,170 million, and $1,028 million for 2007, 2006 and 2005, respectively. Advertising vendor income that offset advertising expenses was approximately $123 million, $118 million, and $110 million for 2007, 2006 and 2005, respectively. Newspaper circulars and media broadcast made up the majority of our advertising costs in all three years.

9. Accounts Receivable

Accounts receivable are recorded net of an allowance for expected losses. The allowance, recognized in an amount equal to the anticipated future write-offs, was $570 million at February 2, 2008, and $517 million at February 3, 2007. We estimate future write-offs based on delinquencies, risk scores, aging trends, industry risk trends and our historical experience. Substantially all accounts continue to accrue finance charges until they are written off. Total accounts receivable past due ninety days or more and still accruing finance charges were $235 million at February 2, 2008, and $160 million at February 3, 2007. Accounts are written off when they become 180 days past due.

As a method of providing funding for our accounts receivable, we sell on an ongoing basis all of our consumer credit card receivables to Target Receivables Corporation (TRC), a wholly owned, bankruptcy-remote subsidiary. TRC then transfers the receivables to the Target Credit Card Master Trust (the Trust), which from time to time will sell debt securities to third parties either directly or through a related trust. These debt securities represent undivided interests in the Trust assets. TRC uses the proceeds from the sale of debt securities and its share of collections on the receivables to pay the purchase price of the receivables to Target.

The accounting guidance for such transactions, SFAS No. 140, "Accounting for Transfers and Servicing of Financial Assets and Extinguishments of Liabilities (a replacement of SFAS No. 125)," requires the inclusion of the receivables within the Trust and any debt securities issued by the Trust, or a related trust, in our Consolidated Statements of Financial Position. Notwithstanding this accounting treatment, the receivables transferred to the Trust are not available to general creditors of Target. Upon termination of the securitization program and repayment of all debt securities issued from time to time by the Trust, or a related trust, any remaining assets could be distributed to Target in a liquidation of TRC.

10. Inventory

Substantially all of our inventory and the related cost of sales are accounted for under the retail inventory accounting method (RIM) using the last-in, first-out (LIFO) method. Inventory is stated at the lower of LIFO cost or market. Cost includes purchase price as adjusted for vendor income. Inventory is also reduced for estimated losses related to shrink and markdowns. The LIFO provision is calculated based on inventory levels, markup rates and internally measured retail price indices. At February 2, 2008, and February 3, 2007, our inventories valued at LIFO approximate those inventories as if they were valued at FIFO.

Under RIM, the valuation of inventory at cost and the resulting gross margins are calculated by applying a cost-to-retail ratio to the retail value inventory. RIM is an averaging method that has been widely used in the retail industry due to its practicality. The use of RIM will result in inventory being valued at the lower of cost or market since permanent markdowns are currently taken as a reduction of the retail value of inventory.

We routinely enter into arrangements with certain vendors whereby we do not purchase or pay for merchandise until the merchandise is ultimately sold to a guest. Revenues under this program are included in sales in the Consolidated Statements of Operations, but the merchandise received under the program is not included in inventory in our Consolidated Statements of Financial Position because of the virtually simultaneous timing of our purchase and sale of this inventory. Sales made under these arrangements totaled $1,390 million, $1,178 million and $872 million for 2007, 2006 and 2005, respectively.

11. Other Current Assets

Other Current Assets (millions)	February 2, 2008	February 3, 2007
Deferred taxes	$ 556	$ 427
Vendor income receivable	244	285
Other receivables (a)	353	278
Other	469	455
Total	$1,622	$1,445

(a) Other receivables relate primarily to pharmacy receivables and merchandise sourcing services provided to third parties.

12. Property and Equipment

Property and equipment are recorded at cost, less accumulated depreciation. Depreciation is computed using the straight-line method over estimated useful lives or lease term if shorter. We amortize leasehold improvements purchased after the beginning of the initial lease term over the shorter of the assets' useful lives or a term that includes the original lease term plus any renewals that are reasonably assured at the date the leasehold improvements are acquired. Depreciation expense for 2007, 2006 and 2005 was $1,644 million, $1,509 million and $1,384 million, respectively. For income tax purposes, accelerated depreciation methods are generally used. Repair and maintenance costs are expensed as incurred and were $592 million, $532 million and $474 million in 2007, 2006 and 2005, respectively. Pre-opening costs of stores and other facilities, including supplies, payroll and other start-up costs for store and other facility openings, are expensed as incurred.

Estimated useful lives by major asset category are as follows:

Asset	Life (in years)
Buildings and improvements	8-39
Fixtures and equipment	3-15
Computer hardware and software	4

Long-lived assets are reviewed for impairment annually and also when events or changes in circumstances indicate that the asset's carrying value may not be recoverable. No material impairments were recorded in 2007, 2006 or 2005 as a result of the tests performed.

13. Other Noncurrent Assets

Other Noncurrent Assets (millions)	February 2, 2008	February 3, 2007
Cash value of life insurance [a]	$ 578	$ 559
Prepaid pension expense	394	325
Interest rate swaps [b]	215	23
Goodwill and intangible assets	208	212
Other	164	93
Total	$1,559	$1,212

[a] Company-owned life insurance policies on approximately 4,000 team members who are designated highly-compensated under the Internal Revenue Code and have given their consent to be insured.

[b] See Notes 20 and 29 for additional information relating to our interest rate swaps.

14. Goodwill and Intangible Assets

Goodwill and intangible assets are recorded within other noncurrent assets at cost less accumulated amortization. Goodwill totaled $60 million at February 2, 2008, and February 3, 2007. Goodwill is not amortized; instead, it is subject to an annual impairment test. Discounted cash flow models are used in determining fair value for the purposes of the required annual impairment analysis. No material impairments were recorded in 2007, 2006 or 2005 as a result of the tests performed.

16. Accrued and Other Current Liabilities

Accrued and Other Current Liabilities (millions)	February 2, 2008	February 3, 2007
Wages and benefits	$ 727	$ 674
Taxes payable [a]	400	450
Gift card liability [b]	372	338
Construction in process accrual	228	191
Deferred compensation	176	46
Workers' compensation and general liability	164	154
Interest payable	153	122
Straight-line rent accrual	152	135
Dividends payable	115	103
Income taxes payable	111	422
Other	499	545
Total	$3,097	$3,180

[a] Taxes payable consist of real estate, team member withholdings and sales tax liabilities.

[b] Gift card liability represents the amount of gift cards that have been issued but have not been redeemed, net of estimated breakage.

19. Net Interest Expense

Net Interest Expense (millions)	2007	2006	2005
Interest expense on debt	$736	$635	$524
Interest expense on capital leases	11	11	8
Capitalized interest	(78)	(49)	(42)
Interest income	(22)	(25)	(27)
Net interest expense	$647	$572	$463

21. Leases

We lease certain retail locations, warehouses, distribution centers, office space, equipment and land. Assets held under capital lease are included in property and equipment. Operating lease rentals are expensed on a straight-line basis over the life of the lease. At the inception of a lease, we determine the lease term by assuming the exercise of those renewal options that are reasonably assured because of the significant economic penalty that exists for not exercising those options. The exercise of lease renewal options is at our sole discretion. The expected lease term is used to determine whether a lease is capital or operating and is used to calculate straight-line rent expense. Additionally, the depreciable life of buildings and leasehold improvements is limited by the expected lease term.

Rent expense on buildings, which is included in selling, general and administrative expenses, includes rental payments based on a percentage of retail sales over contractual levels for certain stores. Total rent expense was $165 million in 2007, $158 million in 2006 and $154 million in 2005, including percentage rent expense of $5 million in 2007, 2006 and 2005. Certain leases require us to pay real estate taxes, insurance, maintenance and other operating expenses associated with the leased premises. These expenses are classified in selling, general and administrative expenses consistent with similar costs for owned locations. Most long-term leases include one or more options to renew, with renewal terms that can extend the lease term from one to more than fifty years. Certain leases also include options to purchase the leased property.

Future minimum lease payments required under noncancelable lease agreements existing at February 2, 2008, were as follows:

Future Minimum Lease Payments (millions)	Operating Leases	Capital Leases
2008	$ 239	$ 12
2009	187	16
2010	173	16
2011	129	16
2012	123	17
After 2012	2,843	155
Total future minimum lease payments	$ 3,694[a]	232
Less: Interest[b]		(105)
Present value of future minimum capital lease payments		$ 127[c]

[a] Total contractual lease payments include $1,721 million related to options to extend lease terms that are reasonably assured of being exercised and also includes $98 million of legally binding minimum lease payments for stores that will open in 2008 or later.
[b] Calculated using the interest rate at inception for each lease.
[c] Includes the current portion of $4 million.

6.19 Candela Corporation Case

Candela Corporation ("Candela" or the "Company") is a pioneer in the development and commercialization of advanced aesthetic laser and light-based systems that allow physicians and personal care practitioners to treat a wide variety of cosmetic and medical conditions including:

- permanent hair reduction on all skin types;
- skin rejuvenation, skin tightening and wrinkle reduction;
- vascular lesions such as rosacea, facial spider veins, leg veins, port wine stains, angiomas and hemangiomas;
- all-color tattoo removal; skin resurfacing scars, stretch marks and warts;
- removal of benign pigmented lesions such as sun spots, age spots, freckles, and Nevus of Ota/Ito;
- acne and acne scars;
- sebaceous hyperplasia;
- beard bumps (PFB);
- psoriasis; and,
- other cosmetic skin treatments.

The growth in the market for using aesthetic laser and light-based products is currently a worldwide phenomenon being driven by an increase in discretionary income of aging baby-boomers, which continues to create new opportunities for Candela. This market demographic places a premium on good health and personal appearance, and has demonstrated a willingness to pay for health and cosmetic products and services. In addition, continuous growth in the popularity of laser and light-based treatments among the general population is also spurring demand for Candela's products. Last year, according to The American Society for Aesthetic Plastic Surgery, Americans spent an estimated $12.2 billion on approximately 11.5 million cosmetic procedures. In particular, lasers and light-based systems are proving an attractive alternative for eliminating unwanted hair. Laser hair-removal procedures were the second most frequent cosmetic procedure performed last year, second only to Botox injections.

Candela is dedicated to developing safe and effective products. Our aesthetic laser and light-based systems are further distinguished by being among the fastest, smallest and most affordable in their respective markets. We believe that we have the largest market share because of these product attributes and we are committed to continual innovation as we meet the needs of our markets.

Candela was incorporated in Massachusetts on October 22, 1970, and subsequently reincorporated in Delaware on July 1, 1985.*

*Source: Candela Corporation 2007 Form 10-K

Required

1. Analyze the firm's financial statements and supplementary information on pages 238–249. Your analysis should include the preparation of common-size financial statements, key financial ratios, and an evaluation of short-term solvency, operating efficiency, capital structure and long-term solvency, profitability, and market measures. (The financial statement analysis template can be accessed and used at www.prenhall.com/fraser.)
2. Using your analysis, list reasons for and against investment in Candela Corporation's common stock.
3. Using your analysis, list reasons for and against loaning Candela Corporation additional funds.

Candela Corporation Consolidated Balance Sheets (in thousands, except per share data)

	June 30, 2007	July 1, 2006
Assets		
Current assets:		
Cash and cash equivalents	$ 27,152	$ 40,194
Restricted cash	48	166
Marketable securities	11,773	27,332
Accounts receivable, net of allowance for doubtful accounts of $1,412 and $1,831 at June 30 and July 1, respectively	38,455	34,273
Notes receivable	1,025	1,611
Inventories, net	21,368	16,666
Other current assets	7,136	5,084
Total current assets	106,957	125,326
Property and equipment, net	3,479	3,302
Deferred tax assets, long-term	6,146	5,294
Goodwill	10,997	—
Acquired intangible assets, net of amortization of $662 at June 30	8,151	—
Marketable securities, long-term	12,260	11,953
Other assets	2,240	3,781
Total assets	$150,230	$149,656
Liabilities and Stockholders' Equity		
Current liabilities:		
Accounts payable	$ 6,922	$ 15,968
Accrued payroll and related expenses	5,344	5,728
Accrued warranty costs, current	5,486	5,868
Income taxes payable	—	933
Sales tax payable	1,161	854
Royalties payable	459	764
Other accrued liabilities	9,554	3,672
Deferred revenue, current	10,000	8,342
Current liabilities of discontinued operations	1,257	1,287
Total current liabilities	40,183	43,416
Deferred tax liability, long-term	2,659	480
Accrued warranty costs, long-term	2,127	3,761
Deferred revenue, long-term	3,751	1,987
Total liabilities	48,720	49,644
Commitments and contingencies		
Stockholders' equity:		
Common stock, $.01 par value, 60,000,000 shares authorized; 26,082,000 and 25,914,000 issued at June 30 and July 1, respectively	261	259
Treasury stock, 3,125,000 and 2,250,000 common shares at June 30 and July 1, respectively, at cost	(22,458)	(12,997)
Additional paid-in capital	69,466	64,234
Accumulated earnings	54,536	48,280
Accumulated other comprehensive (loss) income	(295)	236
Total stockholders' equity	101,510	100,012
Total liabilities and stockholders' equity	$150,230	$149,656

The accompanying notes are an integral part of the consolidated financial statements.

Candela Corporation
Consolidated Statements of Income and Comprehensive Income
For the years ended June 30, 2007, July 1, 2006, and July 2, 2005

	2007	2006	2005
	(in thousands, except per share data)		
Revenue			
Lasers and other products	$113,225	$121,838	$102,323
Product-related service	35,332	27,628	21,578
Total revenue	148,557	149,466	123,901
Cost of sales			
Lasers and other products	49,303	54,748	45,235
Product-related service	24,191	20,869	17,918
Litigation related charges	—	—	4,829
Total cost of sales	73,494	75,617	67,982
Gross profit	75,063	73,849	55,919
Operating expenses:			
Selling, general and administrative	53,562	44,297	40,165
Research and development	18,146	8,879	6,890
Litigation related charges	—	—	773
Total operating expenses	71,708	53,176	47,828
Income from operations	3,355	20,673	8,091
Other income (expense):			
Interest income	2,719	1,748	640
Other income (expense), net	3,725	(19)	(73)
Total other income	6,444	1,729	567
Income from continuing operations before income taxes	9,799	22,402	8,658
Provision for income taxes	3,543	7,468	2,194
Income from continuing operations	6,256	14,934	6,464
Discontinued operations:			
Gain on disposal of skin care center, including revision of leasehold obligations, of $1,374 net of income tax expense of ($515)	—	—	859
Net income	$ 6,256	$ 14,934	$ 7,323
Net income per share of common stock			
Basic:			
Income from continuing operations	$ 0.27	$ 0.65	$ 0.29
Gain from discontinued operations	—	—	0.04
Net income	$ 0.27	$ 0.65	$ 0.33

Diluted:

Income from continuing operations	$ 0.27	$ 0.62	$ 0.28
Gain from discontinued operations	—	—	0.04
Net income	$ 0.27	$ 0.62	$ 0.32

Weighted average shares outstanding:

Basic	23,086	23,017	22,388
Diluted	23,525	23,948	23,073

Net income	$ 6,256	$14,934	$7,323

Other comprehensive income (loss), net of tax:

Foreign currency translation adjustment	246	521	(713)
Unrealized loss on available-for-sales securities, net of tax	(777)	—	—
Comprehensive income	$ 5,725	$15,455	$6,610

The accompanying notes are an integral part of the consolidated financial statements.

Candela Corporation
Consolidated Statements of Cash Flows
For the years ended June 30, 2007, July 1, 2006, and July 2, 2005

	2007	2006	2005
Cash flows from operating activities:			
Net income	$6,256	$14,934	$7,323
Adjustments to reconcile net income to net cash (used by) provided by operating activities:			
(Gain) loss of disposal of discontinued operations	—	—	(859)
Gain on exchange of stock	(3,540)	—	—
Share-based compensation expense	4,125	1,285	—
Depreciation and amortization	1,631	571	755
Provision (benefit) for bad debts	989	1,241	573
Provision for deferred taxes	45	(2,399)	233
Change in restricted cash	118	33	58
Other non-cash items	(144)	95	(180)
Increase (decrease) in cash from working capital, net of acquisitions:	—		
Accounts receivable	(4,943)	(681)	(1,801)
Notes receivable	586	(844)	(19)
Inventories	(4,702)	(3,561)	719
Other current assets	(266)	75	1,335
Other assets	(977)	(2,684)	427
Accounts payable	(10,376)	3,593	4,760
Accrued payroll and related expenses	(438)	882	(567)
Deferred revenue	3,422	2,243	2,731
Accrued warranty costs	(2,016)	620	2,091
Income taxes payable	(2,921)	(779)	(303)
Other accrued liabilities	5,732	(238)	1,698
Net cash (used by) provided by operating activities	(7,419)	14,386	18,974
Cash flows from investing activities:			
Purchases of property and equipment	(763)	(715)	(635)
Maturities of held-to-maturity marketable securities	37,014	4,369	—
Cash proceeds from exchange of stock	994	—	—
Purchases of held-to-maturity marketable securities	(17,706)	(43,654)	—
Acquisition of business, net of cash acquired	(15,986)	—	—
Acquisition of intangible assets	(1,380)	—	—
Net cash provided by (used by) investing activities	2,173	(40,000)	(635)

Cash flows from financing activities:

Proceeds from the issuance of common stock	843	8,122	960
Purchase of treasury stock	(9,461)	—	—
Benefits of tax effects from exercise of stock options	266	811	
Net cash (used by) provided by financing activities	(8,352)	8,933	960
Effect of exchange rates on cash and cash equivalents	556	492	(55)
Net (decrease) increase in cash and cash equivalents	(13,042)	(16,189)	19,244
Cash and cash equivalents at beginning of period	40,194	56,383	37,139
Cash and cash equivalents at end of period	$27,152	$40,194	$56,383

Cash paid during the year for:

Interest	$ —	$ —	$ —
Income taxes	5,451	9,834	2,269

Noncash investing and financing activities:

Stock acquired on exchange of Solx, Inc. investment	$ 2,546	$ —	$ —

The accompanying notes are an integral part of the consolidated financial statements.

Government Regulation

FDA's Premarket Clearance and Approval ("PMA") Requirements.

Unless an exemption applies, each medical device that we wish to market in the U.S. must receive either "510(k) clearance" or PMA in advance from the FDA pursuant to the Federal Food, Drug, and Cosmetic Act. The FDA's 510(k) clearance process usually takes from three to twelve months, but it can last longer. The process of obtaining PMA approval is much more costly, lengthy, and uncertain and generally takes from one to three years or even longer. We cannot be sure that 510(k) clearance or PMA approval will ever be obtained for any product we propose to market.

The FDA decides whether a device must undergo either the 510(k) clearance or PMA approval process based upon statutory criteria. These criteria include the level of risk that the agency perceives is associated with the device and a determination whether the product is a type of device that is similar to devices that are already legally marketed. Devices deemed to pose relatively less risk are placed in either class I or II, which requires the manufacturer to submit a pre-market notification requesting 510(k) clearance, unless an exemption applies. The pre-market notification must demonstrate that the proposed device is "substantially equivalent" in intended use and in safety and effectiveness to a legally marketed "predicate device" that is either in class I, class II, or is a "pre-amendment" class III device (i.e., one that was in commercial distribution before May 28, 1976) for which the FDA has not yet decided to require PMA approval.

After a device receives 510(k) clearance, any modification that could significantly affect its safety or effectiveness, or that would constitute a major change in its intended use, requires a new 510(k) clearance. The FDA requires each manufacturer to make this determination in the first instance, but the FDA can review any such decision. If the FDA disagrees with a manufacturer's decision not to seek a new 510(k) clearance, the agency may retroactively require the manufacturer to submit a pre-market notification requiring 510(k) clearance. The FDA also can require the manufacturer to cease marketing and/or recall the modified device until 510(k) clearance is obtained. We have modified some of our 510(k) cleared devices but have determined that, in our view, new 510(k) clearances are not required. We cannot be certain that the FDA would agree with any of our decisions not to seek 510(k) clearance. If the FDA requires us to seek 510(k) clearance for any modification, we also may be required to cease marketing and/or recall the modified device until we obtain a new 510(k) clearance.

Devices deemed by the FDA to pose the greatest risk such as life-sustaining, life-supporting, or implantable devices, or deemed not substantially equivalent to a legally marketed predicate device, are placed in class III. Such devices are required to undergo the PMA approval process in which the manufacturer must prove the safety and effectiveness of the device to the FDA's satisfaction. A PMA application must provide extensive pre-clinical and clinical trial data and also information about the device and its components regarding, among other things, manufacturing, labeling, and promotion. After approval of a PMA, a new PMA or PMA supplement is required in the event of a modification to the device, its labeling, or its manufacturing process.

A clinical trial may be required in support of a 510(k) submission or PMA application. Such trials generally require an Investigational Device Exemption ("IDE") application approved in advance by the FDA for a limited number of patients, unless the product is deemed a non-significant risk device eligible for more abbreviated IDE requirements. The IDE application must be supported by appropriate data, such as animal and laboratory testing results. Clinical trials may begin once the IDE application is approved by the FDA and the appropriate institutional review boards are at the clinical trial sites.

To date, the FDA has deemed our products to be class II devices eligible for the 510(k) clearance process. We believe that most of our products in development will receive similar treatment. However, we cannot be certain that the FDA will not deem one or more of our future products to be a class III device and impose the more burdensome PMA approval process.

Results of Operations

Fiscal Year Ended June 30, 2007, Compared to Fiscal Year Ended July 1, 2006

Research and Development Expense.   Research and development spending increased approximately $9.2 million to $18.1 million in fiscal 2007 as compared to $8.9 million for fiscal 2006. The increase was attributable primarily to $6.3 million of higher outsourced project-related work utilized to expedite the completion of the new product introduction cycle, $1.1 million of increased project materials expenditures related to the same, and $0.9 million related to increased personnel expenses including share-based compensation. As a percentage of revenue, research and development expenses were approximately 12.2% and 5.9% for fiscal 2007 and 2006, respectively.

Selling, General and Administrative Expense.   Selling, general and administrative expense increased to approximately $53.6 million or 36.0% of revenue during fiscal 2007 as compared to $44.3 million or 30% during fiscal 2006. Of the $9.3 million increase, $3.9 million was due to higher personnel expense for increased headcount, higher commission expense due to increased commissionable revenue, and stock-based compensation. The increase is also attributable to a $0.8 million increase in marketing-related expenses such as customer-related work-shops, advertising, trade shows, and an increase of $2.9 million due to an increase in legal and professional fees.

Other Income/Expense.   Total other income increased approximately $4.7 million for the fiscal 2007 to $6.4 million, from approximately $1.7 million for the fiscal 2006. This increase is primarily attributable to the recognition of a $3.5 million gain on the exchange of common stock of Solx Inc. for cash and common stock of Occulogix Inc. (NasdaqGM: OCCX). The gain was a result of the acquisition of Solx Inc., a privately-held company, by Occulogix Inc., a publicly traded company. The Company held 19.99% of the outstanding common stock of Solx Inc. on an as-converted basis, prior to the merger. As a result of the acquisition of Solx, Inc., the Company received approximately $1.0 million in cash plus approximately 1.3 million shares of common stock in Occulogix Inc.

Income Taxes.   The provision for income taxes results from a combination of activities of both the domestic and foreign subsidiaries. The Company recorded a 36.2% effective tax rate for the year ended June 30, 2007, compared to a 33% effective tax rate for the year ended July 1, 2006. The provision for income taxes for the year ended July 1, 2006, includes a tax provision calculated for taxable income generated at the foreign subsidiaries at rates below that of the United States statutory tax rate.

Fiscal Year Ended July 1, 2006, Compared to Fiscal Year Ended July 2, 2005

Research and Development Expense.   Research and development spending increased $2 million to $8.9 million compared to $6.9 million for fiscal year 2005. This increase was primarily attributable to $1.3 million of higher personnel expense due primarily to increased headcount, stock-based compensation and $0.7 million of other research and development related costs. As a percentage of revenue, research and development expenses were approximately 6% for 2006 and 2005.

Selling, General and Administrative Expense.   Selling, general and administrative expense increased to $44.3 million or 30% of revenue during fiscal 2006 compared to $40.2 million or 32% during fiscal 2005. Of the $4.1 million increase, $2.3 million was due to higher personnel expense for increased headcount, higher commission expense due to increased revenue, and stock-based compensation. The increase is also attributable to a $1 million increase in marketing-related expenses such as customer-related work-shops, advertising, trade shows, and an increase of $1 million due to an increase in legal and audit fees, excluding the litigation related charges for 2005 offset by a decrease in bad debt expense of approximately $0.4 million.

Other Income/Expense.   Total other income increased $1.2 million for the fiscal year 2006 to $1.7 million, from $0.6 million for the fiscal year 2005. This increase is related primarily to interest earned from the increase in our cash and cash equivalents, marketable securities and long-term investments and an increase in interest rates.

Income Taxes. The provision for income taxes results from a combination of activities of both the domestic and foreign subsidiaries. We recorded a 33% effective tax rate for the year ended July 1, 2006, compared to a 25.3% effective tax rate for the year ended July 2, 2005. During the year ended July 2, 2005, the Company recorded a benefit for the utilization of deferred tax assets which was not applicable during the current fiscal year ended 2006.

Liquidity and Capital Resources

Cash used by operating activities amounted to $7.7 million for fiscal 2007 as compared to cash provided by operations of $14.4 million for fiscal 2006. This decrease in cash provided by operating activities was due to: (a) a decrease in year-over-year net income of approximately $8.6 million; (b) a year-over-year increase in inventory of approximately $4.7 million due to the inability to ship new products at year end; and, (c) a year-over-year increase in accounts receivable of approximately $4.7 million due primarily to increases in international receivables that typically have slightly longer payment terms.

Notes to Consolidated Financial Statements

4. **Property and Equipment**
    Property and equipment consist of the following:

	June 30, 2007	July 1, 2006
	(in thousands)	
Leasehold improvements	$ 1,014	$ 920
Office furniture	662	603
Computers, software, and other equipment	10,044	9,236
	$11,720	$10,759
Less: accumulated depreciation and amortization	(8,241)	(7,457)
Property and equipment, net	$ 3,479	$ 3,302

Depreciation expense was approximately $1.0 million, $0.6 million, and $0.8 million for the fiscal years ended 2007, 2006 and 2005, respectively.

5. **Acquisitions**
    On March 6, 2007, we acquired Inolase (2002) Ltd. ("Inolase") a non-public company engaged in the development and manufacture of proprietary devices for the aesthetic light-based treatment industry as well as the development of intellectual property related to medical devices and light sources. The aggregate purchase price was approximately $16.8 million in cash, including $0.3 million of acquisition-related transaction costs. No Candela common stock was issued in the acquisition. The

acquisition-related transactions costs included legal, accounting, and other external costs directly related to the acquisition. Results of operations for Inolase have been included in the accompanying consolidated statement of operations since the date of acquisition.

This acquisition was accounted for as a business combination. Assets acquired and liabilities assumed were recorded as their fair values as of March 6, 2007. The fair value of intangible assets were based on valuations using an income approach, with estimates and assumption provided by management of Inolase and Candela. The excess of the purchase price over the fair value of tangible assets, identified intangible assets, and liabilities assumed were recorded as goodwill.

The agreement to purchase Inolase contains certain earn-out provisions and we are currently assessing the likelihood of their attainment. If we conclude that the outcome of these contingencies is determinable beyond a reasonable doubt, and that they are directly attributable to the purchase price itself, such a conclusion would result in an adjustment to goodwill and the establishment of an additional liability when the purchase-price allocation is finalized. Our final evaluation may also conclude that these provisions are directly attributable to the purchase price itself, but that we are unable to presently calculate the additional future amounts to be paid. If this is our conclusion, any future earn-out payments would represent increases to goodwill in the period(s) in which they are made. The purchase-price allocation is based upon the external valuation, but is preliminary pending our final determination in the above-mentioned area.

Based upon the valuations, the total purchase price was allocated as follows:

	(in thousands)
Goodwill	$10,997
Identifiable intangible assets	7,433
Inventory	214
Accounts receivable & other assets	195
Accounts payable and accrued expenses	(248)
Deferred tax liability	(1,581)
Other liabilities	(201)
Total preliminary purchase price allocation	$16,809

Identifiable intangible assets acquired consisted of patents related to PSF and developed technology related to PSF. Core technology represents a combination of Inolase's processes, inventions and trade secrets related to the design and development of its products. Developed and core technologies totaled $7.4 million and are being amortized over 6 years.

None of the goodwill or intangible assets acquired in the acquisition is deductible for income tax purposes. As a result, and in accordance with SFAS 109, *Income Taxes*, we recorded in the purchase accounting a deferred tax liability of $1.6 million, equal to the tax effect of the amount of the acquired intangible assets other than goodwill.

This transaction resulted in $11.0 million of purchase price that exceeded the estimated fair values of tangible and intangible assets and liabilities, all of which was allocated to goodwill. We believe that such excess in purchase price for accounting purposes was warranted by certain factors, including: (1) the potential to facilitate up-sell and cross-sell opportunities for our products with that of Inolase; (2) the potential to exploit reduced pain applications across our existing and future products; and (3) the potential to leverage Inolase intellectual property into home use applications.

8. Debt, Lease and Other Obligations

Line of Credit. The Company has a renewable $10,000,000 revolving credit agreement with a major bank with interest at the bank's base rate or LIBOR plus 2.25 percent. Any borrowings outstanding under the line of credit are due on demand or according to a payment schedule established at the time funds are borrowed. The line of credit is unsecured. The agreement contains restrictive covenants limiting the establishment of new liens, and the purchase of margin stock. No amounts were outstanding under the line of credit as of June 30, 2007, or July 1, 2006.

Restricted Cash. A financing company used by customers has limited recourse with the Company on a small number of product leases. As such, the Company has placed approximately $0.1 million and $0.2 million in restricted funds at this institution as collateral as of June 30, 2007, and July 1, 2006, respectively. This restricted cash represents the entire exposure under these agreements.

Operating Lease Commitments. The Company leases several facilities and automobiles under non-cancelable lease arrangements. The facility leases may be adjusted for increases in maintenance and insurance costs above specified levels. In addition, certain facility leases contain escalation provisions based on certain inflationary indices. These operating leases expire in various years through fiscal year 2012. These leases may be renewed for periods ranging from one to five years.

Outstanding lease commitments are reflected in the following table as of June 30, 2007:

	Amount (in thousands)
2008	$1,690
2009	856
2010	326
2011	175
2012	18
Thereafter	—
Total minimum lease payments	$3,065

Total rent expense was approximately $1.2 million, $0.9 million, and $1.4 million in fiscal years 2007, 2006, and 2005, respectively.

Schedule II
Candela Corporation
Valuation and Qualifying Accounts
For the years ended June 30, 2007, July 1, 2006, and July 2, 2005

	Balance at Beginning of Period	Additions Charged to Income	Deductions from Reserves	Balance at End of Period
	(In thousands)			
Reserves deducted from assets to which they apply:				
Allowance for doubtful accounts:				
Year ended June 30, 2007	$1,830	$989	$1,407	$1,412
Year ended July 1, 2006	2,065	1,241	1,475	1,831
Year ended July 2, 2005	1,492	2,806	2,233	2,065

APPENDIX A
SUMMARY OF FINANCIAL RATIOS

Ratio	Method of Computation	Significance
Liquidity:		
Current	$$\frac{\text{Current assets}}{\text{Current liabilities}}$$	Measures short-term liquidity, the ability of a firm to meet needs for cash as they arise.
Quick or acid-test	$$\frac{\text{Current assets} - \text{inventory}}{\text{Current liabilities}}$$	Measures short-term liquidity more rigorously than the current ratio by eliminating inventory, usually the least liquid current asset.
Cash flow liquidity	$$\frac{\text{Cash} + \text{marketable securities} + \text{cash flow from operating activities}}{\text{Current liabilities}}$$	Measures short-term liquidity by considering as cash resources (numerator) cash plus cash equivalents plus cash flow from operating activities.
Average collection period	$$\frac{\text{Net accounts receivable}}{\text{Average daily sales}}$$	Indicates days required to convert receivables into cash.
Days inventory held	$$\frac{\text{Inventory}}{\text{Average daily cost of sales}}$$	Indicates days required to sell inventory.
Days payable outstanding	$$\frac{\text{Accounts payable}}{\text{Average daily cost of sales}}$$	Indicates days required to pay suppliers.
Cash conversion or net trade cycle	Average collection period + days inventory held − days payable outstanding	Indicates the days in the normal operating cycle or cash conversion cycle of a firm.
Activity:		
Accounts receivable turnover	$$\frac{\text{Net sales}}{\text{Net accounts receivable}}$$	Indicates how many times receivables are collected during a year, on average.
Inventory turnover	$$\frac{\text{Cost of goods sold}}{\text{Inventories}}$$	Measures efficiency of the firm in managing and selling inventory.
Payables turnover	$$\frac{\text{Cost of goods sold}}{\text{Accounts payable}}$$	Measures efficiency of the firm in paying suppliers.
Fixed asset turnover	$$\frac{\text{Net sales}}{\text{Net property, plant, and equipment}}$$	Measures efficiency of the firm in managing fixed assets.
Total asset turnover	$$\frac{\text{Net sales}}{\text{Total assets}}$$	Measures efficiency of the firm in managing all assets.

Ratio	Method of Computation	Significance
Leverage:		
Debt ratio	$$\frac{\text{Total liabilities}}{\text{Total assets}}$$	Shows proportion of all assets that are financed with debt.
Long-term debt to total capitalization	$$\frac{\text{Long-term debt}}{\text{Long-term debt} + \text{stockholders' equity}}$$	Measures the extent to which long-term debt is used for permanent financing.
Debt to equity	$$\frac{\text{Total liabilities}}{\text{Stockholders' equity}}$$	Measures debt relative to equity base.
Financial leverage index	$$\frac{\text{Return on equity}}{\text{Adjusted return on assets}}$$	Indicates whether a firm is employing debt successfully.
Times interest earned	$$\frac{\text{Operating profit}}{\text{Interest expense}}$$	Measures how many times interest expense is covered by operating earnings.
Cash interest coverage	$$\frac{\text{Cash flow from operating activities} + \text{interest paid} + \text{taxes paid}}{\text{Interest paid}}$$	Measures how many times interest payments are covered by cash flow from operating activities.
Fixed charge coverage	$$\frac{\text{Operating profit} + \text{lease payments}}{\text{Interest expense} + \text{lease payments}}$$	Measures coverage capability more broadly than times interest earned by including operating lease payments as a fixed expense.
Cash flow adequacy	$$\frac{\text{Cash flow from operating activities}}{\text{Capital expenditures} + \text{debt repayments} + \text{dividends paid}}$$	Measures how many times capital expenditures, debt repayments, and cash dividends are covered by operating cash flow.
Profitability:		
Gross profit margin	$$\frac{\text{Gross profit}}{\text{Net sales}}$$	Measures profit generated after consideration of cost of products sold.
Operating profit margin	$$\frac{\text{Operating profit}}{\text{Net sales}}$$	Measures profit generated after consideration of operating expenses.
Effective tax rate	$$\frac{\text{Income taxes}}{\text{Earnings before income taxes}}$$	Measures the percentage the company recognizes as tax expense relative to income before taxes.
Net profit margin	$$\frac{\text{Net profit}}{\text{Net sales}}$$	Measures profit generated after consideration of all expenses and revenues.

Cash flow margin	$$\dfrac{\text{Cash flow from operating activities}}{\text{Net sales}}$$	Measures the ability of the firm to generate cash from sales.
Return on total assets	$$\dfrac{\text{Net earnings}}{\text{Total assets}}$$	Measures overall efficiency of firm in managing assets and generating profits.
Return on equity	$$\dfrac{\text{Net earnings}}{\text{Stockholders' equity}}$$	Measures rate of return on stockholders' (owners') investment.
Cash return on assets	$$\dfrac{\text{Cash flow from operating activities}}{\text{Total assets}}$$	Measures the return on assets on a cash basis.

Market:

Earnings per common share	$$\dfrac{\text{Net earnings}}{\text{Average common shares outstanding}}$$	Shows return to common stock shareholders for each share owned.
Price to earnings	$$\dfrac{\text{Market price of common stock}}{\text{Earnings per share}}$$	Expresses a multiple that the stock market places on a firm's earnings.
Dividend payout	$$\dfrac{\text{Dividends per share}}{\text{Earnings per share}}$$	Shows percentage of earnings paid to shareholders.
Dividend yield	$$\dfrac{\text{Dividends per share}}{\text{Market price of common stock}}$$	Shows the rate earned by shareholders from dividends relative to current price of stock.

APPENDIX B
SOLUTIONS TO SELF-TESTS

Chapter 1

1. (d)
2. (c)
3. (a)
4. (d)
5. (d)
6. (b)
7. (a)
8. (c)
9. (d)
10. (b)
11. (d)
12. (d)
13. (d)
14. (d)
15. (1) c
    (2) b
    (3) a
    (4) c
    (5) b
    (6) a
    (7) d
    (8) b
    (9) d
    (10) a or b

Chapter 2

1. (b)
2. (a)
3. (c)
4. (b)
5. (b)
6. (a)
7. (d)
8. (c)
9. (b)
10. (c)
11. (d)
12. (a)
13. (c)
14. (b)
15. (d)

16. (a)
17. (c)
18. (b)
19. (b)
20. (d)
21. (d)
22. (c)
23. (a) NC
    (b) C
    (c) C
    (d) C or NC
    (e) NC
    (f) C
    (g) C
    (h) C
    (i) NC
    (j) NC
24. (a) 4
    (b) 5
    (c) 8
    (d) 7
    (e) 1
    (f) 2
    (g) 2
    (h) 5
    (i) 8
    (j) 5
    (k) 3
    (l) 2
    (m) 1
    (n) 6
    (o) 8
25. (a) 7
    (b) 1
    (c) 5
    (d) 9
    (e) 4
    (f) 6
    (g) 10
    (h) 2
    (i) 3
    (j) 8

Chapter 3

1. (c)
2. (d)
3. (a)
4. (c)
5. (d)
6. (a)
7. (c)
8. (d)
9. (d)
10. (b)
11. (b)
12. (a)
13. (d)
14. (c)
15. (d)
16. (c)
17. (b)
18. (d)
19. (a) 4
    (b) 9
    (c) 13
    (d) 8
    (e) 5
    (f) 14
    (g) 1
    (h) 6
    (i) 11
    (j) 2
    (k) 10
    (l) 12
    (m) 3
    (n) 7
20. (1) c
    (2) d
    (3) a
    (4) c
    (5) d
    (6) a
    (7) e
    (8) c
    (9) c

(10) b
(11) d
(12) c

Chapter 4

1. (d)
2. (a)
3. (b)
4. (a)
5. (c)
6. (d)
7. (b)
8. (c)
9. (c)
10. (b)
11. (b)
12. (c)
13. (a)
14. (d)
15. (d)
16. (c)
17. (d)
18. (d)
19. (b)
20. (d)
21. (c)
22. (b)
23. (a)
24. (b)
25. (a)
26. (d)

Chapter 5

1. (c)
2. (a)
3. (b)
4. (d)
5. (b)
6. (b)
7. (c)
8. (a)

9. (d)
10. (c)
11. (a)
12. (b)
13. (d)
14. (c)
15. (d)
16. (a)
17. (d)
18. (c)
19. (b)
20. (a)

Chapter 6

1. (c)
2. (a)
3. (d)
4. (c)
5. (d)
6. (d)
7. (a)
8. (b)
9. (d)
10. (c)
11. (a)

12. (c)
13. (d)
14. (b)
15. (a)
16. (d)
17. (c)
18. (d)
19. (a)
20. (b)
21. (c)
22. (a)
23. (c)

24. (b)
25. (d)
26. (b)
27. (a)
28. (c)
29. (a)
30. (c)
31. (b)
32. (d)
33. (a)
34. (c)
35. (a)

APPENDIX C
GLOSSARY

Accelerated Cost Recovery System The system established by the Economic Recovery Tax Act of 1981 to simplify depreciation methods for tax purposes and to encourage investment in capital by allowing rapid write-off of asset costs over predetermined periods, generally shorter than the estimated useful lives of the assets. The system remains in effect for assets placed in service between 1981 and 1986 but was modified by the Tax Reform Act of 1986 for assets placed in service after 1986. *See* Modified Accelerated Cost Recovery System.

Accelerated depreciation An accounting procedure under which larger amounts of expense are apportioned to the earlier years of an asset's depreciable life and lesser amounts to the later years.

Accounting period The length of time covered for reporting accounting information.

Accounting principles The methods and procedures used in preparing financial statements.

Accounts payable Amounts owed to creditors for items or services purchased from them.

Accounts receivable Amounts owed to an entity, primarily by its trade customers.

Accounts receivable turnover *See* Summary of financial ratios, Appendix A.

Accrual basis of accounting A method of earnings determination under which revenues are recognized in the accounting period when earned, regardless of when cash is received, and expenses are recognized in the period incurred, regardless of when cash is paid.

Accrued liabilities Obligations resulting from the recognition of an expense prior to the payment of cash.

Accumulated depreciation A balance sheet account indicating the amount of depreciation expense taken on plant and equipment up to the balance sheet date.

Accumulated other comprehensive income or loss An account that includes unrealized gains or losses in the market value of investments of marketable securities classified as available for sale, specific types of pension liability adjustments, certain gains and losses on derivative financial instruments, and foreign currency translation adjustments resulting when financial statements from a foreign currency are converted into U.S. dollars.

Acid-test ratio *See* Summary of financial ratios, Appendix A.

Activity ratio A ratio that measures the liquidity of specific assets and the efficiency of the firm in managing assets.

Additional paid-in-capital The amount by which the original sales price of stock shares sold exceeds the par value of the stock.

Adverse opinion Opinion rendered by an independent auditor stating that the financial statements have not been presented fairly in accordance with generally accepted accounting principles.

Allowance for doubtful accounts The balance sheet account that measures the amount of outstanding accounts receivable expected to be uncollectable.

Amortization The process of expense allocation applied to the cost expiration of intangible assets.

Annual report The report to shareholders published by a firm; contains information required by generally accepted accounting principles and/or by specific Securities and Exchange Commission requirements.

Asset impairment The decline in value of assets.

Assets Items possessing service or use potential to owner.

Auditor's report Report by independent auditor attesting to the fairness of the financial statements of a company.

Average collection period *See* Summary of financial ratios, Appendix A.

Average cost method A method of valuing inventory and cost of products sold; all costs, including those in beginning inventory, are added together and divided by the total number of units to arrive at a cost per unit.

Balance sheet The financial statement that shows the financial condition of a company on a particular date.

Balancing equation Assets = Liabilities + Stockholders' equity.

Basic earnings per share The earnings per share figure calculated by dividing net earnings available to common shareholders by the average number of common shares outstanding.

Book value *See* Net book value.

Calendar year The year starting January 1 and ending December 31.

Capital assets *See* Fixed assets.

Capital in excess of par value *See* Additional paid-in-capital.

Capital lease A leasing arrangement that is, in substance, a purchase by the lessee, who accounts for the lease as an acquisition of an asset and the incurrence of a liability.

Capital structure The permanent long-term financing of a firm represented by long-term debt, preferred stock, common stock, and retained earnings.

Capitalize The process whereby initial expenditures are included in the cost of assets and allocated over the period of service.

Cash basis of accounting A method of accounting under which revenues are recorded when cash is received and expenses are recognized when cash is paid.

Cash conversion cycle The amount of time (expressed in number of days) required to sell inventory and collect accounts receivable, less the number of days credit extended by suppliers.

Cash equivalents Security investments that are readily converted to cash.

Cash flow adequacy *See* Summary of financial ratios, Appendix A.

Cash flow from financing activities On the statement of cash flows, cash generated from/used by financing activities.

Cash flow from investing activities On the statement of cash flows, cash generated from/used by investing activities.

Cash flow from operating activities On the statement of cash flows, cash generated from/used by operating activities.

Cash flow from operations The amount of cash generated from/used by a business enterprise's normal, ongoing operations during an accounting period.

Cash flow liquidity ratio *See* Summary of financial ratios, Appendix A.

Cash flow margin *See* Summary of financial ratios, Appendix A.

Cash flow return on assets *See* Summary of financial ratios, Appendix A.

Cash interest coverage *See* Summary of financial ratios, Appendix A.

Commercial paper Unsecured promissory notes of large companies.

Commitments Contractual agreements that will have a significant impact on the company in the future.

Common-size financial statements A form of financial ratio analysis that allows the comparison of firms with different levels of sales or total assets by introducing a common denominator. A common-size balance sheet expresses each item on the balance sheet as a percentage of total assets, and a common-size income statement expresses each item as a percentage of net sales.

Common stock Shares of stock representing ownership in a company.

Complex capital structure Capital structures including convertible securities, stock options, and warrants.

Comprehensive income The concept that income should include all revenues, expenses, gains, and losses recognized during an accounting period, regardless of whether they are the results of operations.

Conservatism The accounting concept holding that in selecting among accounting methods the choice should be the one with the least favorable effect on the firm.

Consolidation The combination of financial statements for two or more separate legal entities when one company, the parent, owns more than 50% of the voting stock of the other company or companies.

Contingencies Potential liabilities of a company.

Contra-asset account An account shown as a deduction from the asset to which it relates in the balance sheet.

Convertible securities Securities that can be converted or exchanged for another type of security, typically common stock.

Core earnings *See* Pro forma earnings.

Cost flow assumption An assumption regarding the order in which inventory is sold; used to value cost of goods sold and ending inventory.

Cost method A procedure to account for investments in the voting stock of other companies under which the investor recognizes investment income only to the extent of any cash dividends received.

Cost of goods sold The cost to the seller of products sold to customers.

Cost of goods sold percentage The percentage of cost of goods sold to net sales.

Cost of sales *See* Cost of goods sold.

Cumulative effect of change in accounting principle The difference in the actual amount of retained earnings at the beginning of the period in which a change in accounting principle is instituted and the amount of retained earnings that would have been reported at that date if the new accounting principle had been applied retroactively for all prior periods.

Current (assets/liabilities) Items expected to be converted into cash or paid out in cash in one year or one operating cycle, whichever is longer.

Current maturities of long-term debt The portion of long-term debt that will be repaid during the upcoming year.

Current ratio *See* Summary of financial ratios, Appendix A.

Days inventory held *See* Summary of financial ratios, Appendix A.

Days payable outstanding *See* Summary of financial ratios, Appendix A.

Debt ratio *See* Summary of financial ratios, Appendix A.

Debt to equity ratio *See* Summary of financial ratios, Appendix A.

Deferred credits *See* Unearned revenue.

Deferred taxes The balance sheet account that results from temporary differences in the recognition of revenue and expense for taxable income and reported income.

Depletion The accounting procedure used to allocate the cost of acquiring and developing natural resources.

Depreciation The accounting procedure used to allocate the cost of an asset, which will benefit a business enterprise for more than a year, over the asset's service life.

Derivatives Financial instruments that derive their value from an underlying asset or index.

Diluted earnings per share The earnings per share figure calculated using all potentially dilutive securities in the number of shares outstanding.

Direct method On the statement of cash flows, a method of calculating cash flow from operating activities that shows cash collections from customers; interest and dividends collected; other operating cash receipts; cash paid to suppliers and employees; interest paid; taxes paid; and other operating cash payments.

Disclaimer of opinion Independent auditor could not evaluate the fairness of the financial statements and, as a result, expresses no opinion on them.

Discontinued operations The financial results of selling a major business segment.

Discretionary items Revenues and expenses under the control of management with respect to budget levels and timing.

Dividend payout ratio *See* Summary of financial ratios, Appendix A.

Dividend yield *See* Summary of financial ratios, Appendix A.

Double-declining balance method An accounting procedure for depreciation under which the straight-line rate of depreciation is doubled and applied to the net book value of the asset.

Du Pont System An analytical technique used to evaluate the profitability and return on equity for a firm.

EBITDA Earnings before interest, taxes, depreciation, and amortization. *See* Pro forma earnings.

Earnings before income taxes The profit recognized before the deduction of income taxes.

Earnings before interest and taxes The operating profit of a firm.

Earnings per common share *See* Summary of financial ratios, Appendix A.

Earnings statement *See* Income statement.

Effective tax rate *See* Summary of financial ratios, Appendix A.

Equity *See* Stockholders' equity.

Equity method The procedure used for an investment in common stock when the investor company can exercise significant influence over the investee company; the investor recognizes investment income of the investee's net income in proportion to the percentage of stock owned.

Expenses Cost incurred to produce revenue.

Extraordinary transactions Items that are unusual in nature and not expected to recur in the foreseeable future.

Financial Accounting Standards Board (FASB) The private-sector organization primarily responsible for establishing generally accepted accounting principles.

Financial leverage The extent to which a firm finances with debt, measured by the relationship between total debt and total assets.

Financial leverage index *See* Summary of financial ratios, Appendix A.

Financial ratios Calculations made to standardize, analyze, and compare financial data; expressed in terms of mathematical relationships in the form of percentages or times.

Financial statements Accounting information regarding the financial position of a firm, the results of operations, and the cash flows. Four statements comprise the basic set of financial statements: the balance sheet, the income statement, the statement of stockholder's equity, and the statement of cash flows.

Financing activities On the statement of cash flows, transactions that include borrowing from creditors and repaying the principal; obtaining resources from owners and providing them with a return on the investment.

Finished goods Products for which the manufacturing process is complete.

First-in, first-out (FIFO) A method of valuing inventory and cost of goods sold under which the items purchased first are assumed to be sold first.

Fiscal year A 12-month period starting on a date other than January 1 and ending 12 months later.

Fixed assets Tangible, long-lived assets that are expected to provide service benefit for more than one year.

Fixed asset turnover *See* Summary of financial ratios, Appendix A.

Fixed charge coverage *See* Summary of financial ratios, Appendix A.

Foreign currency translation effects Adjustment to the equity section of the balance sheet resulting from the translation of foreign financial statements.

Form 10-K An annual document filed with the Securities and Exchange Commission by companies that sell securities to the public.

Form 10-Q A quarterly report filed with the Securities and Exchange Commission by companies that sell securities to the public.

Generally accepted accounting principles The accounting methods and procedures used to prepare financial statements.

Goodwill An intangible asset representing the unrecorded assets of a firm; appears in the accounting records only if the firm is acquired for a price in excess of the fair market value of its net assets.

Gross margin *See* Gross profit.

Gross profit The difference between net sales and cost of goods sold.

Gross profit margin *See* Summary of financial ratios, Appendix A.

Historical cost The amount of cash or value of other resources used to acquire an asset; for some assets, historical cost is subject to depreciation, amortization, or depletion.

Income statement The financial statement presenting the revenues and expenses of a business enterprise for an accounting period.

Indirect method On the statement of cash flows, a method of calculating cash flow from operating activities that adjusts net income for deferrals, accruals, and noncash and nonoperating items.

Industry comparisons Average financial ratios compiled for industry groups.

In-process research and development One-time charges taken at the time of an acquisition to write-off amounts of research and development that are not considered viable.

Intangible assets Assets such as goodwill that possess no physical characteristics but have value for the company.

Integrated disclosure system A common body of information required by the Securities and Exchange Commission for both the 10-K Report filed with the Securities and Exchange Commission and the annual report provided to shareholders.

Interim statements Financial statements issued for periods shorter than one year.

International Accounting Standards Board (IASB) The international organization responsible for establishing accounting standards and promoting worldwide acceptance of those standards.

International Financial Reporting Standards (IFRS) The accounting standards established by the International Accounting Standards Board.

Inventories Items held for sale or used in the manufacture of products that will be sold.

Inventory turnover *See* Summary of financial ratios, Appendix A.

Investing activities On the statement of cash flows, transactions that include acquiring and selling or otherwise disposing of (1) securities that are not cash equivalents and (2) productive assets that are expected to benefit the firm for long periods of time; lending money and collecting on loans.

Last-in, first-out (LIFO) A method of valuing inventory and cost of goods sold under which the items purchased last are assumed to be sold first.

Leasehold improvement An addition or improvement made to a leased structure.

Leverage ratio A ratio that measures the extent of a firm's financing with debt relative to equity and its ability to cover interest and other fixed charges.

Liabilities Claims against assets.

Line of credit A prearranged loan allowing borrowing up to a certain maximum amount.

Liquidity The ability of a firm to generate sufficient cash to meet cash needs.

Liquidity ratio A ratio that measures a firm's ability to meet needs for cash as they arise.

Long-term debt Obligations with maturities longer than one year.

Long-term debt to total capitalization *See* Summary of financial ratios, Appendix A.

Lower of cost or market method A method of valuing inventory under which cost or market, whichever is lower, is selected for each item, each group, or for the entire inventory.

Management Discussion and Analysis (MD&A) of the Financial Condition and Results of Operation A section of the annual and 10-K report that is required and monitored by the Securities and Exchange Commission in which management presents detailed coverage of the firm's liquidity, capital resources, and operations.

Mandatorily redeemable preferred stock Securities that have characteristics of both debt and equity.

Market ratio A ratio that measures returns to stockholders and the value the marketplace puts on a company's stock.

Marketable securities Cash not needed immediately in the business and temporarily invested to earn a return; also referred to as short-term investments.

Matching principle The accounting principle holding that expenses are to be matched with the generation of revenues to determine net income for an accounting period.

Merchandise inventories Goods purchased for resale to the public.

Minority interest Claims of shareholders other than the parent company against the net assets and net income of a subsidiary company.

Modified accelerated cost recovery system (MACRS) A modification of the accelerated tax recovery system (ACRS) in the Tax Reform Act of 1986 for assets placed in service after 1986.

Multiple-step format A format for presenting the income statement under which several intermediate profit measures are shown.

Net assets Total assets less total liabilities.

Net book value of capital assets The difference between original cost of property, plant, and equipment and any accumulated depreciation to date.

Net earnings The firm's profit or loss after consideration of all revenue and expense reported during the accounting period.

Net income *See* Net earnings.

Net profit margin *See* Summary of financial ratios, Appendix A.

Net sales Total sales revenue less sales returns and sales allowances.

Net trade cycle *See* Cash conversion cycle and Summary of financial ratios, Appendix A.

Noncurrent assets/liabilities Items expected to benefit the firm for/with maturities of more than one year.

Notes payable A short-term obligation in the form of a promissory note to suppliers or financial institutions.

Notes to the financial statements Supplementary information to financial statements that explain the firm's accounting policies and provide detail about particular accounts and other information such as pension plans.

Off–balance-sheet financing Financial techniques for raising funds that do not have to be recorded as liabilities on the balance sheet.

Operating activities On the statement of cash flows, transactions that include delivering or producing goods for sale and providing services; the cash effects of transactions and other events that enter into the determination of income.

Operating cycle The time required to purchase or manufacture inventory, sell the product, and collect the cash.

Operating efficiency The efficiency of a firm in managing its assets.

Operating expenses Costs related to the normal functions of a business.

Operating lease A rental agreement wherein no ownership rights are transferred to the lessee at the termination of the rental contract.

Operating profit Sales revenue less the expenses associated with generating sales. Operating profit measures the overall performance of a company on its normal, ongoing operations.

Operating profit margin *See* Summary of financial ratios, Appendix A.

Options *See* Stock options.

Par value The floor price below which stock cannot be sold initially.

Payables turnover *See* Summary of financial ratios, Appendix A.

Plant and equipment *See* Fixed assets.

Preferred stock Capital stock of a company that carries certain privileges or rights not carried by all outstanding shares of stock.

Premature revenue recognition Recording revenue before it should be recorded in order to increase earnings.

Prepaid expenses Expenditures made in the current or prior period that will benefit the firm at some future time.

Price-earnings ratio *See* Summary of financial ratios, Appendix A.

Principal The original amount of a liability.

Prior period adjustment A change in the retained earnings balance primarily resulting from the correction of errors made in previous accounting periods.

Pro forma earnings Alternative earnings numbers that adjust net income in some way for items not expected to be part of ongoing business operations.

Pro forma financial statements Projections of future financial statements based on a set of assumptions regarding future revenues, expenses, level of investment in assets, financing methods and costs, and working capital management.

Profitability ratio A ratio that measures the overall performance of a firm and its efficiency in managing assets, liabilities, and equity.

Property, plant, and equipment *See* Fixed assets.

Proxy statement A document required by the SEC that companies use to solicit shareholders' votes and that contains information about directors, director and executive compensation plans, and the audit committee report.

Public Company Accounting Oversight Board (PCAOB) A private, nonprofit organization with the authority to register, inspect, and discipline auditors of all publicly owned companies.

Publicly held companies Companies that operate to earn a profit and issue shares of stock to the public.

Qualified opinion An opinion rendered by an independent auditor when the overall financial statements are fairly presented "except for" certain items (which the auditor discloses).

Quality of financial reporting A subjective evaluation of the extent to which financial reporting is free of manipulation and accurately reflects the financial condition and operating success of a business enterprise.

Quick ratio *See* Summary of financial ratios, Appendix A.

Raw materials Basic commodities or natural resources that will be used in the production of goods.

Replacement cost The estimated cost of acquiring new and substantially equivalent property at current prices.

Reported income The net income published in financial statements.

Reserve accounts Accounts used to estimate obligations, recorded as accrued liabilities; also to record declines in asset values, recorded as contra-asset accounts.

Restructuring charges Costs to reorganize a company.

Retained earnings The sum of every dollar a company has earned since its inception, less any payments made to shareholders in the form of cash or stock dividends.

Return on equity *See* Summary of financial ratios, Appendix A.

Return on investment *See* Return on total assets.

Return on total assets *See* Summary of financial ratios, Appendix A.

Revenue The inflow of assets resulting from the sale of goods or services.

Reverse stock split Decreasing the number of shares of outstanding stock to existing stockholders in proportion to current ownership, usually to increase the market price of a firm's stock.

Sales allowance A deduction from the original sales invoice price.

Sales return A cancellation of a sale.

Salvage value The amount of an asset estimated to be recoverable at the conclusion of the asset's service life.

Sarbanes-Oxley Act of 2002 Legislation passed by the U.S. Congress in hopes of ending future accounting scandals and renewing investor confidence in the marketplace.

Securities and Exchange Commission (SEC) The public-sector organization primarily responsible for establishing generally accepted accounting principles.

Selling and administrative expenses Costs relating to the sale of products or services and to the management function of the firm.

Short-term Generally indicates maturity of less than a year.

Single-step format A format for presenting the income statement under which all items of revenue are grouped together and then all items of expense are deducted to arrive at net income.

Stated value The floor price below which stock cannot be sold initially; *see also* par value.

Statement of cash flows The financial statement that provides information about the cash inflows and outflows from operating, financing, and investing activities during an accounting period.

Statement of financial position *See* Balance sheet.

Statement of retained earnings The financial statement that presents the details of the transactions affecting the retained earnings account during an accounting period.

Statement of stockholders' equity A financial statement that summarizes changes in the shareholders' equity section of the balance sheet during an accounting period.

Stock dividends The issuance of additional shares of stock to existing shareholders in proportion to current ownership.

Stock options A contract that conveys the right to purchase shares of stock at a specified price within a specified time period.

Stock splits The issuance of additional shares of stock to existing shareholders in proportion to current ownership, usually to lower the market price of a firm's stock.

Stockholders' equity Claims against assets by the owners of the business; represents the amount owners have invested including income retained in the business since inception.

Straight-line depreciation An accounting procedure under which equal amounts of expense are apportioned to each year of an asset's life.

Structural analysis Analysis looking at the internal structure of a business enterprise.

Summary of financial ratios *See* Summary of financial ratios, Appendix A.

Tangible Having physical substance.

Taxable income The net income figure used to determine taxes payable to governments.

Temporary differences Differences between pretax accounting income and taxable income caused by reporting items of revenue or expense in one period for accounting purposes and in an earlier or later period for income tax purposes.

Times interest earned *See* Summary of financial ratios, Appendix A.

Total asset turnover *See* Summary of financial ratios, Appendix A.

Treasury stock Shares of a company's stock that are repurchased by the company and not retired.

Trend analysis Evaluation of financial data over several accounting periods.

Unearned revenue A liability caused by receipt of cash in advance of earning revenue.

Units-of-production method An accounting method under which depreciation expense is based on actual usage.

Unqualified opinion An opinion rendered by an independent auditor of financial statements stating that the financial statements have been presented fairly in accordance with generally accepted accounting principles.

Unqualified opinion with explanatory language An opinion rendered by an independent auditor of financial statements stating that the financial statements have been presented fairly in accordance with generally accepted accounting principles, but there are items which the auditor wishes to explain to the user.

Unrealized gains (losses) on marketable equity securities The gains (losses) disclosed in the equity section resulting from the accounting rule that requires investments in marketable equity securities to be carried at the lower of cost or market value.

Warrant A certificate issued by a corporation that conveys the right to buy a stated number of shares of stock at a specified price on or before a predetermined date.

Work-in-process Products for which the manufacturing process is only partially completed.

Working capital The amount by which current assets exceed current liabilities.

INDEX

A

Accelerated Cost Recovery System (ACRS). *See* Modified Accelerated Cost Recovery System
Accelerated depreciation. *See* Depreciation
Accounting changes, 88, 92, 96, 115, 148
  effect on earnings, 115
  impact on earnings quality, 149, 150, 153
Accounting estimates, 21, 79, 148
Accounting for income taxes, 55, 57, 59, 90–91, 106, 167, 245, 246
Accounting for investments in debt and equity securities, 41–42, 88, 94
Accounting for postemployment benefits, 60–61
Accounting for postretirement benefits other than pensions, 60–61
Accounting period, 37
Accounting policies. *See* Accounting principles
Accounting principles, 3–4, 22–29
  accrual basis of accounting, 89
  conservatism, 23
  cumulative effect of changes, 92, 96
  matching, 22–23, 55
Accounting Principles Board Opinion No. 18, 89
Accounting Principles Board Opinion No. 20, 92
Accounting Series Releases (ASRs), 4
Accounting Trends and Techniques, 47, 50, 114
Accounts payable, 35, 52–53, 57, 113, 116, 121, 122, 146, 173, 192–193, 205
  effect of change on cash flow, 115, 116
Accounts payable turnover, 193, 204
Accounts receivable, 19, 23, 42–44, 55, 113, 116, 121, 123, 144, 150, 153, 154, 171, 173, 189, 190, 192, 193, 194, 201, 204, 205, 233
  effect of change on cash flow, 115, 116
  impact on earnings quality, 42
Accounts receivable turnover, 192, 194, 201
Accrual basis of accounting, 89

Accrued liabilities, 52, 54, 57, 113, 146
  effect of change on cash flow, 114, 115, 116
Accumulated depreciation. *See* Depreciation
Accumulated other comprehensive income or loss. *See* Comprehensive income
Acid-test ratio. *See* Quick ratio
Activity ratio, 186, 189
Additional paid-in capital, 62, 94, 111
  effect of change on cash flow, 117–118
Administrative expenses, 85
Adverse opinion, 15, 182
Advertising expenses, 85–86, 87, 159
Allowance for doubtful accounts, 42–44, 55, 153, 161
  impact on earnings quality, 149, 153
American Institute of Certified Public Accountants (AICPA), 47, 50, 114
Amortization, 51, 85, 86–87, 92, 96, 114–116, 146, 170
  bond discounts and premiums, 116
Analytical tools and techniques, 3, 214
Annual reports, 2–4, 14, 18, 23, 64, 79
Annual Statement Studies, 45, 73, 183, 203
Apple Inc., 20
Applied Materials, Inc., 57, 93, 167–168
Asset impairment, 160–161
Assets
  current, 40–42
  fixed, 49, 51–52
  noncurrent, 52, 57, 235
Auditor's Report, 10, 15, 182
  adverse opinion, 15, 182
  disclaimer of opinion, 15, 182
  qualified, 15, 182
  unqualified, 14–15, 16
Average collection period, 190–191, 193, 201
Average cost method. *See* Inventory, Average cost method

B

Bad debt expense, 42, 153, 154
Balance sheet, 36–64
  common size, 37–40, 204
  comparative data, 37

consolidation, 37
  date, 37
  quality of financial reporting, 171
Balancing equation, 37
Bally, 150–151
Bankruptcy, 123–124,
Base LIFO layer liquidations, 48, 157–158
  impact on earnings quality, 149, 157–158
Basic earnings per share. *See* Earnings per share
Book value, 49, 52
Buildings, 50–52
Business combinations, 52
Business Week, 20

C

Calendar year, 37
Candela Corporation, 84, 237, 239, 240, 242, 249
Capital assets. *See* Fixed assets
Capital in excess of par value. *See* Additional paid-in capital
Capital lease, 60, 61, 172
Capital structure, 40, 62, 92–93, 194, 195, 205–209
Capitalized lease. *See* Capital lease
Cash, 41–42, 110, 118
Cash basis of accounting, 21, 22, 54
Cash conversion cycle, 191–192, 193, 201, 204
Cash equivalents. *See* Cash
Cash flows, 107–127
Cash flow adequacy, 196–197, 201, 209
Cash flow from financing activities, 117–118
Cash flow from investing activities, 116–117
Cash flow from operating activities, 113–116
  direct method, 114, 144
  indirect method, 114–116
Cash flow from operations. *See* Cash flow from operating activities
Cash flow liquidity ratio, 189–190, 201, 204
Cash flow margin, 198, 201, 210
Cash interest coverage, 195, 209
Cash return on assets, 198–199, 201, 210
Caterpillar, 173
CFO, 5, 16–17
Change in accounting principle. *See* Accounting changes
Checklist of earnings quality, 149

Cisco, 140, 161
CNN Financial Network, 184
Commercial paper, 41, 110
Commitments, 61, 106, 172
Common size financial statements, 37–38, 81, 185–186, 201
balance sheet, 36–64
income statement, 79–94
Common stock, 62, 92–93, 94, 169–170
effect of change on cash flows, 117
impact on earnings quality, 93
Common stock in treasury. *See* Treasury stock
Communications Consulting Worldwide, Inc., 20
Comparative data, 37
Complex capital structure, 92–93
Comprehensive income, 63–64, 81, 93–94
Computer Associates, 151
Concert.com, 151
Conservatism, 23
impact on earnings quality, 23
Consolidated statements, 34
Consolidated financial statements for R.E.C. Inc., 12, 75, 88–89, 142, 231–238
Consumer Price Index, 82, 155
Contingencies, 61, 106, 172
Convertible securities, 92–93
Core earnings. *See* Pro forma earnings
Cost flow assumptions, 46, 48, 83
impact on earnings quality, 156, 158
Cost method, 46, 64, 89, 92
Cost of goods sold, 45–47, 83, 84, 116, 156–159
Cost of goods sold percentage, 83–84
Cost of sales. *See* Cost of goods sold
Cumulative effect of change in accounting principle, 92, 96
Cumulative translation adjustment, 64
Current assets, 40–41
Current liabilities, 52
Current maturities of long-term debt, 54
effect of change on cash flows, 117
Current ratio, 188–189, 190, 201

D

Days inventory held, 191, 193, 201
Days payable outstanding, 191, 193, 201
Debt financing and coverage. *See* Leverage ratios
Debt ratio, 194–195, 206
Debt to equity ratio, 195
Debt securities, 41, 233
Deferred credits, 55

Deferred federal income taxes. *See* Deferred taxes
Deferred taxes, 55–57
Dell, 151
Depletion, 86
Depreciation
accelerated, 49, 50, 55, 159–160
accumulated, 50, 51, 111, 113, 116, 146
double declining balance, 49
effect of change on cash flow, 114–115
impact on earnings quality, 160
straight-line, 49, 50, 55, 159–160
units of production, 50
Derivatives, 94
Diluted earnings per share. *See* Earnings per share
Dilution, 93
Direct method, 114, 144
Disclaimer of opinion, 15, 182
Discontinued operations, 79, 91, 168
Discretionary items, 23, 159
long-run impact of reductions, 159
Dividends
cash, 89–90
effect of change on cash flow, 111
stock, 62, 95
Dividend payout ratio, 199, 200
Dividend yield, 199, 200
Dollar-value LIFO, 48
Double-declining balance method. *See* Depreciation
Dun & Bradstreet, Inc., 183, 184, 203

E

Early extinguishment of debt, 168
EBITDA, 96, 170
Earnings before income taxes, 90
Earnings before interest and taxes. *See* Operating profit
Earnings per common share, 92–93, 199
Earnings per share, 93, 169, 199
basic, 93
diluted, 93
Earnings quality. *See* Quality of financial reporting
Earnings statement. *See* Income statement
Eastman Kodak Company. *See* Kodak
Effective tax rate, 90–91
Enron, 5, 16, 17, 21, 172, 199
Equipment. *See* Property, plant and equipment
Equity income, 167
impact on earnings quality, 111
Equity method, 89–90, 116, 167
Equity securities, 41–42, 88, 111, 160
Expenses
administrative, 85
advertising, 85–86, 87, 159

amortization, 55–57, 85, 86–87, 114–116, 159–160
bad debt, 42
cost of goods sold, 45–47, 83, 84, 116, 156–159
depreciation, 49–51, 55–57, 85, 86–87, 114–116, 146, 159–160
interest, 88
leases, 86
operating, 85, 159–160
repairs and maintenance, 85, 87
research and development, 87
selling, 83, 85
Extraordinary transactions, 79, 91, 168–169
impact on earnings quality, 172–173, 174

F

F.A.S.B. *See* Financial Accounting Standards Board
FIFO. *See* Inventory, FIFO
Financial Accounting Standards Board
Statement of Financial Accounting Concepts No. 3, 92
Statement of Financial Accounting Standards No. 4, 169
Statement of Financial Accounting Concepts No. 6, 81
Statement of Financial Accounting Standards No. 13, 60, 169
Statement of Financial Accounting Standards No. 44, 169
Statement of Financial Accounting Standards No. 52, 94
Statement of Financial Accounting Standards No. 64, 169
Statement of Financial Accounting Standards No. 87, 162
Statement of Financial Accounting Standards No. 95, 107, 231
Statement of Financial Accounting Standards No. 96, 55
Statement of Financial Accounting Standards No. 106, 60
Statement of Financial Accounting Standards No. 109, 55, 56
Statement of Financial Accounting Standards No. 112, 60
Statement of Financial Accounting Standards No. 115, 88, 89, 94
Statement of Financial Accounting Standards No. 123, 5
Statement of Financial Accounting Standards No. 130, 63
Statement of Financial Accounting Standards No. 131, 21
Statement of Financial Accounting Standards No. 133, 94

Statement of Financial Accounting Standards No. 144, 161
Statement of Financial Accounting Standards No. 145, 168
Statement of Financial Accounting Standards No. 146, 54
Statement of Financial Accounting Standards No. 150, 61
Statement of Financial Accounting Standards No. 154, 92
Statement of Financial Accounting Standards No. 159, 42
Financial Analysts Journal, 119, 162
Financial leverage, 194–209, 211–212
Financial leverage index, 206
Financial ratios, 186–188
Financial Reporting Rulings (FRRs), 4
Financial statements
 analysis, 180–214
 balance sheet, 7, 36–64
 complexity, 21–22
 income statement, 79–94
 notes to, 7–10
 objectives, 180–181
 obstacles to understanding, 1–3
 statement of cash flows, 7, 107–127, 144–147
 statement of retained earnings, 7
 statement of stockholders' equity, 7, 94–96
 supplementary information, 9, 20–21
Financing activities. *See* Cash flow from financing activities
Finished goods, 44
First-in-first-out. *See* FIFO
Fiscal year, 37
Fixed assets
 gain/losses on sales, 116
 impact on earnings quality, 116–117
 loss recognition on write-downs, 158–159
Fixed asset turnover ratio, 205
Fixed charge coverage ratio, 195, 196, 209
Forbes, 184
Ford Motor Company, 158, 173
Foreign currency translation, 10, 64, 94
Form 8-K, 6
Form 10-K, 6, 44, 183
Form 10-Q, 183
Fortune, 184
Functional currency, 94

G

Gale Research, Inc., 183, 184
General Electric Company, 19, 91
Generally accepted accounting principles. *See* Accounting principles

General Motors Corporation, 136
Goodwill, 52
Goodyear Tire & Rubber Company, 166–167
Google, 152–153
Gross basis, 152
Gross margin. *See* Gross profit
Gross profit, 83
Gross profit margin, 83–84, 158, 197, 210
 effect of loss recognition on write-downs of inventory, 158
Growth rate, 43

H

Hasbro, Inc., 160
Held to maturity, 41
Hoover's Corporate Directory, 184

I

IASC. *See* International Accounting Standards Committee
Income statement, 79–94
 multiple-step, 79
 single-step, 79
Income taxes, 33, 106, 167, 245, 246
Indirect method, 114–116
Industry comparison, 185
Infotrak—General Business Index, 183
In-process research and development, 162
Intangible assets, 52, 86, 160–161, 235
Intel Corporation, 55
Interest expense, 33, 88, 147
Interest income, 33, 88, 166
 impact on earnings quality, 169
Interest rate assumptions. *See* Pension accounting
Interim statements, 37
Internal Revenue Service (IRS), 55, 146
International accounting standards, 22
International Accounting Standards Committee, 5
Interpretations, 4
Inventory
 average cost method, 46, 92, 156
 base LIFO layer liquidation, 48, 157–158
 cost flow assumption, 46, 48, 83, 156–157
 dollar-value LIFO, 48
 effect of change on cash flow, 116
 FIFO, 46–48, 83, 96, 156–158
 finished goods, 44
 LIFO, 46–48, 83, 96, 156–158
 loss recognition on write-downs, 158
 raw materials, 44

 turnover, 192, 201
 valuation, 48
 work-in-process, 44
Inventory turnover, 192, 201
Investing activities. *See* Cash flow from investing activities
Investments
 cost method, 89–90
 equity method, 89–90, 116, 167
 unconsolidated subsidiaries, 116, 167

J

Journal of Accountancy, 5, 17, 56, 189

K

Kennametal, Inc., 163–165
Key financial ratios. *See* Financial ratios
Kodak, 28, 75, 104, 137, 156, 157, 179, 227

L

Land, 50–51
Last-in-first-out. *See* LIFO
Leases
 capital, 60
 operating, 60, 61, 172
Leasehold improvements, 51
Leverage
 financial, 194–209, 211–212
 ratios, 172, 186, 194–197
Liabilities, 36, 52–62
 accrued, 54
 current, 52–54
 long-term, 59–62
LIFO. *See* Inventory, LIFO
Line of credit, 34, 54, 248
Liquidity
 analysis, 36, 203–204, 205
 ratios, 34, 186, 188–190, 204
 specific assets. *See* Activity ratios
Long-lived assets. *See* Fixed assets
Long-term debt, 59–60, 113, 117, 126, 171
 current maturities, 54
 effect of change on cash flow, 117
Long-term debt to total capitalization, 194–195
Long-term investments, 52
Long-term liabilities. *See* Liabilities
Long-term solvency, 202, 205–209
Loss recognition on write-downs
 assets, 160
 inventories, 158–159
Lower of cost or market, 48, 168, 233

M

Management's Discussion and Analysis of the Financial Condition and Results of Operations, 3, 6, 30–35, 159, 163

Mandatorily redeemable preferred stock, 61
Market ratios, 199
Marketable securities, 41–42, 88, 110, 118, 166, 170, 185, 193, 203
Marketing expenses. *See* Advertising expenses
Market Watch, 184
Matching principle, 22
Mattel, Inc., 160
Micron Technology, Inc., 155
Microsoft, 20, 169–170
Minority interest, 37
Moody's Investor Service, Inc., 184
Morningstar, 184
Motorola, Inc., 140
Multiple-step format, 79

N

Net basis, 116, 151
Net earnings, 92
Net income. *See* Net earnings
Net profit margin, 92, 197–198
Net sales, 81
Net trade cycle. *See* Cash conversion cycle
Net working capital. *See* Working capital
Nonoperating items, 88, 114, 197
Notes payable, 53–54, 113, 117–118
   effect of change on cash flow, 117–118
Notes to the financial statements, 7–10

O

Objectives of financial analysis, 180–181
Off-balance sheet financing, 61, 172, 195
Operating activities. *See* Cash flow from operating activities
Operating cycle, 40, 41
Operating efficiency, 202, 205
Operating expenses, 87, 146, 159–165
Operating lease, 61, 85, 172, 196
Operating profit, 79, 87–88
Operating profit margin, 88, 197
Options. *See* Stock options
Owner's equity. *See* Stockholders' equity

P

Paid-in capital. *See* Additional paid-in capital
Parmalat, 5, 171
Par value method, 64
Pension accounting
   impact on earnings quality, 162–165

interest rate assumptions, 162–165
Pensions, 56, 163
Permanent differences, 56
Pfizer, Inc., 19, 63, 64, 172
Plant and equipment. *See* Fixed assets
Postretirement benefits other than pensions, 60–61
Preferred stock, 61–62, 63–64
Premature revenue recognition, 150–151
Prepaid expenses, 48, 116, 188, 189
Price-to-earnings ratio, 199
Prior period adjustment, 96
Pro forma earnings, 96, 170, 213
Pro forma financial statements, 212–213
Profitability
   analysis, 209–211
   ratios, 186, 197–199
Projections, 212–213
Property, plant, and equipment. *See* Fixed assets
Provision for doubtful accounts. *See* Allowance for doubtful accounts
Proxy statement, 19–20, 182
Public Company Accounting Oversight Board, 16

Q

Qualified opinion, 15
Quality of financial reporting, 21, 22–23, 171–173
   manipulation, 21
Quick ratio, 189–190, 204

R

Raw materials, 44
Repairs and maintenance, 85, 87
Research and development, 23, 87, 159, 162
Reserve accounts, 54–55, 161
Retained earnings, 62–63, 94, 95, 96, 117
Return on total assets. *See* Return on investment
Return on equity, 198, 208, 210, 211, 212
Return on investment, 198–199, 211
Reuters, 184
Revenues. *See* Sales
Reverse stock split, 93, 95–96
Risk, 194–195, 205–206
Risk Management Association, 45, 51, 73, 83, 183, 203

S

Sales, 81, 148–156
   allowance, 81
   impact of manipulation on earnings quality, 88, 148–150

price vs. volume increase, 155
   real vs. nominal growth, 155–156
   net, 81–93
   return, 81
Salvage value, 49, 50
Sarbanes-Oxley Act of 2002, 10, 14, 16–17
Securities and Exchange Commission, 3–6, 9, 16–17, 19, 21, 37, 44, 92, 150, 152, 170, 173, 182, 183
   EDGAR database, 6, 7, 183
   Staff Accounting Bulletin No. 101, 152
Securities available for sale, 41–42
Selling and administrative expenses, 85
Shareholders' equity. *See* Stockholders' equity
Short-term solvency. *See* Liquidity ratios
Single-step format, 79
Stated value. *See* Par value
Statement of cash flows, 7, 107–127, 144–147
   financing activities, 110, 111–113, 117–118
   investing activities, 110, 111, 116–118
   operating activities, 110, 111, 113–116, 122–124
Statement of changes in financial position, 107
Statement of financial position. *See* Balance sheet
Statement of retained earnings, 7
Statement of stockholders' equity, 7, 79, 94–96
Statements of Financial Accounting Standards. *See* Financial Accounting Standards Board
Stock compensation, 5
Stock dividends, 62, 95
Stock options, 4–5, 92–93
Stock splits, 93, 95
Stockholders' equity, 42, 62–64
Straight-line depreciation. *See* Depreciation
Structural analysis, 40, 81, 185

T

Tangible fixed assets. *See* Fixed assets
Target Corporation, 20, 228
Taxable income, 47, 55–56
Temporary differences, 55–57
Times interest earned ratio, 195–196
Total asset turnover ratio, 193, 212
Trading securities, 41, 88

Treasury stock, 64, 169
  cost method, 64
  impact on earnings quality, 169
  par value method, 64
Trend analysis, 185

U

Unearned revenue, 55
Units-of-production method of
  depreciation. *See* Depreciation
Unqualified opinion, 16, 182

V

Valuation allowance, 56
Valuation and Qualifying
  Accounts Schedule, 44

Value Line, Inc., 184
Vendor financing, 173

W

W.T. Grant, 119
Walgreen Company, 172
Wal-Mart, 20
Warrant, 92–93
Waste Management, 168
Work-in-process, 44
Working capital, 41
WorldCom, 5, 16, 160, 172, 199

Y

Yahoo!, 152–153
Year, 37

calendar, 37
fiscal, 37

Z

Zack's Investment Research,
  Inc., 184